un Vernon 25 . 9ber

have had the pleasure
etters from you since
in France, and can
rquis de la Fayette
it an acknowledge:
altho' his doing it is
the same time am sur
Company —
have a little more
ever should be) I
all the occurrences
that have come under

The Founding Fathers

The Founding Fathers

GEORGE WASHINGTON

A Biography in His Own Words

VOLUME 2

Edited by

RALPH K. ANDRIST

JOAN PATERSON KERR
Picture Editor

NEWSWEEK
New York

ISBN: Clothbound Edition 0-88225-037-X; ISBN: Deluxe Edition 0-88225-038-8
Library of Congress Catalog Card Number 72-76000
Copyright © 1972 by Newsweek, Inc.
All rights reserved. Printed and bound in the United States of America
Endpapers: Washington to David Humphreys, Nov. 25, 1784;
HENRY E. HUNTINGTON LIBRARY AND ART GALLERY

Arms of the United States, 1786

Chapter 7

"I Resign with Satisfaction"

When the British marched out of Yorktown to give up their arms, their band played in dirge time a popular song of the day, "The World Turned Upside-down." If the song expressed something of the astonishment and humiliation of the King's troops at surrendering to the ragged rebel forces, it also said something for the emotions in the hearts of the American troops, who were probably hard-put to realize that the scene was actually taking place, after all the years of defeat and privation and false hopes. That only the help of a French army and fleet had made the victory possible diminished their satisfaction very little. Washington had scant time to pause and savor his victory. The Army had to be established near the main British force in New York again. And he had a myriad of duties to attend to before he could leave Yorktown. Troops had to be sent south to reinforce Nathanael Greene in South Carolina. Care had to be provided for enemy sick and wounded. Arrangements had to be made either to use or store matériel captured from the enemy. The list went on and on—and only so much could be left to subordinates. Affairs were enough in hand to let Washington depart on November 5, 1781. But the next day he was sending a message to his secretary, Jonathan Trumbull, Jr., explaining that he had been tragically delayed and asking Trumbull to send the rest of Washington's staff on to Mount Vernon.

> Eltham [Virginia], November 6, 1781
> I came here in time to see Mr. Custis breathe his last. About Eight o'clock yesterday Evening he expired. The deep and solemn distress of the Mother, and affliction of the Wife of this amiable young Man, requires every comfort in my power to afford them; the last rights of the deceased I must also see performed; these will take me three or four days; when I shall proceed with Mrs. Washington and Mrs. Custis to Mount Vernon.

As the dirty tavern you are now at cannot be very comfortable; and in spite of Mr. Sterne's [novelist Laurence Sterne] observation the House of Mourning not very agreeable; it is my wish, that all of the Gentn. of my family, except yourself, who I beg may come here and remain with me; may proceed on at their leizure to Mount Vernon, and wait for me there. Colo. Cobb will join you on the road at the Tavern we breakfasted at (this side Ruffens).

John Parke Custis had joined his stepfather in Yorktown and had served briefly as a civilian aide. His belated gesture cost him his life; he had contracted "camp fever"—probably typhus—and had gone to Eltham, the home of his uncle Burwell Bassett, some thirty miles from Yorktown. His wife, mother, and oldest daughter, only five, had been summoned; Washington had arrived only hours before he died. After the funeral and other melancholy duties had been taken care of, Washington went on to Mount Vernon. He had looked forward to a few days of quiet at home, but Jack's death had cast a pall over the household, and with two grieving women about, he was probably happy to have his staff with him to keep him busy. One letter, with some observations on the future of the war, went to the Marquis de Lafayette, who was about to leave America and return to his home in France.

Mount Vernon Virga. Novr. 15th. 1781. Not 'till the 5th. My dear Marquis, was I able to leave York; providing for the detachment that was to go Southerly; Embarking the Troops that were to go Northerly; making a distribution of the Ordnance and Stores for various purposes; and disposing of the Officers and other Prisoners to their respective places of destination would not admit of my leaving that part of the Country sooner. . . .

As you expressed a desire to know, My sentiments respecting the operations of next Campaign before your departure for France, I will without a tedious display of reasoning, declare in one Word, that the advantages of it to America and the honour and Glory of it to the allied Arms in these States, must depend *absolutely* upon the Naval force which is employed in these Seas, and the time of its appearance, next year. No Land force can act decisively, unless it is accompanied by a Maritime superiority; nor can more than negative advantages be expected without it; For proof of this, we have only to

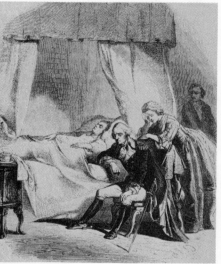

Life of George Washington, HEADLEY

A highly romantic rendering of the death in 1781 of John Parke Custis

recur to the instances of the ease and facility with which the British shifted their Ground, as advantages were to be obtained at either extremity of the Continent, and to their late heavy loss the moment they failed in their naval superiority. To point out the further advantages which might have been obtained in the course of this Year if Count de Grasse could have waited and would have covered a further operation to the Southward, is unnecessary; because a doubt did not, nor does at this moment remain upon any Mans mind of the total extirpation of the British force in the Carolina's and Georgia, if he could have extended his co-operation two Months longer.

It follows then as certain as that Night succeeds the day, that without a decisive Naval force we can do nothing definitive; and with it every thing honourable and glorious. A constant naval superiority would terminate the War speedily; without it, I do not know that it will ever be terminated honourably. If this force should appear early, we shall have the whole Campaign before us. The Months of June to September inclusive, are well adapted for operating in any of the States to the Northward of this; and the remaining Months are equally well suited to those South of it; In which time with such means, I think much, I will add, every thing, might be expected.

How far the policy of Congress may carry them, towards filling their Continental Battalions does not lay with me to determine. This measure (before and since the capitulation) has been strongly recommended [to] me. Should it be adopted by that Body, and executed with energy in the several States, I think our force (comprehending the Auxiliary Troops now here) will be fully competent to all the purposes of the American War, provided the British force on this Continent remains nearly as it now is; but as this is a contingency which depends very much upon political manoeuvres in Europe, and as it is uncertain how far *we* may be in a State of preparation at the opening of the next Campaign, the propriety of augmenting the present Army under the command of Count de Rochambeau is a question worthy of consideration, but as it lies with Congress to determine, I shall be silent on the subject.

If I should be deprived of the pleasure of a personal

interview with you, before your departure, permit me, my dear Marquis, to adopt this method of making you a tender of my ardent Vows for a propitious Voyage, a gracious reception from your Prince, an honourable reward for your services, a happy meeting with your Lady and friends and a safe return in the Spring to My Dear Marquis....

His victory had made Washington a hero; even many who had once called him incompetent joined in the paeans. While he was at Mount Vernon he was already finding himself busy replying to eulogistic letters from Congress and other well-wishers. To his neighbors at Alexandria, Virginia, went a letter of thanks that differed from most only in being a bit more personal.

[Mount Vernon] November 20th. 1781.

I accept with peculiar satisfaction the very kind and affectionate address of the citizens of Alexandria, the long acquaintance which in former times I have had of their Sincerity and cordiality, stamps it with particular Value, and permit me to say, that to make a peaceful return to this agreeable Society of my Fellow Citizens, is among the most ardent of my Wishes, and would prove my greatest comfort for all the toils and Vicissitudes which I have experienced during my absence.

The great director of events has carried us through a variety of Scenes, during this long and bloody Contest, in which we have been for Seven Campaigns most nobly strugling. The present prospect is pleasing. The late success at York Town is very promising, but on our own improvement depend its future good consequences. A vigorous prosecution of this success, will, in all probability procure us what we have so long wished to secure, an establishment of peace, Liberty and Independence. A Relaxation of our exertions at this moment may cost us many more toilsome Campaigns, and be attended with the most unhappy consequences.

Your condolence for the loss of that amiable youth Mr. Custis, affects me most tenderly; [his] loss, I trust, will be compensated to you, in some other Worthy representative.

Amidst all the Vicissitudes of time or fortune, be assured Gentlemen, that I shall ever regard with particular affection the Citizens and Inhabitants of Alexandria.

Companion likenesses of Martha and George Washington drawn in 1782 are among earliest engraved portraits.

On November 20 George and Martha Washington left Mount Vernon. The next day they were in Annapolis, where for two days Washington was wined and dined and addressed by the mayor, the governor and legislature of Maryland, and groups of citizens. Then they proceeded to Philadelphia and more acclaim. Even at the theater Washington sat through laudatory prologues in painful embarrassment. While the Army went into winter quarters again, at Newburgh on the Hudson, Washington remained in Philadelphia, for Congress had many things to discuss with him about the future of the war. Most of the problems involved recruiting men or raising money. In March of 1781 the thirteen states had at last united formally under the Articles of Confederation. The union was a weak one; Congress, its only executive body, could make war but could obtain the necessary men and money only by asking the states for them—with no power to compel any state to comply. The Commander in Chief sent a circular letter to the chief executives of all thirteen states.

Philadelphia 22 Janry. 1782.

Although it may be somewhat out of my province, to address your Excellency on a subject not immediately of a Military nature, yet I consider it so nearly connected with and so essential to the operations under my direction, that I flatter myself my interference will not be deemed impertinent.

Upon applying to the Superintendant of Finance to know how far I might depend upon him for the Pay, feeding and Clothing of the Army for the current year, and for the Sums necessary to put it and keep it in motion, he very candidly laid open to me the State of our Monied affairs, and convinced me, that although the assistances we had derived from abroad were considerable, yet they would be by no means adequate to our expences. He informed me further: that to make up the deficiency, the States had been called upon by Congress, for eight Million of Dollars for the service of the Year 1782, and shewed me the copy of a Circular letter from himself to the several Legislatures, in which he had so fully and clearly pointed out the necessity of a compliance with the requisition, that it is needless for me to say more on that head, than that I Intirely concur with him in opinion, so far as he has gone into the matter. But there are other reasons which could not be so well known to him as they are to me, as having come under my immediate observation and which therefore I shall take the liberty to mention.

Your Excellency cannot but remember the ferment

BOTH: MOUNT VERNON LADIES' ASSOCIATION OF THE UNION

Engraved after drawings by Benjamin Blyth, these hand-colored portraits were published by J. Coles in Boston.

into which the whole Army was thrown twelve Months ago, for the want of pay and a regular supply of Clothing and Provisions: and with how much difficulty they were brought into temper, by a partial supply of the two first, and a promise of more regular supplies of all in future. Those promises the Soldiery now begin to claim and although we shall be able to satisfy them tolerably in respect to Clothing, and perfectly in regard to Provision (if the Financier is enabled to comply with his Contracts) yet there is no prospect of obtaining pay, until part of the money required of the States can be brought into the public Treasury. You cannot conceive the uneasiness which arises from the total want of so essential an Article as Money, and the real difficulties in which the officers in particular are involved on that account. The favourable aspect of our affairs, and the hopes that matters are in a train to afford them relief contributes to keep them quiet but I cannot answer for the effects of a disappointment. . . .

To bring this War to a speedy and happy conclusion, must be the fervent wish of every lover of his Country; & sure I am, that no means are so likely to effect these as vigorous preparations for another Campaign. Whether then we consult our true interest, Substantial oeconomy, or sound policy, we shall find that relaxation and langour are of all things to be avoided. Conduct of that kind on our part will produce fresh hopes and new exertions on that of the Enemy; whereby the War, which has already held beyond the general expectation, may be protracted to such a length, that the people groaning under the burthen of it and despairing of success, may think any change, a change for the better.

I will close with a request, that your Excelly. will be good enough to take the first opportunity of laying these my sentiments before the Legislature of your State. From the attention they have [ever] been pleased to pay to any former requisitions or representations of mine, I am encouraged to hope that the present, which is equally important with any I have ever made, will meet with a favourable reception.

A detail from a cartoon of 1782, "The Horrors of War," shows America with a dagger in her breast begging an indifferent England to "forego this bloody warfare."

As spring neared, Washington expected a resurgence of enemy military activity and was increasingly concerned about the failure of the states to prepare for that time. One of those to whom he expressed his concern was James McHenry, aide to Lafayette until three months earlier, when he had resigned to serve in the Maryland legislature.

Philadelphia March 12th. 1782.

Never, since the commencement of the present revolution, has there been, in my judgment, a period when vigorous measures were more consonant with sound policy than the present. The Speech of the British King and the Addresses of the Lords and Commons are evincive proofs to my Mind of two things, namely their wishes to prosecute the American War, and their fears of the consequences. My Opinion, therefore, of the matter is, that the Minister will obtain supplies for the current Year, prepare vigorously for another Campaign, and then prosecute the War or treat of Peace as circumstances and fortuitous events may justify; and that nothing will contribute more to the first, than a relaxation, or apparent supineness on the part of these States. The debates upon the addresses evidently prove what I have here advanced to be true. For these addresses, as explained, are meant to answer any purpose the Ministers may have in view. What madness then can be greater, or policy and oeconomy worse, than to let the Enemy again rise upon our folly and want of exertion? Shall we not be justly chargeable for all the Blood and Treasure which shall be wasted in a lingering War, procrastinated by the false expectation of Peace, or timid measures for the prosecution of it? Surely we shall, and much is to be lamented that our endeavours do not at all times accord with our wishes; each State is anxious to see the end of our Warfare accomplished, but shrinks when it is called upon for the means: and either withholds them altogether, or grants them in such [a] way as to defeat the End. Such, it is to be feared, will be the case in many instances respecting the requisitions of Men and Money.

I have the pleasure, however, to inform you, that the Assembly of this State [Pennsylvania], now setting, have passed their supply Bill without a dissenting voice, and that a laudable spirit seems to pervade all the members of that Body; but I fear notwithstanding, they will be deficient of their Quota of Men. It is idle, at this late period of the War, when enthusiasm is cooled, if not done away; when the Minds of that class of Men who are

Another 1782 cartoon shows the reconciliation between America and her "Dear Mama," Britannia.

proper subjects for Soldiers, are poisoned by the high Bounties which have been given; and the knowledge of the distresses of the Army so generally diffused through every State; to suppose that our Battalions can be compleated by voluntary enlistment; the attempt is vain and we are only deceiving ourselves and injuring the cause by making the experiment. There is no other *effectual* method to get Men suddenly, but that of classing the People, and compelling each Class to furnish a Recruit. Here every Man is interested; every Man becomes a recruiting Officer. If our necessities for Men did not press, I should prefer the mode of voluntary Inlistment to all others to obtain them; as it does, I am sure it will not answer, and that the Season for enterprise will be upon us long ere we are ready for the Field.

The anxious state of suspense in which we have been for some time, and still remain, respecting the Naval engagement in the West Indies and attempt upon Brimstone Hill in the Island of St. Kitts, is disagreeable beyond description. The issue of these must be very interesting and may give a very unfavourable turn to affairs in that Quarter, and to America in its consequences.

Only six days after Washington had given McHenry such a categorical statement of the aggressive plans of the British Crown, he had obtained fresher news that made him modify his views of enemy intentions and caused him to write in a different vein to Nathanael Greene, the talented commander of American forces in the South.

> Philadelphia 18th. March 1782.
> It gives me the more pain to hear of your distresses for want of Clothing or other necessaries, as you are at so great a distance that you cannot be suddenly relieved, even if we had the means. I am not however without hopes, that should the War be continued to the Southward (of which I have my doubts, for reasons which I shall presently give) matters will be put into much better train than they have hitherto been. The arrangements made already by the Superintendant of Finance have been attended with infinite public advantages, and he is extending those arrangements as fast as circumstances will possibly admit. . . .
> By late advices from Europe and from the declara-

Lord North as caricatured by Sayers

tions of the British Ministers themselves, it appears, that they have done with all thoughts of an excursive War, and that they mean to send small if any further reinforcements to America. It may be also tolerably plainly seen, that they do not mean to hold all their present Posts, and that New York will be occupied in preference to any other. Hence, and from other indications, I am induced to believe that an evacuation of the Southern States will take place. Should this happen, we must concentre our force as the Enemy do theirs: You will therefore, upon the appearance of such an event, immediately make preparations for the march of the army under your command to the northward. What Troops shall in that case be left in the Southern States will be a matter of future discussion.

The information that Washington sent to Greene was accurate. The British had had their fill of the fight to subdue the Colonies. On February 27, 1782, the House of Commons voted against carrying on the war in America and a few days later authorized the Government to negotiate a peace settlement. On March 20 came the resignation of Lord North, Prime Minister since 1770, whose coercive acts had driven the Colonies into revolt. He was replaced by Lord Rockingham, who had long advocated American independence. There was a shake-up in the military, too; Sir Guy Carleton, long-time commander in Canada, replaced Sir Henry Clinton as British Commander in Chief in America and arrived in New York on May 5. In spite of these changes, Washington remained very skeptical of British intentions, as he told Governor George Clinton.

[Newburgh] May 7th. 1782.

It seems we are coming to a period, when we are exceedingly in danger of being imposed upon by the Insiduous measures of our Enemy. You have doubtless seen the Intelligence from New York and the Debates in Parliament upon the American War, which the Country it seems are catching at as a prelude to a speedy peace, upon principles of Independence. I will only mention to your Excellency that I have perused the several motions which have been made and the Debates thereon with great attention, and upon serious consideration am obliged to say, that the whole appears to me merely delusory, calculated to quiet the Minds of their own people, & to lull the exertions of ours, and that finding themselves hard pushed in other quarters, they want to amuse us in America, whilst they attend to other parts of their Empire; which being secured, they will have time and means to revert to this continent again, with hopes of success.

An idea of American Independence, on its true principles, dont appear thro' the whole debates; but an idea of reconnecting us to the British Nation, by dissolving our connexion with France, is too prevalent.

Washington's mistrust in no way lessened when on May 9 he received from General Carleton a letter saying that Carleton and Admiral Robert Digby, the British naval commander, were joined "in the commission of peace." Washington continued to denounce accounts from England as an "opiate to increase that stupor into which we have fallen." While most Americans relaxed at the prospect of peace, he worked out a comprehensive and grandiose strategy for winning the war with attacks on Canada, New York, Charleston, Savannah, and perhaps even Bermuda. But the Army did not march, and Washington had other problems.

GENERAL ORDERS

Head Quarters Newburgh Thursday 16 May 82
Parole. Signs.

The General is extremely concerned to learn that an Article so salutary as that of distilled Liquors was expected to be when properly used, and which was designed for the comfort and refreshment of the troops has been in many instances productive of very ill consequences. He calls the attention of officers of every grade to remedy these abuses and to watch over the health of their men, for which purpose he suggests the expedient of keeping liquor Rolls in every Corps, from which the Name of every soldier shall be struck off who addicts himself to drunkenness or injures his Constitution by intemperence. Such soldiers as are Struck off are not to draw liquor on any occasion, but are to receive other articles in lieu thereof. The Quarter Masters upon receiving such commuted Articles are to receipt for the ful amount of the rations included in the returns: that there may be no irregularity in the Accounts.

On May 22 Washington received from Colonel Lewis Nicola, a respected officer, a long letter in which Nicola discussed the sad situation of the unpaid Army, blamed the situation on the inefficiency of

Congress and of republican government in general, and proposed the solution: make Washington a king. Possibly some other designation might be wise, Nicola conceded, because "some people have so connected the ideas of tyranny and monarchy as to find it very difficult to seperate them." Washington replied at once.

The War of Independence, LOSSING

Washington's headquarters, Newburgh, New York

Newburgh May 22d. 1782.

With a mixture of great surprise and astonishment, I have read with attention the sentiments you have submitted to my perusal. Be assured, Sir, no occurrence in the course of the War, has given me more painful sensations than your information of there being such Ideas existing in the Army as you have expressed, and I must view with abhorrence and reprehend with severity. For the present the communication of them will rest in my own bosom, unless some further agitation of the matter, shall make a disclosure necessary.

I am much at a loss to conceive, what part of my conduct, could have given encouragement to an address, which to me seems big with the greatest mischiefs that can befall my Country. If I am not deceived in the knowledge of myself, you could not have found a person to whom your schemes are more disagreeable: At the same time, in justice to my own feelings, I must add, that no Man possesses a more sincere wish to see ample justice done to the Army than I do, and as far as my powers and influence, in a constitutional way, extend, they shall be employed to the utmost of my abilities to effect it, should there be any occasion. Let me conjure you then, if you have any regard for your Country; concern for yourself, or posterity, or respect for me, to banish these thoughts from your Mind, and never communicate, as from yourself, or any one else, a sentiment of the like Nature.

Washington might reprove Nicola, but this would not stop the talk. More and more officers and men would become convinced during the days ahead that only by retaining their weapons when peace came, and brandishing them if necessary, would they obtain the months of back pay owing to them. Washington would meet the problem again. As for the prospects for peace, Washington continued skeptical. His attitude toward British peace proposals is well typified by the way he let them pass with only a perfunctory mention in a letter to the Comte de Rochambeau, still with the French army in Virginia.

Head Quarters 28th. May 1782.
Since the information I conveyed to your Excellency by the Baron Closen, the amusement of Peace, held out by our Enemies, has been much augmented by the arrival of Sir Guy Carleton in New York, who announces himself as Commander in Chief in America, with powers of conciliation to these States. These Ideas, pleasing as their first prospect might have been, are now, I believe, beginning to be generally viewed in their proper Colours; as merely delusory and vain, and I hope will not be attended with such consequences as the Enemy seem to flatter themselves with.

The Alliance Frigate you will hear is safe arrived in New London. A Cutter also from France in 25 Days passage, is in at Salem. Her dispatches are gone to Congress You will probably know their contents as early as I shall.

Our accounts of the action in the West Indies between the two Fleets remain very uncertain and vague. From repeated publications in New York, compared with those I collected from other parts, I confess, I form too many reasons to fear, that the matter has not passed so favorably to our friend the Count de Grasse as you seem to imagine A little time will disclose the whole to us; and I sincerely hope it may dispel my apprehensions.

The action between French and British fleets to which Washington had referred had gone badly for the French. It was a new reason for foreboding; Washington was certain that a victorious Britain would lose interest in peace. Meanwhile, the Army had little to do, and Washington filled the void, as commanders always have, with drill and spit and polish.

GENERAL ORDERS

Head Quarters Newburgh Saturday June 8. 82
The General was highly pleased with the appearance of the first Massachusetts Brigade yesterday under Arms, and was very well satisfied with their Manoeuvering: the firing might have been better, and he fears the Locks or flints of the Musketts were in bad order, as many of them missed fire. The Officers commanding the Light Infantry should impress upon the men the necessity of taking deliberate Aim whenever they fire and see that they do it when it is in their power. It is the effect of the shot not the report of the Gun that can discomfit the Enemy and

if a bad habit is acquired at exercise it will prevail in real Action and so vice versa.

Although Washington continued to argue that the enemy's talk of peace was designed only to throw Americans off guard, the evidences of an approaching end to hostilities seemed very real. Benjamin Franklin had begun talks with the British in Paris in April. On July 11 the British evacuated Savannah. But when Lord Rockingham died after only a few months as British Prime Minister, Washington predicted to James McHenry that a new ministry would discard Rockingham's peace policy.

The Marquis of Rockingham

Verplanks point Septr. 12th. 1782. Our prospects of Peace is vanishing. The Death of the Marquis of Rockingham, has given a shock to the New Administration, and disordered its whole System. Fox, Burke, Lord John Cavendish, Lord Keppel (and I believe others) have left it; Earl Shelburne takes the lead, as first Lord of the Treasury; to which Office he was appointed by the King, the moment the vacancy happened, by the death of Lord Rockingham. This Nobleman declares, that the Sun of Great Britain will set the moment American Independency is acknowledged, and that no Man has ever heard him give an assent to the measure. The Duke of Richmond, on the other hand, asserts, that the Ministry, of which Lord Shelburne is one, came into Office upon the express condition and pledged to each other, that America should be declared Independent, that he will watch him and the moment he finds him departing therefrom, he will quit Administration, and give it every opposition in his power. That the King will push the War, as long as the Nation will find Men or Money, admits not of a doubt in my Mind. The whole tenor of his conduct, as well as his last proroguing Speech on the 11th. of July, plainly indicate it; and shews, in a clear point of view, the impolicy of relaxation on our parts. If we are wise, let us prepare for the worst; there is nothing which will so soon produce a speedy and honourable Peace as a state of preparation for War, and we must either do this, or lay our account to patch up an inglorious Peace after all the Toil, Blood, and Treasure we have spent. This has been my uniform Opinion. A Doctrine I have endeavoured, amidst the torrent of expectation of an approaching Peace, to inculcate; and what I am sure the event will justify me in.

221

Despite Washington's pessimism, there was no discernible change in British policy. Washington had moved his army to Verplanck's Point on the Hudson, so that French and American armies might camp near each other, ready to cooperate if the British should act. The French, moving up from Virginia, arrived in mid-September. It was an occasion for many reunions of old Yorktown comrades, but American officers were at a great disadvantage in the mutual entertaining that went on — as Washington complained to the Secretary at War in detailing the discontents and grievances eating into the hearts of officers and men.

Head Quarters, [Verplanck's Point]
Octr. 2nd. 1782.

My dear Sir:

Painful as the task is, to describe the dark side of our Affairs, it some times becomes a matter of indispensable necessity. Without disguise or palliation, I will inform you candidly of the discontents which, at this moment, prevail universally throughout the Army.

The complaint of Evils which they suppose almost remediless, are, the total want of Money, or the means of existing from one day to another, the heavy debts they have already incurred, the loss of Credit, the distress of their Families (i.e. such as are married) at home, and the prospect of Poverty and Misery before them. It is vain Sir, to suppose that Military Men will acquiesce *contently* with bare Rations, when those in the Civil Walk of life (unacquainted with half the hardships they endure) are regularly paid the emoluments of Office; while the human Mind is influenced by the same passions, and have the same inclinations to endulge, it cannot be. A Military Man has the same turn to sociability, as a person in Civil Life: He conceives himself equally called upon to live up to his rank; and his Pride is hurt, when circumstances restrain him: Only conceive then, the mortification they (even the General Officers) must suffer when they cannot invite a French Officer, a visiting Friend, or traveling acquaintance to a better repast than stinking Whiskey (and not always that) and a bit of Beef without Vegitables, will afford them.

The Officers also complain of other hardships which they think might and ought to be remedied without delay, vizt. the stopping Promotions where there have been vacancies open for a long time, the withholding Commissions from those who are justly entitled to them and have Warrants, or Certificates of their appointments from the

Detail from a British cartoon, "The Blessings of Peace," showing Peace as a witch on a broom flying toward Great Britain's setting sun

Executives of their States, and particularly the leaving the compensation for their services in a loose equivocal state, without ascertaining their claims upon the public, or making Provision for the future payment of them.

While I premise, that tho' no one that I have seen or heard of, appears opposed to the principle of reducing the Army as circumstances may require; Yet I cannot help fearing the Result of the measure in contemplation, under present circumstances, when I see such a number of Men, goaded by a thousand Stings of reflexion on the past, and of anticipation on the future, about to be turned into the World, soured by penury and what they call the ingratitude of the Public, involved in debts, without one Farthing of Money to carry them home, after having spent the flower of their days and many of them their patrimonies in establishing the freedom and Independence of their Country, and suffered every thing human Nature is capable of enduring on this side of Death. I repeat it, these irritable circumstances, without one thing to sooth their feelings, or *frighten* the gloomy prospects, I cannot avoid apprehending that a train of evils will follow, of a very serious and distressing Nature. On the other hand, could the Officers be placed in as good a situation, as when they came into Service, the contention, I am persuaded, would be, not who should continue in the Field, but who should retire to private Life.

I wish not to heighten the shades of the Picture, so far as the real Life would justify me in doing, or I would give Anecdotes of Patriotism and distress which have scarcely ever been paralleled; never surpassed in the history of Mankind. But you may rely upon it, the patience and long sufferance of this Army are almost exhausted, and that there never was so great a spirit of discontent as at this instant. While in the Field, I think it may be kept from breaking out into acts of outrage; but when we retire into Winter Quarters (unless the Storm is previously dissipated) I cannot be at ease, respecting the consequences. It is high time for a Peace.

To you, My Dear Sir, I need not be more particular in describing my anxiety and the Grounds of it. You are too well acquainted from your own service, with the real sufferings of the Army to require a longer detail: I will therefore only add, that exclusive of the common hardships of a Military life, our Troops have been, and still

Detail from same cartoon of 1783 with Franklin (1) crowning the young republic between her allies, the kings of France and Spain

Trumbull sketch for an unfinished painting of the peace treaty signing at Paris in 1783; Benjamin Franklin is at center.

are obliged to perform more services, foreign to their proper duty, without gratuity or reward, than the Soldiers of any other Army: For example, the immense labours expended in doing the duties of Artificers, in erecting Fortifications and Military Works; the fatigue of Building themselves Barracks, or Huts annually; and of cutting and transporting Wood for the use of all our Posts and Garrisons, without any expence whatever to the public.

Of this Letter, (which from the tenor of it must be considered in some degree of a Private nature) you may make such use as you shall think proper, since the principal objects of it were, by displaying the merits, the hardships, the disposition and critical state of the Army, to give information that might eventually be useful. . . .

Secretary at War Benjamin Lincoln had been a major general in the Continental Army and well understood what Washington was saying. He replied in a private letter, the gist of which was that one cannot get blood from a turnip: Congress could pay the Army only if the states provided the money, and the states were showing no interest in honoring their debts to the men who had given so much for so long. Washington had returned to his Newburgh headquarters in October, and in December the French army left American shores for the West Indies. That same month the British evacuated Charleston, though it would be weeks before Washington learned of the event. And in Paris on November 30, 1782, a provisional treaty of peace had been signed recognizing American independence. Months would pass before that news would reach America, and in the meantime Washington continued to preach caution in accepting British earnests of peaceful intentions. But though he talked preparedness and even planned a little for a campaign in 1784, he too was affected by the general atmosphere of relaxation. He was finding time to write again to Lund Washington about Mount Vernon affairs and even got off a letter to his nephew Bushrod, son of his brother John Augustine. Washington was much given to quoting maxims, usually of his own coining, when he advised the young, and his letter to Bushrod (who would one day be an associate justice of the United States Supreme Court) is a fine example of his use of this prose form.

Newburgh Jany. 15th. 1783.

Dear Bushrod:

You will be surprized perhaps at receiving a Letter from me; but if the end is answered for which it is written, I shall not think my time misspent.

Your Father, who seems to entertain a very favourable Opinion of your prudence, and I hope you merit it; in one or two of his Letters to me, speaks of the difficulty he is under to make you remittances. Whether this arises from the scantiness of his Funds or the extensiveness of your demands, is matter of conjecture with me. I hope it is not the latter, because common prudence, and every other consideration which ought to have weight in a reflecting Mind, is opposed to your requiring more than his conveniency and a regard to his other Children will enable him to pay; and because he holds up no Idea in his Letter, which would support me in the conclusion. Yet when I take a view of the inexperience of Youth; the temptations in, and vices of Cities; and the distresses to which our Virginia Gentlemen are driven by an accumulation of Taxes, and the want of a market; I am almost inclined to ascribe it in part to both. Therefore, as a Friend, I give you the following advice.

Let the object which carried you to Philadelphia, be always before your Eyes. Remember, that it is not the mere study of the Law, but to become eminent in the profession of it, which is to yield honour and profit; the first was your choice, let the second be your ambition: And that dissipation is incompatible with both.

That the Company in which you will improve most, will be least expensive to you; and yet I am not such a Stoick as to suppose you will, or to think it right that you ought, always to be in Company with Senators and Philosophers; but of the Young and Juvenile kind, let me advise you to be choice. It is easy to make acquaintances, but very difficult to shake them off; however irksome and unprofitable they are found, after we have once committed ourselves to them; the indiscretions and scrapes, which very often they involuntarily lead one into, proves equally distressing and disgraceful.

Be courteous to all, but intimate with few, and let those few be well tried before you give them your confidence. True friendship is a Plant of slow Growth, and must undergo and withstand the shocks of adversity before it is entitled to the appellation.

Let your *Heart* feel for the afflictions and distresses of every one, and let your *hand* give in proportion to your Purse; remembering always the estimation of the Widows Mite. But that it is not every one who asketh, that deserveth Charity: All however are worthy of the inquiry or the deserving may suffer.

Mount Vernon, LOSSING

Bushrod Washington

Do not conceive that fine Clothes make fine Men, any more than fine Feathers make fine Birds. A plain genteel Dress is more admired and obtains more credit than Lace and embroidery in the Eyes of the Judicious and Sensible.

The last thing I shall mention, is first of importance; and that is, to avoid Gaming. This is a vice which is productive of every possible evil: Equally injurious to the morals and Health of its votaries. It is the Child of avarice, The Brother of inequity, and Father of mischief. It has been the ruin of many worthy Familys; the loss of many a Man's honour and the cause of Suicide. To all those who enter the lists, it is equally fascinating; The Successful Gamester pushes his good fortune 'till it is over taken by a reverse: The loosing Gamester, in hopes of retrieving past misfortunes, goes on from bad to worse, 'till grown desperate, he pushes at every thing; and looses his all. In a word, few gain by this abominable practice (the profit, if any, being diffused) while thousands are injured.

Perhaps you will say my conduct has anticipated the advice, and that "not one of these cases apply to me." I shall be heartily glad of it. It will add not a little to my happiness, to find those, to whom I am so nearly connected, pursuing the right Walk of life: It will be the sure Road to my Favour, and to those honours, and places of profit, which their Country can bestow, as merit rarely goes unrewarded.

The day after he wrote to Bushrod, Washington sent a letter to his brother Jack—Bushrod's father—and discussed some painful family matters.

Newburgh 16th. Jany. 1783.
Since the letter which Bushrod delivered me in Philadelphia, I have received your favors of the 24th. of July from Westmoreland—and 12th. of Novr. from Berkley.

The latter gave me extreme pain. In Gods name how did my Brothr. Saml. contrive to get himself so enormously in debt? Was it by purchases? By misfortunes? or shear indolence & inattention to business? From whatever cause it proceeded, the matter is now the same, & curiosity only prompts the enquiry—as it does to know what will be saved, & how it is disposed of. In the list of his debts did it appear that I had a claim upon him for the

Samuel Washington

purchase money of the Land I sold Pendleton on Bullskin? I have never received a farthing for it yet, and think I have been informed by him that he was to pay it.

I have heard a favourable acct. of Bushrod, and doubt not but his prudence will direct him to a proper line of Conduct. I have given him my sentiments on this head; & perswade myself that, with the advice of Mr. Wilson, to whose friendship as well as instruction in his profession I recommended him and the admontion of others, he will stand as good a chance as most youth of his age to avoid the Vices of large Cities, which have their advantages & disadvantages in fitting a Man for the great theatre of public Life.

I have lately received a letter from my Mother in which she complains much *of the Knavery of the Overseer at the little Falls Quarter*—that She says she can get nothing from him. It is pretty evident I believe, that I get nothing from thence, while I have the annual rent of between Eighty & an hundred pounds to pay. *The whole profit of the Plantation according to her Acct. is applied to his own use*—which is rather hard upon me as I had no earthly inducement to meddle with it but to comply with her wish, and to free her from care. This like every other matter of private concern, with me, has been totally neglected; but it is too much while I am suffering in every other way (and hardly able to keep my own Estate from Sale) to be saddled with all the expence of hers & not be able to derive the smallest return from it. . . .

While I am talking of my Mother and her concerns, I am impelled to mention somethings which has given, and still continues to give me pain. About two years ago a Gentleman of my acquaintance informed me that it was in contemplation to move for a pension for her in the Virginia Assembly—That he did not suppose I knew of the Measure—or that it would be agreeable to me to have it done—but wished to know my sentiments on it. I instantly wrote him that it was new & astonishing to me & begged that he would prevent the motion if possible, or oppose it if made; for I was sure she had not a Child that would not share the last farthing with her & that would not be hurt at the idea of her becoming a Pensioner—or in other Words receiving charity. Since *then* I have heard nothing of *that* matter; but I learn from very good authority that she is upon all occasions, & in all Companies

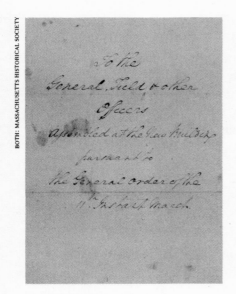

Above and opposite, the first two pages of Washington's speech to his officers, Newburgh, March 15, 1783

complaining of the hardness of the times—of her wants & distresses; & if not in direct terms, at least by strong innuendos inviting favors which not only makes *her* appear in an unfavourable point of view but *those* also who are connected with her. That she can have no *real* wants that may not be supplied I am sure of—*imaginary* wants are indefinite, & oftentimes insatiable, because they are boundless & always changing. The reason of my mentioning these matters to you is, that you may enquire into her real wants and see what is necessary to make her comfortable. If the Rent is insufficient to do this, while I have any thing I will part with it to make her so; & wish you to take measures in my behalf accordingly—at the same time I wish you to represent to her in delicate terms the impropriety of her complaints & acceptance of favors even where they are voluntarily offered from any but relations. It will not do to touch upon this subject in a letter to her—& therefore I have avoided it.

Physically, the Army was passing the winter well. In February Washington could write to one of his generals that the troops were "better covered, better Clothed and better fed, than they have ever been in any former Winter Quarters." But morale was low. On March 10 Washington was given a copy of a call to all officers for a mass meeting the next day to consider ways to obtain a just settlement of their grievances. The Newburgh Address, as this appeal to the Army came to be known, was from an anonymous hand (later identified as an aide to General Horatio Gates) and was skillfully and emotionally written. The writer spoke at length of the ingratitude of the country, wondered what the soldiers could expect during peace if they were treated so shabbily while they still bore arms, and finally came to his point: the Army should not disband until it had obtained justice. Dismayed and alarmed at this call for insurgency by the military, Washington denounced it in General Orders the next morning.

Head Quarters Newburgh
Tuesday March 11th. 1783.

The Commander in Chief having heard that a General meeting of the officers of the Army was proposed to be held this day at the Newbuilding in an ananommous paper which was circulated yesterday by some unknown person conceives (altho he is fully persuaded that the good sense of the officers would induce them to pay very little attention to such an irregular invitation) his duty as well as the reputation and true interest of the Army requires his disapprobation of such disorderly proceedings, at the same time he requests the General & Field officers with one officer from each company and a proper representation of the Staff of the Army will assemble at 12 o'clock on Saturday next at the Newbuilding to hear the report of the Committee of the Army to Congress.

After mature deliberation they will devise what further measures ought to be adopted as most rational and best calculated to attain the just and important object in view. The senior officer in Rank present will be pleased to preside and report the result of the Deliberations to the Commander in Chief.

Washington's action headed off the mass meeting of officers, but another Newburgh Address appeared. Its principal argument was that Washington, by the tone of his General Orders, had indicated that he was actually on the side of the insurgents. It became plain to Washington that he would have to appear in person at a new meeting scheduled for March 15. The meeting hall, which Washington referred to as the Newbuilding, was a large structure built by the troops some weeks earlier for use as an assembly and dance hall. It was filled to overflowing with officers, some plainly resentful. After he apologized for finding it necessary to address them and explained that he had put his thoughts in writing because the occasion was too important for misunderstandings, Washington began to read.

[Newburgh, March 15, 1783]

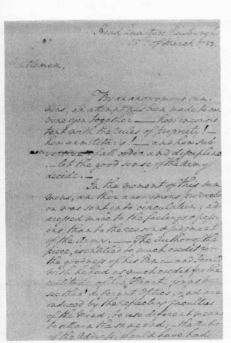

By an anonymous Summons, an attempt has been made to convene you together; how inconsistent with the rules of propriety, how unmilitary, and how subversive of all good order & discipline, let the good sense of the Army decide.

In the moment of this summons, another anonymous production was sent into circulation, addressed more to the feelings and passions, than to the reason and judgment of the Army. The author of the Piece, is entitled to much credit for the goodness of his pen, and I could wish he had as much credit for the rectitude of his heart; for as Men see through different optics, and are induced by the reflecting faculties of the mind, to use different means to obtain the same end, the author of the Address, should have had more Charity, than to mark for suspicion the Man who should recommend moderation & longer forbearance, or in other words, who should not think as he thinks, and act as he advises.

But he had another plan in view, in which candour and liberality of sentiment, regard to justice, and love of Country, have no part; and he was right to insinuate the darkest suspicions, to effect the blackest designs.

That the address is drawn with great art, and is designed to answer the most insidious purposes, that it is calculated to impress the mind, with an idea of premeditated injustice in the Sovereign power of the United States, and rouse all those Resentments which must unavoidably flow from such a belief, that the secret mover of this scheme (whoever he may be) intended to take advantage of the passions, while they were warmed, by the recollection of past distresses without giving time for cool, deliberate thinking, and that composure of mind which is so necessary to give dignity and Stability to measures is rendered too obvious, by the mode of conducting the business to need other proof, than a reference to the proceeding.

Thus much, Gentlemen, I have thought it incumbent on me to observe to you, to shew upon what principles I opposed the irregular & hasty meeting, which was proposed to have been held on Tuesday last and not because I wanted a disposition to give you every opportunity consistent with your own honour, and the dignity of the Army, to make known your grievances. If my conduct heretofore has not evinced to you that I have been a faithful friend to the Army, my declaration of it at this time would be equally unavailing and improper: but as I was among the first who embarked in the cause of our Common Country; as I have never left your side one moment, but when called from you on public duty; as I have been the constant companion & witness of your distresses, and not among the last to feel and acknowledge your Merits; as I have ever considered my own Military reputation as inseparably connected with that of the Army; as my heart has ever expanded with joy, when I have heard its praises, and my indignation has arisen when the mouth of detraction has been opened against it, it can scarcely be supposed, at this late state of War, that I am indifferent to its interests. But how are they to be promoted? The way is plain says the anonymous addresser, if War continues, remove into the unsettled Country; there establish yourselves, and leave an ungrateful Country to defend

At the end of the war Washington submitted his expense account to Congress, including this last item of Mrs. Washington's travel expenses.

*Discharge of a sergeant from the
American Army signed by Washington*

itself. But who are they to defend. Our Wives, our Children, our farms and other property which we leave behind us? Or, in the State of hostile seperation, are we to take the two first (the latter cannot be removed) to perish in a Wilderness with hunger, cold and nakedness? If Peace takes place, never sheath your swords (says he) untill you have obtained full and ample justice. This dreadful alternative, of either deserting our Country, in the extremest hour of distress, or turning our Arms against it (which is the apparent object, unless Congress can be compelled into instant compliance) has something so shocking in it, that humanity revolts at the idea. My God! what can this writer have in view by recommending such measures? Can he be a friend to the Army? Can he be a friend to this Country? Rather is he not an insidious foe? some emissary, perhaps from New York, plotting the ruin of both, by sowing the seeds of discord and separation between the Civil and Military Powers of the Continent, and what a compliment does he pay to our understandings, when he recommends measures, in either alternative, impracticable in their nature. . . .

I cannot . . . in justice to my own belief, & what I have great reason to conceive is the intention of Congress, conclude this address, without giving it, as my decided opinion, that that Honourable body entertain exalted sentiments of the services of the Army, and from a full conviction of its merits and sufferings, will do it complete justice. That their endeavours to discover and establish funds for this purpose, have been unwearied, and will not cease, till they have succeeded, I have no doubt; but like all other large bodies, where there is a variety of different interests to reconcile, their deliberations are slow. Why then should we distrust them? and in consequence of that distrust, adopt measures, which may cast a shade over that glory, which has been so justly acquired and tarnish the reputation of an Army, which is celebrated through all Europe, for its fortitude and Patriotism, and for what is this done; to bring the object we seek nearer? No! most certainly, in my opinion it will cast it at a greater distance. . . .

While I give you these assurances, and pledge myself in the most unequivocal manner, to exert whatever ability I am possessed of, in your favour, let me entreat you Gentlemen, on your part not to take any measures, which, viewed in the calm light of reason, will lessen the dignity, and sully the Glory you have hitherto maintained. Let me request you to rely on the plighted faith of your Country, and place a full confidence in the purity of the intentions of Congress, that previous to your dissolution as an Army, they will cause all your [accounts] to be fairly liquidated, as directed in their Resolutions which were published to you two days ago, and that they will adopt the most effectual measures in their power, to render ample justice to you for your faithful and meritorious services. And let me conjure you, in the name of our Common Country, as you value your own sacred honour, as you respect the rights of humanity, and as you regard the Military and National character of America, to express your utmost horror and detestation of the Man, who wishes, under any specious pretences, to overturn the liberties of our Country, and who wickedly attempts to open the flood-gates of Civil discord, and deluge our rising Empire in blood. By thus determining, and thus acting, you will pursue the plain and direct road to the attainment of your wishes; you will defeat the insidious designs of our Enemies, who are compelled to resort from open force to secret artifice; you will give one more distinguished proof of unexampled patriotism and patient virtue, rising superior to the pressure of the most complicated sufferings; and you will, by the dignity of your conduct, afford occasion for posterity to say, when speaking of the glorious example you have exhibited to Mankind, had this day been wanting, the World had never seen the last stage of perfection, to which human nature is capable of attaining.

It was an effective exhortation, but the resentment of many officers ran deep, and the intriguers might well have swayed the meeting if Washington had left the hall at the end of his address. Instead, he took a paper from his pocket, saying he would read a letter from a member of Congress to show what the delegates were trying to do for the Army. He began reading, faltered over the cramped text, and then drew out a pair of spectacles as his audience watched in surprise. Only recently had he been fitted for glasses; few of his officers had seen him wearing them. "Gentlemen," he said as he hooked them behind his ears, "you must pardon me. I have grown gray in your service and now find myself growing blind." The simple act and words did more than all eloquence could have achieved and brought tears to the eyes of many in his audience. The officers voted overwhelmingly their confidence in Congress, restated their patriotism, and dissociated themselves from the Newburgh Addresses.

On March 12 a ship at last brought the provisional peace treaty of November 30. But it was an anticlimax; the treaty did not become effective until France and Britain also agreed on peace terms. Word of that happy event came two weeks later, and so Britain and her former Colonies were at peace after eight years—although the formal end to hostilities had to await ratification of the final treaty by Congress. Washington announced that action in General Orders.

Friday April 18th. 1783.

The Commander in Chief orders the Cessation of Hostilities between the United States of America and the King of Great Britain to be publickly proclaimed tomorrow at 12 o'clock at the Newbuilding, and that the Proclamation which will be communicated herewith, be read tomorrow evening at the head of every regiment & corps of the army—After which the Chaplains with the several Brigades will render thanks to almighty God for all his mercies, particularly for his over ruling the wrath of man to his own glory, and causing the rage of war to cease amongst the nations.

Altho the proclamation before alluded to, extends only to the prohibition of hostilities and not to the annunciation of a general peace, yet it must afford the most rational and sincere satisfaction to every benevolent mind—as it puts a period to a long and doubtful contest, stops the effusion of human blood, opens the prospect to a more splendid scene, and like another morning star, promises the approach of a brighter day then hath hitherto illuminated the Western Hemisphere. On such a happy day, a day which is the harbinger of Peace, a day which compleats the eighth year of the war, it would be ingratitude not to rejoice!—it would be insensibility not to participate in the general felicity.

The Commander in Chief far from endeavoring to stifle the feelings of Joy in his own bosom, offers his most cordial Congratulations on the occasion to all the Officers of every denomination—to all the Troops of the United States in General, and in particular to those gallant and persevering men who had resolved to defend the rights of their invaded country so long as the war should continue—For these are the men who ought to

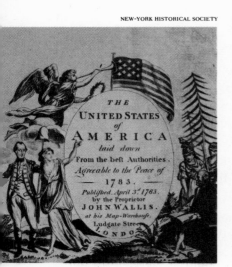

Cartouche from a map of the United States "laid down from the best Authorities Agreeable to the Peace of 1783"; Washington stands at left.

be considered as the [pride] and boast of the American Army; And, who crowned with well earned laurels, may soon withdraw from the field of Glory, to the more tranquil walks of civil life.

Congress, eager to get soldiers off the public payroll, ordered Washington to furlough men even though the drafting and ratification of a definitive peace treaty would not be completed for many months. The Commander in Chief had insisted that men leaving the Army should do so with at least three months' pay in their pockets, but there was no money to make good on the promise, and appeals to the states brought in nothing. The best that Robert Morris, financial wizard of the Revolution, could propose, was that each man be given a note calling on his home state to give him three months' pay. Morris had difficulty even finding money to buy paper on which to print the notes, and many veterans straggled home bearing only their muskets, which Congress had handsomely voted to give them as a parting gift. Disaffection was in the air, and trouble came. Washington wrote to the president of Congress on first hearing of it.

Head Qurs. Newburgh
Evening June 24th. 1783.

It was not until 3 O'Clock this Afternoon that I had the first intimation of the infamous and outrageous Mutiny of a part of the Pennsylvania Troops, it was then I received your Excellency's Letter of the 21st. by your Express, and agreeable to your request contained in it, I instantly ordered three complete Regiments of Infantry and a Detachment of Artillery to be put in motion as soon as possible; this Corps (which you will observe by the Return is a large proportion of our whole force) will consist of upwards of 1500 Effectives. As all the Troops who composed this gallant little Army, as well those who were furloughed, as those who remain in service, are Men of tried fidelity I could not have occasion to make any choice of Corps, and I have only to regret, that there exists a necessity, they should be employed on so disagreeable a service. I dare say, however, they will on this and all other occasions perform their duty as brave and faithful Soldiers.

Silhouette of Robert Morris

Washington was deeply chagrined by mutiny in an army whose loyalty he had defended, but he pointed out that the trouble-makers were "Recruits and Soldiers of a day," most of them having been

in the service for only a brief time and having borne little of the burden
of the war in comparison with the main Army, which had not revolted. He
sent some fifteen hundred troops, almost the entire remaining Army, to take
care of what he euphemistically called "the unhappy Irregularities of the
troops in Philadelphia"; then, left in Newburgh with little to do, he informed
Congress, "I have resolved to wear away a little time in performing a tour
to the northward." Starting on July 18, he visited Saratoga, Lake George,
Lake Champlain, Ticonderoga, and other places made famous by the war
in the North. With the war receding, he was less interested in the strategic
value of the country than in its land values, and he bid on at least three
tracts of upper New York State land. He was back in Newburgh on August
6, to discover Martha ill with a fever and to find a letter from Congress sum-
moning him to Princeton, New Jersey, where Congress had moved because
of the mutiny scare. In the latter part of August, Washington moved his
headquarters to a farmhouse at Rocky Hill near Princeton. He was entertained, spent much time tying up loose ends left by the disbanding of the
Army, and conferred with Congress on the size and organization of a peacetime Army. Martha returned to Virginia, while he finished his business with
Congress. By the middle of November Washington was at West Point,
replying briefly to a letter from Sir Guy Carleton.

> West Point, Novr. 14th. 1783.
> I had the honor yesterday, to receive, by Major Beckwith,
> your Excellency's favor of the 12th. To day I will see the
> Governor of this State, & concert with him the necessary
> arrangements for taking possession of the City of New
> York & other Posts mentioned in your Letter, at the
> times therein specified For the information of which,
> you will please to accept my thanks.

General Carleton had announced that he would evacuate
Manhattan, Long Island, and Staten Island over a period of two or three
days beginning November 21. There were postponements of a few days,
but at last it was accomplished, and Washington led the small remnant of
his army into New York while the British boarded ship. His report to the
president of Congress was of the utmost brevity.

> New York 3d. Decem. 1783.
> In my last Letter to your Excellency, I had the honor
> to acquaint Congress with the arrangement Sir Guy
> Carleton had made for the evacuation of New York on
> the 23d. ulto. I have now to inform you, that the em-
> barkation was postponed two days on account of the
> badness of the weather.
> On the 25th. Novr. the British Troops left this City,

First and last pages of General Washington's farewell address to the Army, his last official document as commander, November 2, 1783

& a Detachment of our army marched into it. The civil power was immediately put in possession, & I have the happiness to assure you that the most perfect regularity & good order have prevailed ever since; on which pleasing events I congratulate your Excellency & Congress.

At noon on December 4, Washington met for the last time with some of his officers in New York's Fraunces Tavern. Only a few were there: three major generals, a single brigadier general, a colonel or two, a number of lower grades. Washington tried to eat something from the table of food but could not manage, then filled a glass with wine and signaled the others to do the same. "With a heart full of love and gratitude, I now take leave of you," he said in a choked voice. "I most devoutly wish that your later days may be as prosperous and happy as your former ones have been glorious and honorable." They drank in silence, then Washington asked each to come to him. Starting with Henry Knox they came, and he embraced each without speaking. Then still too moved to speak, he walked out of the tavern and to the waterfront, where he boarded a waiting boat to be rowed to the New Jersey shore. He was in a hurry, but as he rode south he had to pause to receive the formal expressions of esteem of citizens and politicians: the people of New Brunswick, the legislature of New Jersey, the merchants of Philadelphia, the Executive Council of Pennsylvania, many others. And to each he had to make an appropriate response, as in his remarks at Baltimore.

LIBRARY OF CONGRESS

Washington leaving New York

Baltimore December 18th. 1783.

The acceptable manner in which you have wellcomed my arrival in the Town of Baltimore, and the happy terms in which you have communicated the congratulations of its Inhabitants, lay me under the greatest obligations.

Be pleased, Gentlemen, to receive this last public acknowledgement for the repeated instances of your politeness, and to believe, it is my earnest wish that the Commerce, the Improvements, and universal prosperity of this flourishing Town, may, if possible, encrease with even more rapidity than they have hitherto done.

He finally reached Annapolis, Maryland, to which Congress had taken its deliberations early in November. There were some odds and ends of Army business: several officers had asked to be recommended for service in any peacetime Army that might be formed; an officer wounded and partially disabled in 1776 had asked Washington to present his petition for a pension. There were three days and nights of dinners and balls, and then Congress formally received the Commander in Chief. He was escorted into the chamber, bowed, and read a statement of his purpose in being there.

Annapolis 23d. Decr. 1783.

The great events on which my resignation depended having at length taken place, I have now the honor of offering my sincere congratulations to Congress, & of presenting myself before them to surrender into their hands the trust committed to me, and to claim the indulgence of retiring from the service of my Country.

Happy in the confirmation of our Independence & Sovereignty, & pleased with the opportunity afforded the United States of becoming a respectable Nation, I resign with satisfaction the appointment I accepted with diffidence; a diffidence in my abilities to accomplish so arduous a task, which however was superseded by a confidence in the rectitude of our cause, the support

237

of the Supreme power of the Union, and the patronage of Heaven.

The Successful termination of the War has verified the most sanguine expectations, & my gratitude for the interposition of Providence, & the assistance I have received from my Countrymen, encreases with every review of the momentous Contest.

While I repeat my obligations to the army in general, I should do injustice to my own feelings not to acknowledge in this place the peculiar services & distinguished merits of the Gentlemen who have been attached to my person during the war. It was impossible the choice of confidential officers to compose my family, should have been more fortunate; permit me, Sir, to recommend in particular, those who have continued in Service to the present moment, as worthy of the favorable notice & patronage of Congress.

I consider it an indispensable duty to close this last solemn act of my official life, by commending the interests of our dearest Country to the protection of Almighty God, & those who have the superintendence of them, to his holy keeping.

Having now finished the work assigned me, I retire from the great Theatre of Action; & bidding an affectionate farewell to this August Body under whose orders I have so long acted, I here offer my Commission & take my leave of all the employments of public life.

At the close of his address Washington drew from his pocket the commission he had received in 1775 and handed it to the president of Congress. He was no longer Commander in Chief but simply George Washington, Virginia planter. His horse was waiting when he left Congress shortly after noon. He rode hard the rest of that day and most of the next, and turned into the driveway of Mount Vernon well before the early winter twilight of Christmas Eve had fallen.

Broadside of a circular letter from Washington to the governors of the states on resigning his command

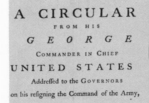

A Picture Portfolio

A Lifetime Haven

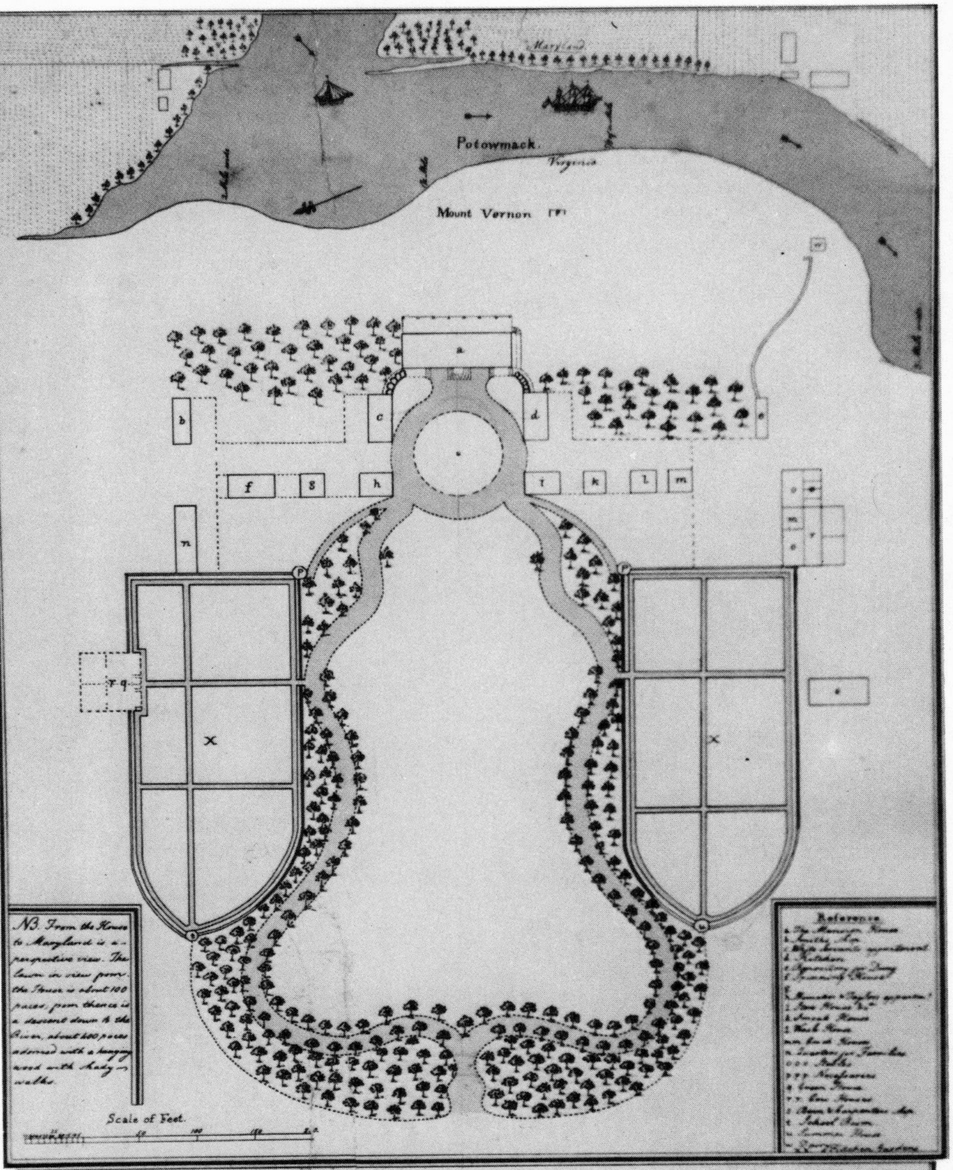

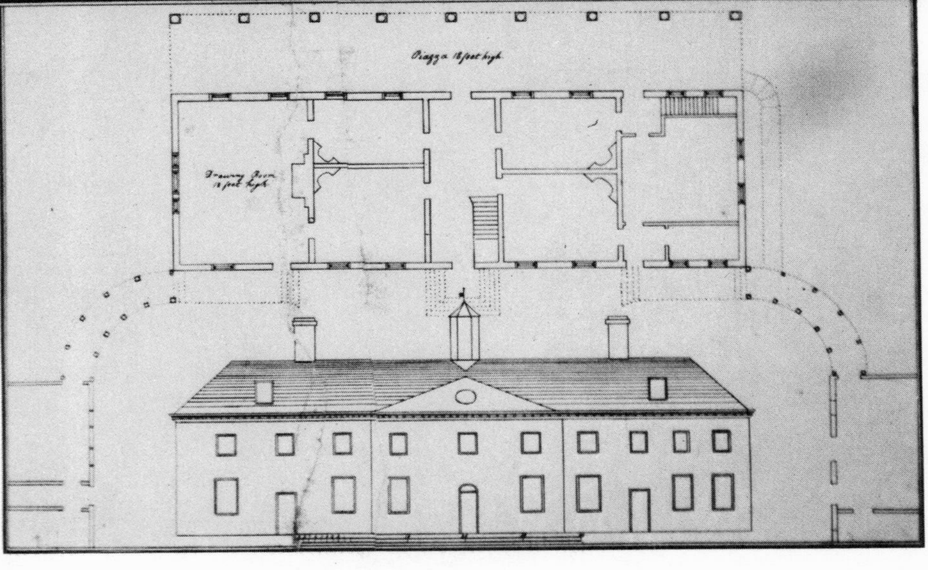

"THE SIMPLICITY OF RURAL LIFE"

George Washington first saw the quiet acres of what was to become Mount Vernon, sloping down to the broad Potomac (below), when his father moved the family there from a farm farther south. He was three years old. The plantation was not to be his until some years after the untimely death, in 1751, of his older half-brother and "best friend" Lawrence (right), who had himself inherited it. Mount Vernon blossomed under Washington's meticulous and loving supervision. The plan at left shows the handsome layout of the house and grounds in 1787. Despite its comfort, Washington, in extending an invitation to a European visitor, offered only "the simplicity of rural life."

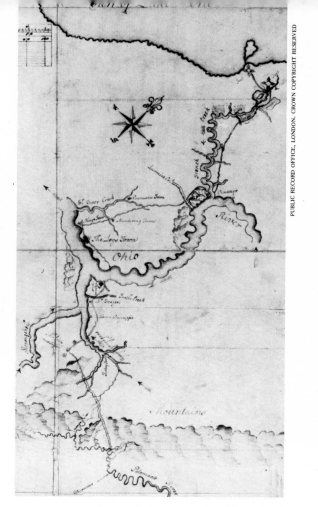

A RUGGED MANHOOD

Before Lawrence died, George, not yet twenty-one and with no qualifications except that of a surveyor (above), applied for his brother's job as Adjutant General of Virginia. And when Virginia was divided into four districts, he was appointed one of the four adjutants with the rank of major. Thus commenced the military career that was to bring him fame. Charles Willson Peale's portrait (left) shows him in the uniform he had designed for his regiment; he was described by a friend of those early manhood days as "straight as an Indian, measuring six feet two inches in his stockings and weighing 175 pounds.... His movements and gestures are graceful, his walk majestic, and he is a splendid horseman." Almost immediately he was sent by Virginia's governor to determine the strength of the French forces at the Forks of the Ohio. His own map of this mission (right, above) indicates his rigorous route. That he kept up both his surveying and mapmaking is attested by the survey map he made of Mount Vernon in 1766 (right).

The George Washington Atlas, WASHINGTON, D.C., 1932. N.Y. PUBLIC LIBRARY

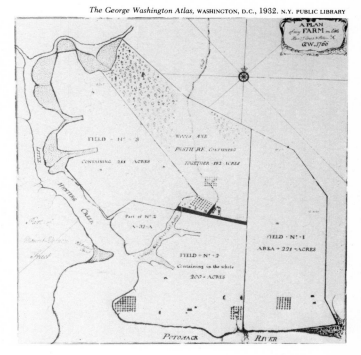

AN ENDURING RELATIONSHIP

Washington's marriage to the widow Martha Dandridge Custis, when both were twenty-seven, was—like the house to which he brought her—a lifetime haven. Seen in a portrait the year before her marriage (left, above), Martha was a plump and tiny woman, barely five feet tall. She ran the large establishment at Mount Vernon, viewed from the west front in this 1792 painting, with skill and good humor, and she made it into a home to which Washington always longed to return. If there was any dark side to their married life, it was in the fact that they had no children together. Martha had brought to the marriage two small children (left). Overindulged by both mother and stepfather, "Jackie" was described later as "exeedingly indolent." "Patsy," an epileptic, died at seventeen.

245

SOUTHERN HOSPITALITY

The Washingtons enjoyed company, and throughout the pleasant years at Mount Vernon there was always a great deal of it. In the 1780's Washington conceived of the long porch with its graceful two-story pillars as a splendid spot from which to watch for guests arriving by boat and to entertain them. Lafayette, a frequent and favorite house guest, is seen below in an idealized painting, chatting with his adopted father, while Martha, her grandchildren, servants, and dogs complete the tranquil scene. The architect Benjamin Latrobe visited Mount Vernon in 1796 and drew the family at tea one afternoon on the spacious piazza—a view complete with Washington peering through a telescope between the lofty pillars (right). He then sketched the aging Virginia planter's profile (right, below) "while he was looking to discover a distant vessel in the Potomac, in which he expected some of his friends from Alexandria."

Sketch of General Washington, Stolen at Mount Vernon while he was looking to discover a distant Vessel in the Po-towmac; in which he expec-ted some of his friends from Alexandria.

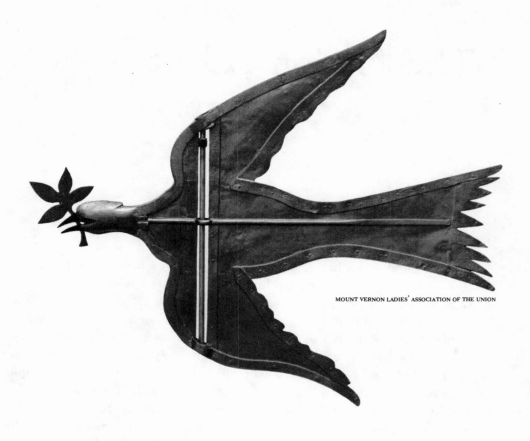

A CROWNING DOVE

Washington suffered two long and painful periods of separation from his beloved Mount Vernon. First were the years of the Revolution, when he took no leave of any kind and saw his home and four unknown grandchildren for the first time in seven years on his way south to Yorktown. The second, and perhaps harder, wrench came after an all-too-satisfying respite when his country called upon him to become its first President in 1789, as commemorated in the painting by Frederick Kemmelmeyer at left. Once again, as Washington confided to his diary, "I bade adieu to Mount Vernon, to private life, and to domestic felicity, and with a mind oppressed with more anxious and painful sensation than I have words to express, set out...." Before this last personal sacrifice, Washington had crowned his lovely house with a Dove of Peace weathervane (above) that was to welcome him home for good in 1797, after two strenuous terms of office devoted to setting the nation on the road to its destiny.

249

Chapter **8**

The Nation Adrift

After eight and a half years as Commander in Chief, when it had often seemed that few besides himself much cared whether the war was won or lost, Washington was at last free to do the things he had so long dreamed of. He hunted fox, he visited old neighbors, he took stock of the condition of his fields and buildings, he made plans for the future. Lund Washington had managed Mount Vernon probably to the best of his ability, but Lund was no hand at bookkeeping, and Mount Vernon had become a large operation. Its lands extended ten miles along the Potomac and inland as much as four miles. Besides the main, or mansion house, establishment, which amounted to a community in itself, there were five smaller dependent farms. Plantation operations included a flour mill, a ferry, looms, carpentry and blacksmith shops, a fishery, later a distillery. There were herds of horses and cattle, flocks of sheep, and an unknown number of swine, which ran wild in the woods. To work this huge establishment, Washington had two hundred or more slaves, both black and white overseers, artisans, and technicians of one kind or another. Lund also had an aversion to travel, and thus had not collected rents from tenants on Washington's lands in the West. Furthermore, Washington's papers were in disorder; they had become jumbled during several hurried removals on alarms that British raiders were coming, and so Washington had no way of determining just where his accounts stood. But he did know that he had lost a great deal of money. Those things would have to be taken care of in good time. First, almost immediately on arriving home, he turned his attention to the house. In 1774 he had added a south wing; in 1776 he had had Lund add a balancing north wing, whose interior was still unfinished. He wrote to Samuel Vaughan of London, then visiting in Philadelphia, for advice on one point.

Mot. Vernon 14th. Jany. 1784.

The torpid state into which the severity of the season has thrown things—the interruption of the post, occasioned by bad roads, and frozen rivers—& a want of other conveyance consequent thereof, must plead my excuse for not thanking you sooner for the polite attention you were pleased to shew me, while I was in Philada.; & for the friendly offers you obligingly made me, before I left that city. But though my acknowledgements of them come late, I pray you to be persuaded that they are not less sincere, nor are they less gratefully offered on that account.

Colo. Humphreys (one of my late Aid de Camp's) who accompanied me to Virginia, & is now on his return home, will do me the favor of presenting this letter to you, & of handing Mr. Higgins's observations on Cements, which you were pleased to lend me, & from which I have extracted such parts as I mean to carry into practice.

I found my new room, towards the completion of which you kindly offered your house-joiner, so far advanced in the wooden part of it, the Doors, Windows & floors being done, as to render it unnecessary to remove your workman with his Tools (the distance being great) to finish the other parts; especially as I incline to do it in [stucco], (which, if I understood you right, is the present taste in England), & more especially as you may find occasion for him in the execution of your own purposes as the Spring advances. And now my good sir, as I have touched upon the business of stuccoing, permit me to ask you if the rooms with which it is encrusted are painted, generally; or are they left of the natural colour which is given by the cement made according to Mr. Higgins's mode of preparing it? And also, whether the rooms thus finished are stuccoed below the surbase (chair high) or from thence upwards only?

These are trifling questions to trouble you with, but I am sure you will have goodness enough to excuse, & answer them. Please to make a tender of my best respects to Mrs. Vaughan & the rest of the family, & accept the compliments of the season from Mrs. W——n & myself who join in expression of the pleasure we shou'd feel in seeing you under our roof.

Washington's bookplate was engraved for him in 1772 by S. Valliscure of London. The Metropolitan Museum has the original copper plate.

Although Washington might cry poverty, he did not let his debts interfere with his style of living, and not until 1787 was the north wing completed to his satisfaction; it was given over almost entirely to a two-story banqueting hall. Even while enjoying to the utmost his return to the role of Virginia country gentleman, Washington could not put aside his concern for the nation he had done so much to create. Less than a month after returning home he was writing to Benjamin Harrison, Governor of Virginia, to express himself on what could be a fatal weakness in the Government.

Mount Vernon 18th. Jany. 1784.

I have just had The pleasure to receive your letter of the 8th. For the friendly & affectionate terms in which you have welcomed my return to this Country & to private life; & for the favourable light in which you are pleased to consider, & express your sense of my past services, you have my warmest & most grateful acknowledgments.

That the prospect before us is, as you justly observe, fair, none can deny; but what use we shall make of it, is exceedingly problematical; not but that I believe, all things will come right at last; but like a young heir, come a little prematurely to a large inheritance, we shall wanton and run riot until we have brought our reputation to the brink of ruin, & then like him shall have to labor with the current of opinion when *compelled* perhaps, to do what prudence & common policy pointed out as plain as any problem in Euclid, in the first instance.

The disinclination of the individual States to yield competent powers to Congress for the Fœderal Government, their unreasonable jealousy of that body & of one another & the disposition which seems to pervade each, of being all-wise and all-powerful within itself, will, if there is not a change in the system be our downfal as a Nation. This is as clear to me as the A, B, C; & I think we have opposed Great Britain, & have arrived at the present state of peace & independency, to very little purpose, if we cannot conquer our own prejudices. The powers of Europe begin to see this, & our newly acquired friends the British, are already & professedly acting upon this ground; & wisely too, if we are determined to persevere in our folly. They know that individual opposition to their measures is futile, & *boast* that we are not sufficiently united as a Nation to give a general one! Is not the indignity alone, of this declaration, while we are in the very act of peace-making & conciliation, sufficient to stimulate us to vest more extensive & adequate powers in the sovereign of these United States? For my

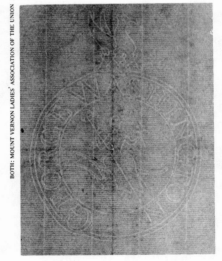

A watermark on Washington's stationery shows Britannia holding a sprig of foliage and sitting on a plough.

Decorative motifs from a china set, derived from the Society of the Cincinnati, the select group of Revolutionary officers, headed by George Washington

own part, altho' I am returned to, & am now mingled with the class of private citizens, & like them must suffer all the evils of a Tyranny, or of too great an extension of foederal powers; I have no fears arising from this source; in my mind, but I have many, & powerful ones indeed which predict the worst consequences from a half-starved, limping Government, that appears to be always moving upon crutches, & tottering at every step. Men, chosen as the Delegates in Congress are, cannot officially be dangerous—they depend upon the breath—nay, they are so much the creatures of the people, under the present Constitution, that they can have no views (which could possibly be carried into execution) nor any interests, distinct from those of their constituents. My political creed therefore is, to be wise in the choice of Delegates—support them like Gentlemen while they are our representatives—give them competent powers for all federal purposes—support them in the due exercise thereof—& lastly, to compel them to close attendance in Congress during their delegation. These things under the present mode for, & termination of elections, aided by annual instead of constant Sessions, would, or I am exceedingly mistaken, make us one of the most wealthy, happy, respectable & powerful Nations, that ever inhabited the terrestrial Globe—without them, we shall in my opinion soon be every thing which is the direct reverse of them.

I shall look for you, in the first part of next month, with such other friends as may incline to accompany you, with great pleasure, being with best respects to Mrs. Harrison, in which Mrs. Washington joins me....

Despite his continuing deep interest in the course of the nation, there is little doubt that Washington was quite convinced that his days in public life were over. A number of his letters echo this conviction. One such went to the Marquis de Chastellux, French philosopher and writer, who had been a major general in Rochambeau's army during the war and had become a close friend to Washington.

Mount Vernon 1st. Feby. 1784.
I have had the honor to receive your favor of the 23d. of August from L'Orient. I hope this Letter will find you in the circle of your friends at Paris, well recovered from the fatigues of your long & wearisome inspection on

In 1784 Washington was admitted to membership in Charleston's library.

The Order of the Cincinnati, worn by Society members

the frontiers of the Kingdom.

I am at length become a private citizen of America, on the banks of the Patowmac; where under my own Vine & my own Fig tree — free from the bustle of a camp & the intrigues of a Court, I shall view the busy world, "in the calm light of mild philosophy" — & with that serenity of mind, which the Soldier in his pursuit of glory, & the Statesman of fame, have not time to enjoy. I am not only retired from all public employments; but I am retiring within myself & shall tread the private walks of life with heartfelt satisfaction.

After seeing New York evacuated by the British Forces on the 25th. of Novembr., & civil Government established in the city, I repaired to Congress, & surrendered into their hands, all my powers, with my Commission on the 23d. of Decemr. and arrived at this Cottage on Christmas eve, where I have been close locked up ever since in Frost & Snow.

Actually, when Washington wrote to Chastellux, he still had not found the serenity about which he wrote. For years his life had been the life of the army camp, and he had lived by its rhythms, from the first drumbeat of reveille in the morning to the sound of tattoo at night. Each morning during those years he had waked to face seemingly insoluble problems: could he feed his men, where could he obtain clothing for them, dare he face the British with his inferior numbers, would he even have an army in two or three months? In a letter to Major General Henry Knox, soon to be appointed Secretary at War, he revealed how long it had taken him to stop thinking as Commander in Chief.

> Mount Vernon 20th. Feby. 1784.
>
> The bad weather, & the great care which the Post riders take of themselves, prevented your Letters of the 3d. & 9th. of last month from getting to my hands 'till the 10th. of this. Setting off next morning for Fredericksburg to pay my duty to an aged mother, & not returning 'till yesterday, will be admitted I hope, as a sufficient apology for my silence until now.
>
> I am much obliged by the trouble you have taken to report the state of the Garrison & Stores, together with the disposition of the Troops at West-Point, to me; and think the allowance of rations, or subsistence money, to such Officers as could not retire at that inclement season, was not only perfectly humane, but perfectly just also—and that it must appear so to Congress....
>
> I am just beginning to experience that ease, & freedom from public cares which, however desireable, takes some time to realize; for strange as it may seem, it is never the less true, that it was not 'till lately, I could get the better of my usual custom of ruminating as soon as I waked in the morning, on the business of the ensuing day —& of my surprize at finding, after having revolved many things in my mind, that I was no longer a public Man, or had any thing to do with public transactions.
>
> I feel now however, as I conceive a wearied traveller must do, who after treading many a painful step with a heavy burthen on his shoulders, is eased of the latter, having reached the haven to which all the former were directed; & from his house-top is looking back & tracing with an eager Eye, the meanders by which he escaped the Quicksands & mires which lay in his way; & into which, none but the all-powerful guide, & great dispencer of human events could have prevented his falling.

The Marquis de Chastellux

INDEPENDENCE NATIONAL HISTORICAL PARK COLLECTION

The problems of having to hold together and lead an army were, of course, replaced by other knotty questions. Washington found it difficult to put the affairs of Mount Vernon in order because of the confused state of his papers. He wrote here and there seeking information that would help him get some grip on things, especially the status of his land holdings in the West. A letter to John Stephenson, a business acquaintance, was a masterpiece in combining condolences, a request for information, and a dun for payment of a debt.

Fredericksg. 13th. Feby. 1784.

After condoling with you on the unhappy fate of your Brother William, which I do very sincerely; & upon the Death of your brother Vale., I should be glad to get a copy from both their Books, or Memos. of the accounts as they stand between us; which are of long standing, & I fear not a little intricate. I write to you Sir, because I do not know (if you are not one yourself) who are the Executors or Administrators of those deceased Gentlemen. There were also some Land transactions, in partnership & otherwise between your Brother William & me, which I wish to have an account of. If it is in your power therefore, or you should have come across any warrants, Entries, Memoms. or papers relative to this business, which can give me insight into the matter, I shall be much obliged to you for the information.

There is also a Bond in my possession from your deceased brother Hugh (for whose Death I am also very much concerned) with your name, or that of your brother James's to it (I am not certain which as I am from home, & have accidentally met with this good and direct opportunity) for a Sum of money due to me from your Fathers Estate; which I wish to know when it can be settled & paid, as the situation of my private Affairs makes it absolutely necessary to close my Accounts & to receive payment as soon as possible.

Fielding Lewis, Washington's nephew

When Washington's nephew Fielding Lewis, son of his sister Betty, wrote asking for a loan, Washington's answer was definite and a bit sharp.

Mount Vernon 27th. Feby. 1784.

Dear Fieldg.:

You very much mistake my circumstances when you suppose me in a condition to advance money. I made no money from my Estate during the nine years I was absent from it, & brought none home with me. Those who owed me, for the most part, took advantage of the depreciation & paid me off with six pence in the pound. Those to whom I was indebted, I have yet to pay, without other means, if they will not wait, than selling part of my Estate; or distressing those who were too honest to take advantage of the tender Laws to quit scores with me.

This relation of my circumstances, which is a true one, is alone sufficient (without adding that my living under the best oeconomy I can use, must unavoidably be expensive,) to convince you of my inability to advance money.

I have heard with pleasure that you are industrious. Convince people by your mode of living that you are sober & frugal also; and I persuade myself your creditors will grant you every indulgence they can. It would be no small inducement to me, if it should ever be in my power, to assist you. Your Father's advice to you in his Letter of the 8th. of October 1778 is worthy the goodness of his own heart, & very excellent to follow; if I could say anything to enforce it, it should not be wanting.

I shall always be glad to see you here. Your Aunt joins me in best wishes & I am, &ca.

P.S. There was a great space between the 23d. of September 1778, when you were called upon by your Father for a specific list of your Debts, & his death: how happen'd it that in all that time you did not comply with his request? And what do they amount to now? His Letters to you are returned, & I hope will get safe to hand.

Tobias Lear, a portrait by Sharples

In time Washington's records were put in order. During 1786 he hired as his secretary Tobias Lear, a New Hampshire Yankee, who was to serve him through his first term as President and again during the last year of his life. Lear performed the small miracle of reorganizing Washington's papers. The result was not encouraging; his records showed that Washington had lost some ten thousand pounds sterling, partly because many of his debtors had taken advantage of wartime inflation to pay him off in near-worthless money, partly because most of the debts still owing him had become uncollectible. Mount Vernon was constantly bulging with visitors, some of them friends Washington welcomed, most of them strangers. Many were only travelers caught by the night, for the public road to Alexandria ran nearby, and there was no inn. A few were people who had simply come to see the famous man, to gawk like spectators at a zoo. There were painters and sculptors to immortalize him on canvas or in marble, and would-be historians and biographers wanting to look at his papers. His diary lists only a fraction of the visitors: those who were friends or who came with recommendations from friends or were notable for some reason. He was occasionally exasperated by strangers demanding favors.

Monday, 10th [October, 1785]. A Mr. Jno. Lowe, on his way to Bishop Seabury [Samuel Seabury, first

Protestant Episcopal Bishop of Connecticut] for Ordination, called & dined here. Could not give him more than a general certificate founded on information, respecting his character; having no acquaintance with him, nor any desire to open a Corrispondence with the *new* ordained Bishop.

The boldness and presumption of some of these self-invited guests is past understanding. Because Washington was a public figure, he was considered fair game for all manner of outrageous demands from those who happened by Mount Vernon.

> *Saturday, 5th* [November, 1785]. ...Mr. Robert Washington of Chotanck, Mr. Lund Washington & Mr. Lawrence Washington dined here, as did Colo. Gilpin and Mr. Noah Webster. The 4 first went away afterwards. The last stayed all Night. In the afternoon a Mr. Lee came here to sollicit Charity for his Mother who represented herself, as having nine children — a bad husband — and no support. He also stayed the Evening.

His account book for the date shows that Washington gave this dubious beggar the generous sum of two pounds, eight shillings. There is no way of knowing how often Washington was taken advantage of by charlatans. Probably most of the uninvited were just who they claimed to be — but not always.

> *Sunday, 19th* [March, 1786]. ... A Gentleman calling himself the Count de Cheize D'arteignan Officer of the French Guards came here to dinner; but bringing no letters of introduction, nor any authentic testimonials of his being either; I was at a loss how to receive, or treat him. He stayed dinner and the evening.

The count, of whom Washington continued to be suspicious, remained for two days, then went on. He was obviously a fraud, for the French army lists of that day contain no such name. Most of these visitors had horses that had to be stabled and fed at Washington's expense; many had servants who also drew on the food resources of the plantation. Washington once said that Mount Vernon could be compared to "a well-resorted tavern." He fed his guests generously, and they always joined the Washington family for the midday meal. The table was almost always filled, often with a dozen or more: family, friends, and strangers. As a Virginia gentleman, Washington would accept no pay, not even from chance travelers caught at his door by storm or nightfall. Besides the visitors who came to his door, he received endless letters asking for favors, endorsement of books, a kind word about limping odes dedicated to him, and the like. He wrote to David Humphreys, his wartime aide-de-camp, complaining about the endless demands on his time and patience.

> Mount Vernon, February 7, 1785.
>
> My dear Humphreys:
>
> In my last, by the Marquis de la Fayette, I gave you reason to believe that when I was more at leizure, you should receive a long letter from me; however agreeable this might be to my wishes, the period it is to be feared, will never arrive. I can with truth assure you, that at no period of the war have I been obliged to write half as much as I now do, from necessity. I have been enquiring for sometime past, for a person in the character of Secretary or clerk to live with me [the position eventually filled by Tobias Lear]; but hitherto unsuccessfully. What with letters (often of an unmeaning nature) from foreigners. Enquiries after Dick, Tom, and Harry who *may have been* in some part, or at *sometime*, in the Continental service. Letters, or certificates of service for those who want to go out of their own State. Introductions; applications for copies of Papers; references of a thousand old matters with which I *ought* not to be troubled, more than the Great Mogul, but which must receive an answer of some kind, deprive me of my usual exercise; and without relief, may be injurious to me as I already begin to feel the weight, and oppression of it in my head, and am assured by the *faculty*, if I do not change my course, I shall certainly sink under it.

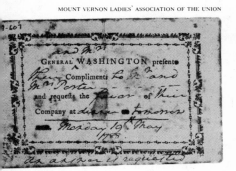

A printed invitation to dine, sent in 1788 to Mr. and Mrs. Thomas Porter, newlyweds from Alexandria

On September 1, 1784, Washington set out upon a journey to the West. He had three main purposes: to revisit his lands on the Kanawha River, which he had last seen in 1770 when he had gone down the Ohio to select bounty lands for himself and other veterans of the Fort Necessity campaign; to take care of a couple of irritating situations of long standing on his lands in Pennsylvania; and to find a point where a navigable headwater of the Potomac closely approached a navigable headwater of the Ohio. With Washington were his nephew Bushrod, Dr. James Craik, who had been his companion in 1770, and Craik's son William. By the morning of the third day they were sixty miles from Mount Vernon. Following is an extract from Washington's diary.

3d [September, 1784]. Having business to transact with my Tenants in Berkeley; & others, who were directed to meet me at my Brother's (Colo. Charles Washington's), I left Doctr. Craik and the Baggage to follow slowly, and set out myself about Sunrise for that place—where after Breakfasting at Keys' ferry I arrived about 11 Oclock—Distant abt. 17 Miles.

Colo. Warner Washington [George's uncle], Mr. Wormeley, Genl. Morgan, Mr. Snickers and many other Gentlemen came here to see me—& one object of my journey being to obtain information of the nearest and best communication between the Eastern & Western Waters; & to facilitate as much as in me lay the Inland Navigation of the Potomack; I conversed a good deal with Genl. Morgan on this subject, who said, a plan was in contemplation to extend a road from Winchester to the Western Waters to avoid if possible an interference with any other State—but I could not discover that Either himself, or others, were able to point it out with precision. He seemed to have no doubt but that the Counties of Frederk., Berkeley & Hampshire would contribute freely towards the extension of the Navigation of Potomack; as well as towards opening a road from East to West.

4th. Having finished my business with my Tenants (so far at least as partial payments could put a close to it)— and provided a waggon for the transportation of my Baggage to the Warm springs (or Town of Bath) to give relief to my Horses, which from the extrem[e] heat of the weather began to rub & gaul, I set out after dinner, and reached Captn. Stroads a Substantial farmers betwn. Opeckon Creek & Martinsburgh—distant by estimation 14 Miles from my Brothers.

Finding the Captn. an intelligent Man, and one who had been several times in the Western Country—tho' not much on the communication between the North Branch of Potomack, & the Waters of Monongahela—I held much conversation with him—the result of which, so far as it respected the object I had in view, was,—that there are two Glades which go under the denomination of the Great glades—one, on the Waters of the Yohiogany, the other on those of Cheat River; and distinguished by the name of the Sandy Creek Glades—that the Road to the first goes by the head of Patterson Creek—that from the Accts. he has had of it, it is rough;—the distance he knows not—that there is a way to the Sandy Creek Glades from the great crossing of Yohiogany (on Braddocks Road) & a very good one; but how far the Waters of Potomack above Fort Cumberland, & the Cheat river from its Mouth are navigable, he professes not to know— and equally ignorant is he of the distance between them.

He says that old Captn. Thos. Swearengen has informed him, that the navigable water of the little Kanhawa comes within a small distance of the Navigable Waters of the Monongahela, & that a good road, along a ridge, may be had between the two—& a young Man who we found at his House just (the Evening before) from Kentucke, told us, that he left the Ohio River at Weeling (Colo. David Shepperds), & in about 40 Miles came to red stone old Fort on the Monongahela, 50 Miles from its Mouth.

Two pages from the diary kept by Washington on his journey west

There was more in the same vein. Washington was pursuing the problem of finding a practical route from the Potomac to the

Ohio. The headwaters of the two rivers almost interlace in the Allegheny Mountains, but the region was still largely wilderness, and he had to depend on often conflicting accounts by local inhabitants. Washington was not moved by some sudden enthusiasm; he knew that if settlers west of the mountains were not kept tied to the East by communications and commerce, then inevitably their trade would go down the west-flowing rivers to the Mississippi, and the United States would in time become two nations. The next day he arrived at Berkeley Springs, or Bath, as it had been renamed in 1776, where he had once taken his doomed brother Lawrence and later his stepdaughter Patsy in their vain searches for health.

> *5th* [September, 1784]. Dispatched my Waggon (with the Baggage) at daylight; and at 7 Oclock followed it. Bated [Baited, stopped for food] at one Snodgrasses, on Back Creek—and dined there; About 5 Oclock P.M. we arrived at the Springs, or Town of Bath after travelling the whole day through a drizling rain, 30 Miles.

> *6th.* Remained at Bath all day and was shewed the Model of a Boat constructed by the ingenious Mr. Rumsey, for ascending rapid currents by mechanism; the principles of this were not only shewn, & fully explained to me, but to my very great satisfaction, exhibited in practice in private, under the injunction of Secresy, untill he saw the effect of an application he was about to make to the assembly of this State, for a reward.

> The model, & its operation upon the water, which had been made to run pretty swift, not only convinced me of what I before thought next to, if not quite impracticable, but that it might be turned to the greatest possible utility in inland Navigation; and in rapid currents; that are shallow—and what adds vastly to the value of the discovery, is the simplicity of its works; as they may be made by a common boat builder or carpenter, and kept in order as easy as a plow, or any common impliment of husbandry on a farm.

> Having obtained a Plan of this Town (Bath) and ascertained the situation of my lots therein, which I examined; it appears that the disposition of a dwelling House; Kitchen & Stable cannot be more advantageously placed than they are marked in the copy I have taken from the plan of the Town; to which I refer for recollection, of my design; & Mr. Rumsey being willing to undertake those Buildings, I have agreed with him to have them finished by the 10th. of next July. The

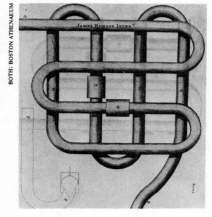

Engraving from Columbian Magazine, *in Washington's library, of a boiler invented by James Rumsey*

dwelling House is to be 36 feet by 24....

Meeting with the Revd. Mr. Balmain at this place, he says the distance from Staunton to the Sweet Springs is 95 Miles; that is, 50 to what are commonly called the Augusta Springs & 45 afterwards. This differs widely from Captn. Strodes Acct., and both say they have travelled the Road.

From Colo. Bruce whom I also found at this place, I was informed that he had travelled from the North Branch of Potomack to the Waters of Yaughiogany, and Monongahela—that the Potomk. where it may be made Navigable—for instance where McCulloughs path crosses it, 40 Miles above the old fort (Cumberland), is but about 6 Miles to a pretty large branch of the Yohiogany, but how far it is practicable to make the latter navigable he knows not, never having explored it any length downwards.

The copy of Columbian Magazine *also contained "Plan for Mr. Fitch's Steam Boat," an early competitor to the "ingenious" Rumsey's boat.*

Again Washington noted much more about the navigability of this or that tributary of the Potomac and the Ohio, and of the feasibility of roads to connect them. James Rumsey, whom Washington met at Bath, had showed him a model of an odd craft, an arrangement of two hulls with a paddle wheel between them. The current of the stream turned the paddle wheel, which in turn activated poles that pushed against the bottom of the stream and forced the craft against the current. Washington, enthusiastic, was certain it was the solution to upriver travel. On September 10 he headed north into Pennsylvania to take care of some matters there before continuing on to his lands on the Kanawha River. His business with Gilbert Simpson was of an annoying nature. Simpson, in a partnership arrangement, was supposed to be operating a gristmill on land owned by Washington. Although Washington claimed to have put twelve hundred pounds into the venture over the years without getting a penny back, his artful partner had always been able to charm him out of his anger.

10th [September, 1784]. Set off a little after 5 Oclock altho' the morning was very unpromising. Finding from the rains that had fallen, and description of the Roads, part of which between the old Town & this place (old Fort Cumberland) we had passed, that the progress of my Baggage would be tedeous, I resolved (it being Necessary) to leave it to follow; and proceed on myself to Gilbert Simpson's, to prepare for the Sale which I had advertised of my moiety of the property in co-partnership with him— and to make arrangements for my trip to the Kanhawa, if the temper & disposition of the Indians should render it advisable to proceed. Accordingly, leaving Doctr. Craik, his Son, and my Nephew with it, I set out with one Servant only. Dined at a Mr. Gwins at the Fork of the Roads leading to Winchester and the old Town, distant from the latter abt. 20 Miles & lodged at Tumbersons at the little Meadows....

The Road from the Old Town to Fort Cumberland we found tolerably good, as it also was from the latter to Gwins, except the Mountain which was pretty long (tho' not steep) in the assent and discent; but from Gwins to Tumberson's it is intolerably bad—there being many steep pinches of the Mountain—deep & Miry places—and very stony ground to pass over. After leaving the Waters of Wills Creek which extends up the Mountain (Alligeny) two or three Miles as the road goes, we fell next on those of George's Creek, which are small—after them upon Savage River which are more considerable; tho' from the present appearance of them, does not seem capable of Navigation....

12th. Left Daughtertys about 6 Oclock,—stopped a while at the Great Meadows [site of Fort Necessity and Washington's defeat; then owned by Washington], and viewed a tenament I have there, which appears to have been but little improved, tho capable of being turned to great advantage, as the whole of the ground called the Meadows may be reclaimed at an easy comparitive expence & is a very good stand for a Tavern. Much Hay may be cut here when the ground is laid down in Grass & the upland, East of the Meadow, is good for grain....

In passing over the Mountains, I met numbers of Persons & Pack horses going in with Ginsang; & for salt & other articles at the Markets below; from most of whom I made enquiries of the Nature of the Country between the little Kanhawa and ten miles Creek (which had been represented as a short and easy portage) and to my surprize found the Accts. wch. had been given were so far from the truth that numbers with whom I conversed assured me that the distance between was very considerable—that ten miles Ck. was not navigable even for Canoes more than a Mile from its mouth and few of them, altho I saw many who lived on different parts of this Creek would pretend to guess at the

Plan of Rumsey's steamboat (above) and his proposals for forming a company to enable him to build it

PROPOSALS
For forming a Company, to enable
JAMES RUMSEY
To carry into Execution, on a Large and Extensive Plan, his
STEAM·BOAT
And sundry other Machines herein after mentioned.

George Washington: The Pictorial Biography BY CLARK KINNAIRD, COPYRIGHT © 1967, BY PERMISSION OF HASTINGS HOUSE, PUBLISHERS

distance.

I also endeavoured to get the best acct. I could of the Navigation of Cheat River, & find that the line which divides the States of Virginia & Pensylvania crosses the Monongahela above the Mouth of it; wch. gives the Command thereof to Pensylvania—that where the River (Cheat) goes through the Laurel hill, the Navigation is difficult; not from shallow, or rapid water, but from an immense quantity of large Stones, which stand so thick as to render the passage even of a short Canoe impracticable—but I could meet with no person who seemed to have any accurate knowledge of the Country between the navigable or such part as could be made so, of this River & the North Branch of Potomack. All seem to agree however that it is rought & a good way not to be found.

The Accts. given by those Whom I met of the late Murders, & general dissatisfaction of the Indians, occasioned by the attempts of our people to settle on the No. West side of the Ohio, which they claim as their territory; and our delay to hold a treaty with them, which they say is indicative of a hostile temper on our part, makes it rather improper for me to proceed to the Kanhawa agreeably to my original intention, especially as I learnt from some of them (one in particular) who lately left the Settlement of Kentucke that the Indians were generally in arms & gone, or going, to attack some of our Settlements below—and that a Party who had drove Cattle to Detroit had one of their Company & several of their Cattle killed by the Indians—but as these Accts. will either be contradicted or confirmed by some whom I may meet at my Sale the 15th. Instt. my final determination shall be postponed 'till then.

13th. I visited my Mill, and the several tenements on this Tract (on which Simpson lives). I do not find the land in *general* equal to my expectation of it. Some part indeed is as rich as can be, some othe[r] part is but indifferent—the levellest is the coldest, and of the meanest quality—that which is most broken is the richest; tho' some of the hills are not of the first quality.

The tenements with respect to buildings, are but indifferently improved—each have Meadow and arable, but in no great quantity. The Mill was quite destitute

Mount Vernon, LOSSING

Silhouette of Dr. James Craik

of Water. The works & House appear to be in very bad condition—and no reservoir of Water—the stream as it runs, is all the resource it has. Formerly there was a dam to stop the Water; but that giving way it is brought in a narrow confined & trifling race to the forebay, wch. and the trunk, which conveys the water to the Wheel are in bad order. In a word, little rent, or good is to be expected from the present aspect of her.

14th. Remained at Mr. Gilbert Simpsons all day. Before Noon Colo. Willm. Butler and the Officer Commanding the Garrison at Fort Pitt, a Capt. Lucket came here. As they confirmed the reports of the discontented temper of the Indians and the Mischiefs done by some parties of them—and the former advised me not to prosecute my intended trip to the Great Kanhawa, I resolved to decline it.

This day also the people who lives on my land on Millers run came here to set forth their pretensions to it; & to enquire into my right. After much conversation, & attempts in them to discover all the flaws they could in my Deed, &ca.—& to establish a fair and up right intention in themselves;—and after much councelling which proceeded from a division of opinion among themselves—they resolved (as all who live on the Land were not here) to give me their definite determination when I should come to the Land, which I told them would probably happen on Friday or Saturday next.

15th. This being the day appointed for the Sale of my moiety of the Co-partnership stock—Many People were gathered (more out of curiosity I believe than from other motives) but no great Sale made. My Mill I could obtain no bid for, altho I offered an exemption from the payment of Rent 15 Months. The Plantation on which Mr. Simpson lives rented well—Viz. for 500 Bushels of Wheat payable at any place with in the County that I, or my Agent should direct. The little chance of getting a good offer in money for Rent, induced me to set it up to be bid for in Wheat. . . .

16th. Continued at Simpsons all day in order to finish the business which was begun yesterday—Gave leases to some of my Tents. on the Land whereon I now am.

17th. Detained here by a settled Rain the whole day—

which gave me time to close my accts. with Gilbert Simpson, & put a final end to my Partnership with him. Agreed this day with a Major Thomas Freeman to superintend my business over the Mountains, upon terms to be inserted in his Instructions.

In settling up with Simpson, Washington apparently got the worst of the deal once again, for in his ledger under Simpson's account is a notation, "Settled [by Simpson] by a payment in depreciated paper Money." This accomplished, Washington was off to another tract of land, the one from which "the people who lives on my land on Millers run," as he noted in his diary, had come to Simpson's to talk to him on September 14. These people, religious dissenters from Europe, had moved onto Washington's land in 1773, virtually evicting the man who was living there to protect Washington's rights.

18th [September, 1784]. Set out with Doctr. Craik for my Land on Miller's run (a branch of Shurtees [Chartier's] Creek). Crossed the Monongahela at Deboirs Ferry—16 miles from Simpsons—bated at one Hamiltons about 4 Miles from it, in Washington County, and lodged at a Colo. Cannons on the Waters of Shurtees Creek—a kind hospitable Man; & sensible.

Most of the Land over which we passed was hilly—some of it very rich—others thin. Between a Colo. Cooks and the Ferry the Land was rich but broken. About Shurtee, & from thence to Colo. Cannons, the soil is very luxurient and very uneven.

19th. Being Sunday, and the People living on my Land, *apparently* very religious, it was thought best to postpone going among them till tomorrow—but rode to a Doctr. Johnsons who had the Keeping of Colo. Crawfords (surveying) records—but not finding him at home was disappointed in the business which carried me there.

20th. Went early this Morning to view my Land, & to receive the final determination of those who live upon it. Having obtained a Pilot near the Land I went ...first to the plantation of Samuel McBride, who has about

5 Acres of Meadow—&
30 of arable Land

under good fencing—a Logged dwelling house with a punchion roof, & stable, or small barn, of the same

267

kind—the Land rather hilly, but good, chiefly white
oak.... [Here follow similar descriptions of the farms
of a dozen other settlers.]

The foregoing are all the Improvements upon this
Tract which contains 2813 acres.

The Land is leveller than is common to be met with
in this Part of the Country, and good; the principal
part of it is white oak, intermixed in many places with
black oak; and is estemed a valuable tract.

Dined at David Reeds, after which Mr. James Scot &
Squire Reed began to enquire whether I would part
with the Land, & upon what terms; adding, that tho'
they did not conceive they could be dispossed, yet to
avoid contention, they would buy, if my terms were
moderate. I told them I had no inclination to sell; however, after hearing a great deal of their hardships, their
Religious principles (which had brought them together
as a society of Ceceders) and unwillingness to seperate
or remove; I told them I would make them a last offer
and this was—the whole tract at 25/. pr. Acre, the money
to be paid at 3 annual payments with Interest;—or to
become Tenants upon leases of 999 years, at the annual
Rent of Ten pounds pr. [   ] pr. Ann.—The former they
had a long consultation upon, & asked if I wd. take
that price at a longer credit, without Interest, and being
answered in the negative they then determined to stand
suit for the Land; but it having been suggested that
there were among them some who were disposed to
relinquish their claim, I told them I would receive their
answers individually; and accordingly calling upon them
as they stood... they severally answered, that they
meant to stand suit, & abide the Issue of the Law.

This business being thus finished, I returned to Colo.
Cannons in company with himself, Colo. Nevil, Captn.
Swearingen (high Sherif) & a Captn. Richie, who had
accompanied me to the Land.

21st. Accompanied by Colo. Cannon & Captn. Swearingen who attended me to Debores ferry on the Monongahela which seperates the Counties of Fayette &
Washington, I returned to Gilbert Simpson's in the
Afternoon; after dining at one Wickermans Mill near
the Monongahela.

Colo. Cannon, Captn. Sweringin & Captn. Richie

all promised to hunt up the Evidences which could prove my possession & improvement of the Land before any of the present Occupiers saw it.

Washington was angry and determined to prosecute the case vigorously, for he considered the settlers as squatters who had spurned his fair offer to let them buy or rent. It was not until 1786, however, that the case was finally decided; Washington's 1771 survey was somehow missing from land office records, and other records had flaws. Eventually, though, he won his case. But that lay in the future. Now, with his business concluded and the trip to the Kanawha canceled by Indian hostility, he started for home, still gathering voluminous information on Potomac-Ohio routes and even going so far as to work out combinations of streams and portages by which the fur trade of the Northwest could be funneled through Detroit and down into Virginia. He arrived home on October 4, 1784, and soon was lobbying to urge the legislatures of Maryland and Virginia to authorize improvement of navigation on the Potomac, which the two states shared as a common boundary. He later described the results to his friend former Major General Benjamin Lincoln.

Mount Vernon 5th. Feby. 1785.
We have nothing stirring in this quarter worthy of observation, except the passing of two Acts by the Assemblies of Virginia & Maryland (exactly similar) for improving & extending the navigation of the river Potomac from tide water, as high up as it shall be found practicable, & communicating it by good roads with the nearest navigable waters to the Westward: which acts in their consequences, may be of great political, as well as commercial advantages: the first to the confederation, as it may tie the Settlers of the Western Territory to the Atlantic States by interest, which is the only knot that will hold. Whilst those of Virginia & Maryland will be more immediately benefited by the large field it opens for the latter. Books for receiving subscriptions are to be opened at Alexandria & other places the 8th. instant, & continue so until the 10th. of May; as the navigable part of the business is to be undertaken by a company to be incorporated for the purpose.

Major General Benjamin Lincoln

The Potomac Company was formed, and Washington was named its president. That same summer, 1785, he and the other directors made the first of several inspections, beginning just above the Great

Falls of the Potomac, not far upstream from where the city of Washington would rise. His diary detailed the difficulties they found.

Wednesday, 3d [August, 1785]. ... Having provided Canoes and being joined by Mr. Rumsay the principal Manager, & Mr. Stewart an Assistant to him, in carrying on the Works, we proceeded to examine the falls [Seneca Falls]; and beginning at the head of them went through the whole by water, and continued from the foot of them to the Great fall—After which, returning back to a Spring on the Maryland Side between the Seneca & Great Falls, we partook (about 5 O'clock) of another cold Collation which a Colo. Orme a Mr. Turner & others of the Neighbourhood, had provided and returned back by the way of Mr. Bealls Mill to our old Quarters at Mr. Goldsboroughs—The distance as estimated 8 Miles.

The Water through these Falls is of sufficient depth for good Navigation; and as formidable as I had conceived them to be; but by no means impracticable. The principal difficulties lye in rocks which occasion a crooked passage. These once removed, renders the passage safe without the aid of Locks & may be effected for the sum mentioned in Mr. Jno. Ballendine's estimate (the largest extant) but in a different manner than that proposed by him. It appearing to me, and was so, unanimously determined by the Board of Directors, that a channel through the bed of the river in a strait direction, and as Much in the course of the current as may be, without a grt. increase of labour & expence, would be preferable to that through the Gut which was the choice of Mr. Ballendine for a Canal with Locks—the last of which we thought unnecessary, & the first more expensive in the first instance, besides being liable to many inconveniences which the other is not as it would, probably be frequently choaked with drift wood—Ice—and other rubbish which would be thrown therein through the several inlets already made by the rapidity of the currts. in freshes and others which probably would be made thereby; whereas a navigation through the bed of the river when once made will, in all probability, remain forever, as the currt. here will rather clear than contribute to choak the passage. It is true, no track path [towpath] can be had in a navigation thus ordered, nor does there appear a necessity for it. Tracking, constitutes a large part of Mr. Ballendine's

The Great Falls of the Potomac, a formidable but not "impracticable" obstacle to Washington's canal

estimate—The want of which, in the rapid parts of the river, (if Mr. Rumsey's plan for working Boats against stream by the force of mechanical powers should fail) may be supplied by chains buoyed up to haul by which would be equally easy, more certain, and less dangerous than setting up with Poles....

Thursday, 4th. In order to be more certain of the advantages and disadvantages of the Navigation proposed by Mr. Ballendine, through the Gut, we took a more particular view of it—walking down one side & returning on the other and were more fully convinced of the impropriety of its adoption first, because it would be more expensive in the first instance—and secondly because it would be subject to the ravages of freshes &ca. as already mentioned without any superiority over the one proposed through the bed of the River unless a track path should be preferable to hauling up by a Chain with buoys.

Engaged nine labourers with whom to *commence* the Work.

Friday, 5th. ...After Breakfast, and after directing Mr. Rumsey when he had marked the way and set the labourers to Work to meet us at Harpers ferry on the Evening of the morrow at Harpers Ferry (at the conflux of the Shannondoah with the Potomack) myself and the Directors set out for the same place by way of Frederick Town (Maryland). Dined at a Dutch man's 2 Miles above the Mo[uth] of Monocasy & reached the former about 5 Oclock. Drank Tea—supped—and lodged at Govr. Johnsons.

In the Evening the Bells rang, & Guns were fired; & a Committee waited upon me by order of the Gentlemen of the Town to request that I wd. stay next day and partake of a public dinner which the Town were desirous of giving me—But as arrangements had been made, and the time for examining the Shannondoah Falls, previous to the day fixed for receiving labourers into pay, was short I found it most expedient to decline the honor.

The group went up the Potomac as far as Harpers Ferry. Although the Potomac canal long remained a project close to Wash-

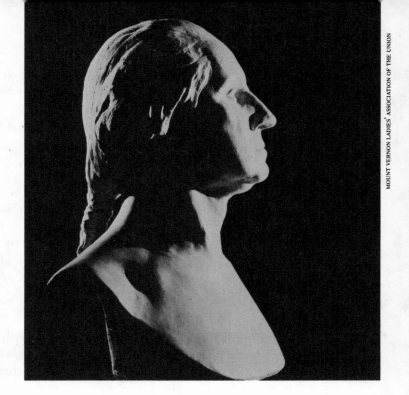

Bust of Washington made by the famous sculptor Houdon in 1785; persons familiar with Washington thought it the best likeness.

ington's heart, it was never to amount to anything during his lifetime. James Rumsey's self-poling boat proved impracticable, and canal building was difficult and expensive beyond the resources of the company. Earlier that same year Washington had made a poignant little pilgrimage; he had ridden over to the ruins of Belvoir, onetime home of George William Fairfax and his wife Sally, who had once bewitched the young George Washington. The Fairfaxes now lived in England; Belvoir, empty, had burned during the war years. Within its halls, as an awkward teen-ager, Washington had first come in contact with the exciting world of Virginia society. Now he wrote to Fairfax, expressing the wistful hope that he and his wife might return to Belvoir.

> Mount Vernon 27th. Feby. 1785.
>
> I cannot at this moment recur to the contents of those letters of mine to you which I suspect have miscarried; further than that they were all expressive of an earnest wish to see you & Mrs. Fairfax once more fixed in this country; & to beg that you would consider Mt. Vernon as your home until you could build with convenience — in which request Mrs. Washington joins very sincerely. I never look towards Belvoir, without having this upper most in my mind. But alas! Belvoir is no more! I took a ride there the other day to visit the ruins, & ruins indeed they are. The dwelling house & the two brick buildings in front, underwent the ravages of the fire; the walls of which are very much injured: the other

Houses are sinking under the depredation of time & inattention, & I believe are now scarcely worth repairing. In a word, the whole are, or very soon will be a heap of ruin. When I viewed them—when I considered that the happiest moments of my life had been spent there—when I could not trace a room in the house (now all rubbish) that did not bring to my mind the recollection of pleasing scenes; I was obliged to fly from them; & came home with painful sensations, & sorrowing for the contrast. Mrs. Morton still lives at your Barn quarter. The management of your business is entrusted to one Muse (son to a Colonel of that name, whom you cannot have forgotten)—he is, I am told, a very active & industrious man; but in what sort of order he has your Estate, I am unable to inform you, never having seen him since my return to Virginia.

Despite his enthusiasm for canals and the time he gave to a wide-ranging correspondence, Washington was, above all, a farmer. He continued endlessly to try new plants and new methods, and to go about it as scientifically as he knew how. His diaries recorded agricultural experiments, as they had before the war.

Monday, 25th [April, 1785]. ...Got the ground, on the North side of the gate—between the outer ditch & the Sweet brier hedge in a proper state of preparation to receive grass seed; and for making a compleat experimt. of the Plaister of Paris as a manure. Accordingly, I divided it into equal sections; by a line from the Center of the old gate, between the New Gardon Houses, stretched to the outer ditch at which they were 18 1/2 feet apart and 16 apart at the outer edge of the Holly berries by the Sweet brier hedge. Each of these Sections contained 655 square feet. On the 1st. that is, the one next the road I sprinkled 5 pints of the Plaister in powder—on the 2d. 4 pints—on the 3d. 3 pints—on the 4th. 2 pts. on the 5th. one pint—and on the 6th. none. On the 7th. 8th. 9th. 10th. & 11th. 5, 4, 3, 2 & 1 pints again; and on the 12th. nothing—and on the 13th. 14th. 15. 16 & 17th.—5, 4, 3, 2 & 1 in the same manner as before. On these three grand divisions (as they may be called) I sowed Orchard Grass Seed. But before I did this, I harrowed the first grand division with a heavy Iron toothed harrow. The 2d. grand division was gone over with a Bush harrow (without the Iron harrow)—and the third grand division was only rolled without either of the above harrowings. The whole of this ground was, in quality, as nearly alike as ground cou'd well be—and this experiment, if the grass seed comes up well, will show first, what quantity is most proper for an acre (the above [amt.] being, as nearly as may be, in the proportion of 1, 2, 3, 4, & 5 Bushels to the acre)—and secondly, whether burying the Powder of Paris deep (as a heavy harrow will do it)—shallow—or spreading it on the surface only, is best.

But alas! for all Washington's efforts, Mount Vernon never quite lived up to his hopes. Before the war, he had given up growing tobacco, partly because his harvest always brought prices lower than the prevailing rate and partly because it exhausted the land and renewing it with organic manures was more expensive than buying new land. He had done better with crops such as wheat and corn, but his best expectations were always disappointed. In 1785 it was drought and an infestation of chinch bugs that gave him a severe setback.

Friday, 22d. [July]. ...Rid to the Ferry—Dogue run and Muddy hole Plantations.

Mr. Lund Washington & his wife dined here. And Mr. Thompson went away after Breakfast.

The leaves of the locust Trees this year, as the last, began to fade, & many of them dye. The Black Gum Trees which I had transplanted to my avenues or Serpentine Walks, & which put out leaf and looked well at first, are all dead, so are the Poplars, and most of the Mulberrys. The Crab apple trees also, which were transplanted into the Shrubberies & the Papaws are also dead, as also the Sassafras in a great degree—The Pines wholly—& several of the Cedars—as also the Hemlock almost entirely. The live Oak which I thought was dead is putting out shoots from the bottom and have appearances of doing well. ...

Thursday, 11th [August]. ...The Drought, the effects of which were visible when I left home, had, by this (no rain having fallen in my absence) greatly affected vegetation. The grass was quite burnt & crisp under foot—Gardens parched—and the young Trees in my Shrubberies, notwithstanding they had been watered

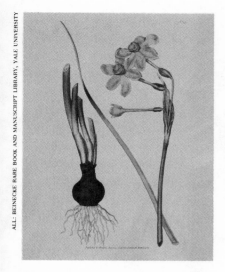

Washington subscribed to England's Botanical Magazine *(left), in which these plates of the Jonquil (top) and the Sessile Trillium appeared.*

(as it is said) according to my direction were much on the decline. In a word nature had put on a melancholy look—everything seeming to droop....

Saturday, 13th. ...Rid to my Muddy hole and Neck Plantations; and beheld Corn in a melancholy situation, fired in most places to the Ear with little appearance of yielding if rain should soon come & a certainty of making nothing if it did not. Attempts had been made at both these Plantations to sow Wheat, but stirring the ground in the parched condition it was in, had so affected the Corn as to cause well grounded apprehensions that it would die if not restored by seasonable & sufficient Rains. This put a stop to further seeding which is almost as bad as the injury done by it to the Corn as latter sowing in old Corn ground seldom produces. At the first mentioned place about 30 Bushels had been sowed—at the latter less.

The two kinds of Chinese Seeds which had appeared before I left home were destroyed either by the drought or insects. That between the 8th. & 9th. stakes in the 2d. row was entirely eradicated—indeed some kind of fly, or bug, had begun to prey up on the leaves before I left home. The other was broke of near the ground & cannot I fear recover....

Monday, 15th. ...Rid to my Plantations at the Ferry, Dogue run and Muddy hole. Found the two first were suffering as I had described the other two on Saturday—and that both had discontinued sowing of Wheat after putting about 30 Bushels at each place in the ground.

My Overseer at the Ferry (Fairfax) ascribes the wretched condition of his Corn to the bug which has proved so destructive to both Wheat and Corn on James River and elsewhere equally with the drought & shewed me hundreds of them & their young under the blades at the lower joints of the stock. The Corn is effected by their sucking the juices which occasions a gradual decline of the whole plant. He also shewed me a piece of course grass that was quite killed by them, by the same kind of operation.

When other Potomac plantations were still green and fruitful, Washington's trees died and his crops wilted in dry weather, for the hard truth was that Mount Vernon was set on mediocre land. Its topsoil overlay heavy clay into which water was slow to soak. Heavy rains ran off instead of sinking in, eroding precious topsoil, while in spring the fields were so slow to absorb standing water that they were always late in being worked and planted. In such a situation Washington's efforts to restore fertility accomplished little. Mount Vernon had also become overburdened with excess workers. Washington's diary for February, 1786, listed 216 slaves of all ages at Mount Vernon and its five dependent farms. He had adopted the humane policy of rarely selling a slave unless the slave was willing, and since Washington was a good, if strict, master, few left. The birth rate was high, and as a result there were more hands to feed than the plantation could profitably employ. Moreover, Washington was troubled by slavery. As a Southerner he had once accepted it as part of the normal order of things, but time had brought doubts. His mixed feelings on the subject appeared in a letter to Robert Morris of Philadelphia.

Mt. Vernon, 12th. April 1786.

I give you the trouble of this letter at the instance of Mr. Dalby of Alexandria; who is called to Philadelphia to attend what he conceives to be a vexatious law-suit respecting a slave of his, which a Society of Quakers in the city (formed for such purposes) have attempted to liberate. The merits of this case will no doubt appear upon trial; but from Mr. Dalby's state of the matter, it should seem that this Society is not only acting repugnant to justice so far as its conduct concerns strangers, but, in my opinion extremely impolitickly with respect to the State—the City in particular; & without being able, (but by acts of tyranny & oppression) to accomplish their own ends. He says the conduct of this society is not sanctioned by Law: had the case been otherwise, whatever my opinion of the Law might have been, my respect for the policy of the State would on this occasion have appeared in my silence; because against the penalties of promulgated Laws one may guard; but there is no avoiding the snares of individuals, or of private societies—and if the practice of this Society of which Mr. Dalby speaks, is not discountenanced, none of those whose *misfortune* it is to have slaves as attendants, will visit the City if they can possibly avoid it; because by so doing they hazard their property—or they must be at the expence (& this will not always succeed) of providing servants of another description for the trip.

I hope it will not be conceived from these observations, that it is my wish to hold the unhappy people, who are

Details from two nineteenth-century paintings include slaves at Mount Vernon as domestics in the house (above) and field hands (opposite).

the subject of this letter, in slavery. I can only say that there is not a man living who wishes more sincerely than I do, to see a plan adopted for the abolition of it—but there is only one proper and effectual mode by which it can be accomplished, & that is by Legislative authority; and this, as far as my suffrage will go, shall never be wanting. But when slaves who are happy & content to remain with their present masters, are tampered with & seduced to leave them; when masters are taken unawares by these practices; when a conduct of this sort begets discontent on one side and resentment on the other, & when it happens to fall on a man whose purse will not measure with that of the Society, & he loses his property for want of means to defend it—it is oppression in the latter case, & not humanity in any; because it introduces more evils than it can cure.

I will make no apology for writing to you on this subject; for if Mr. Dalby has not misconceived the matter, an evil exists which requires a remedy; if he has, my intentions have been good though I may have been too precipitate in this address.

As 1786 wore on, Washington became increasingly concerned about the state of the nation. Under the Articles of Confederation the United States was little more than a collection of thirteen quasi nations. States levied import duties on each other's commerce and issued their own money. Congress was impotent; it could not tax, and its only means of income was to beg from the states, which seldom responded. By 1786, Congress was no longer able to pay even the interest on the national debt. Washington's somber outlook was typified by the following extract from a letter to the Marquis de Lafayette.

Mount Vernon, May 10, 1786.
It is one of the evils of democratical governments, that the people, not always seeing & frequently misled, must often feel before they can act right—but then evils of this nature seldom fail to work their own cure. It is to be lamented nevertheless that the remedies are so slow, & that those who may wish to apply them seasonably are not attended to before they suffer in person, in interest & in reputation. I am not without hopes that matters will soon take a more favourable turn in the fœderal Constitution. The discerning part of the community have long since seen the necessity of giving adequate powers to

The State House at Annapolis

Congress for national purposes; & the ignorant & designing must yield to it 'ere long. Several late acts of the different Legislatures have a tendency thereto; among these, the Impost which is now acceded to by every State in the Union, (tho' clogged a little by that of New York) will enable Congress to support the national credit in pecuniary matters better than it has been; whilst a measure, in which this state [Virginia] has taken the lead at its last session, will it is to be hoped give efficient powers to that Body for all commercial purposes. This is a nomination of some of its first characters to meet other Commissioners from the several States in order to consider of & decide upon such powers as shall be necessary for the sovereign power of them to act under; which are to be reported to the respective Legislatures at their autumnal sessions for, it is to be hoped, final adoption: thereby avoiding those tedious & futile deliberations, which result from recommendations & partial concurrences; at the same time that it places it at once in the power of Congress to meet European Nations upon decisive & equal ground. All the Legislatures which I have heard from, have come into the proposition, & have made very judicious appointments. Much good is expected from this measure, and it is regretted by many that more objects were not embraced by the meeting. A General Convention is talked of by many for the purpose of revising & correcting the defects of the fœderal government; but whilst this is the wish of some, it is the dread of others from an opinion that matters are not yet sufficiently ripe for such an event.

The meeting of commissioners from the several states to which Washington referred was to be held at Annapolis. Virginia and Maryland, after having reached agreement on navigation of the Potomac, had joined in inviting all the states to send delegates to try in the same spirit to solve their mutual trade problems. Only five states were represented when the meeting convened in September, 1786, and nothing could be accomplished. Undaunted, the delegates issued a call for all the states to send delegates to Philadelphia the following May for a much broader purpose: to discuss all matters necessary "to render the constitution of the Federal Government adequate to the exigencies of the Union."

Not long after getting a report of the disappointing outcome of the Annapolis Convention, Washington received distressing news from Massachusetts. In the postwar depression, many New England farmers and small property owners were having their property seized to satisfy claims for unpaid debts and taxes. In Massachusetts, when petitions for relief were ignored by the legislature, the protesters in late August began mass demonstrations to intimidate courts and prevent legal action against debtors. Then, afraid they might be indicted for treason, the insurgents marched on Springfield to frighten the state's Supreme Court. Violence was avoided when both insurgents and militia agreed to go home. Washington, receiving his news in bits and pieces, got an overly sensational picture of the situation. He poured out his feelings to Henry ("Light-Horse Harry") Lee, one of his wartime officers and soon to be Governor of Virginia, who had suggested that Washington go to Massachusetts and use his influence to end the rebellion.

Mount Vernon 31st. Octr. 1786.
I am indebted to you for your several favors of the 1st., 11th. & 17th. of this inst. & shall reply to them in the order of their dates; but first let me thank you for the interesting communications imparted by them.

The picture which you have exhibited, & the accounts which are published of the commotions, & temper of numerous bodies in the Eastern States, are equally to be lamented & deprecated. They exhibit a melancholy proof of what our trans-Atlantic foe has predicted; & of another thing perhaps, which is still more to be regretted, & is yet more unaccountable, that mankind when left to themselves are unfit for their own Government. I am mortified beyond expression when I view the clouds which have spread over the brightest morn that ever dawned upon any Country. In a word, I am lost in amazement when I behold what intrigue, the interested views of desperate characters, ignorance & jealousy of the minor part, are capable of effecting, as a scourge on the major part of our fellow Citizens of the Union; for it is hardly to be supposed that the great body of the people, tho' they will not act, can be so short sighted, or enveloped in darkness as not to see rays of a distant sun thro' all this mist of intoxication & folly.

You talk, my good Sir, of employing influence to appease the present tumults in Massachusetts. I know not where that influence is to be found; and if attainable, that it would be a proper remedy for the disorders. Influence is no Government. Let us have one by which our lives, liberties & properties will be secured; or let us know the worst at once. Under these impressions,

"Light-Horse Harry" Lee

The Critical Period in American History BY JOHN FISKE, 1898

House in which Shays was captured

my humble opinion is, that there is a call for decision. Know precisely what the insurgents aim at. If they have *real* grievances, redress them if possible; or acknowledge the justice of them, & your inability to do it in the present moment. If they have not, employ the force of government against them at once. If this is inadequate, *all* will be convinced that the superstructure is bad, or wants support. To be more exposed in the eyes of the world, and more contemptible than we already are, is hardly possible. To delay one or the other of these, is to exasperate on the one hand, or give confidence on the other, & will add to their numbers; for, like snowballs, such bodies encrease by every movement, unless there is something in the way to obstruct & crumble them before the weight is too great & irresistible.

These are my sentiments. Precedents are dangerous things—let the reins of government then be braced & held with a steady hand, & every violation of the Constitution be reprehended: if defective, let it be amended, but not suffered to be trampled upon whilst it has an existence.

The protest, which had become known as Shays' Rebellion from its leader, Daniel Shays, a captain during the Revolution, flared up again in late December when the insurgents returned to Springfield planning to seize arms from the national arsenal there. Early in the new year they were dispersed by troops under Benjamin Lincoln. Shays fled to Vermont; he and a number of other leaders were condemned to death, and large numbers of others were disfranchised, a punishment that Washington considered too severe. Writing to Lincoln, Washington commented on the outcome.

Mount Vernon March 23d. 1787.
Ever since the disorders in your State began to grow serious I have been peculiarly anxious to hear from that quarter; General Knox has, from time to time, transmitted to me the state of affairs as they came to his hands; but nothing has given such full and satisfactory information as the particular detail of events which you have been so good as to favor me with, and for which you will please to accept my warmest and most grateful acknowledgements. Permit me also, my dear Sir, to offer you my sincerest congratulations upon your success. The suppression of those tumults

Governor James Bowdoin

and insurrections with so little bloodshed, is an event as happy as it was unexpected; it must have been peculiarly agreeable to you, being placed in so delicate and critical a situation. I am extremely happy to find that your sentiments upon the disfranchising act [are] such as they are; upon my first seeing it, I formed an opinion perfectly coincident with yours, viz., that measures more generally lenient might have produced equally as good an effect without entirely alienating the affections of the people from the government; as it now stands, it affects a large body of men, some of them, perhaps, it deprives of the means of gaining a livelihood; the friends and connections of those people will feel themselves wounded in a degree, and I think it will rob the State of a number of its inhabitants if it produces nothing worse.

It gives me great pleasure to hear that your Eastern settlements succeeds so well. The sincere regard which I have for you will always make your prosperity a part of my happiness.

In Massachusetts, Governor James Bowdoin was defeated in the next election, Shays and other condemned leaders were soon pardoned, and the harassed debtors obtained through the ballot the changes they had failed to win by marching. Although conservatives took Shays' Rebellion as proof that a republican government was unworkable, most thinking Americans saw it as an indication of the need for a stronger government, one that could handle, or better yet, prevent, such crises. The rebellion thus unintentionally created strong sentiment in favor of the approaching convention to review the confederation. Washington wanted no personal part in the convention, and many of his close friends urged him not to go; if it should be a failure, his reputation, more than that of any other man, would suffer. But once again he answered the call of duty. In early May, 1787, as the time for his departure for Philadelphia neared, he wrote to Robert Morris to politely decline a thoughtful invitation.

Mount Vernon May 5th. 1787.

When your favor of the 23d. Ult. was sent here from the Post Office, I was at Fredericksburg (to which place I had been called, suddenly, by Express) to bid, as I was prepared to expect, the last adieu to an honoured parent, and an affectionate Sister whose watchful attention to my Mother during her illness had brought to deaths door. The latter I hope is now out of danger, but the former

The Morris house in Philadelphia, in which Washington made his home

cannot long Survive the disorder which had reduced her to a Skeleton, tho' she is somewhat amended.

I do not know how, sufficiently, to express my thankfulness to Mrs. Morris and you for your kind invitation to lodge at your house, and though I could not be more happy any where, yet as there is great reason to apprehend that the business of the Convention (from the tardiness of some States, and the discordant opinions of others) will not be brought to a speedy conclusion, I cannot prevail on my self to give so much trouble to a private family as such a length of time must do. I hope therefore that Mrs. Morris and you will not take it a miss that I decline the polite and obliging offer you have made me.

Mrs. Washington is become too Domestick, and too attentive to two little Grand Children to leave home, and I can assure you, Sir, that it was not until after a long struggle I could obtain my own consent to appear again in a public theatre. My first remaining wish being, to glide gently down the stream of life in tranquil retirement till I shall arrive at the world of Spirits.

Washington left Mount Vernon on May 9, 1787. Almost immediately on arriving in Philadelphia he accepted Robert Morris's renewed invitation and moved into the financier's mansion. When he arrived at the State House (today called Independence Hall) on May 14 for the opening session, only the Pennsylvania and Virginia delegations were present — hardly a quorum. While foreboding grew in Washington's heart, delegates from other states leisurely drifted in during the following days. Meanwhile, the Virginia delegation, ignoring the fact that the convention had been called only to revise the Articles of Confederation, drafted a plan for a completely new form of government to be presented to the convention. At last Washington was able to record in his diary that the meeting to revise the Articles of Confederation had been convened.

Friday, 25th [May, 1787]. Another Delegate coming in from the State of New Jersey gave it a representation and encreased the number to Seven which forming a quoram of the 13 the Members present resolved to organize the body; when, by a unanimous vote I was called up to the Chair as President of the body. Majr. William Jackson was appointed Secretary — and a Comee. was chosen consisting of (Mr. Wythe, Mr. Hamilton and Mr. Chs. Pinkney chosen) 3 Members to

prepare rules & regulations for conducting the business—
and after appointing door keepers the Convention
adjourned till Monday, (10 oclock) to give time to the
Comee. to report the matters referred to them.

Returned many visits (in the forenoon) today. Dined
at Mr. Thos. Willings—and sp[en]t the evening at my
lodgings.

Unfortunately for posterity, the delegates voted to keep
their deliberations secret, and Washington's diary henceforth reveals little
more than where he dined and had tea. Meanwhile, in what has since become known as the Constitutional Convention, the delegates decided to
scrap completely the Articles of Confederation and then debated through
the hot summer over the form of the new government. In 1787 they had
no precedents. The Virginia Plan, calling for judicial, legislative, and
executive branches of the national government, was accepted as the basis
for discussion. But should the executive be one man or three, a Southerner,
a Westerner, and a Northerner? A one-house legislature or two? Should the
upper house be elected by the people or chosen by the lower house? Should?
—there were a hundred vexing problems. How often Washington despaired
during the deliberations we cannot know. As presiding officer, he carefully kept a neutral stance; moreover, the Revolution had taught him a
great deal about seemingly hopeless causes. At least once he expressed
pessimism in a letter to Alexander Hamilton, who had left the convention
for a time.

*First page of Washington's copy
of the first printed draft of the
Constitution, August 6, 1787*

Philadelphia 10th. July [17]87.

I thank you for your communication of the 3d. When I refer you to the State of the Councils which prevailed at the period you left this City — and add, that they are now, if possible, in a worse train than ever; you will find but little ground on which the hope of a good establishment can be formed. In a word, I *almost* despair of seeing a favourable issue to the proceedings of the Convention, and do therefore repent having had any agency in the business.

The Men who oppose a strong & energetic government are, in my opinion, narrow minded politicians, or are under the influence of local views. The apprehension expressed by them that the *people* will not accede to the form proposed is the *ostensible*, not the *real* cause of the opposition — but admitting that the present sentiment is as they prognosticate, the question ought nevertheless to be, is it or is it not, the best form? If the former, recommend it, and it will assuredly obtain mauger opposition. I am sorry you went away. I wish you were back. The crisis is equally important and alarming, and no opposition under such circumstances should discourage exertions till the signature is fixed. I will not, at this time trouble you with more than my best wishes and sincere regards.

Voting record of convention on the question of a single executive (right), one of the many problems considered before adoption of the Constitution; Washington was the first to sign the document (opposite, above); following this, "Members adjourned to the City Tavern" (far right).

Despite their differences, the men at Philadelphia, from states large and small and representing divergent economic interests, did compromise their many disagreements to create a constitution that—if completely satisfactory to none—all but three delegates present were willing to accept. (Rhode Island, which had stubbornly refused to send delegates to the convention, was not represented at the final signing, and part of the New York delegation had left earlier.) Washington, on the final day, ended his prohibition against mentioning convention proceedings in his diary.

Monday, 17th [September, 1787]. Met in Convention when the Constitution received the Unanimous assent of 11 States and Colo. Hamilton's from New York (the only delegate from thence in Convention) and was subscribed to by every Member present except Govr. [Edmund] Randolph and Colo. [George] Mason from Virginia—& Mr. [Elbridge] Gerry from Massachusetts.

The business being thus closed, the Members adjourned to the City Tavern, dined together and took a cordial leave of each other—after which I returned to my lodgings—did some business with, and received the papers from the secretary of the Convention, and retired to meditate on the momentous w[or]k which had been executed, after not less than five, for a large part of the time Six, and sometimes 7 hours sitting every day, [except] sundays & the ten days adjournment to give a Comee. opportunity & time to arrange the business for more than four Months.

The next day Washington left for Mount Vernon. Although as president of the convention he had taken little part in the debate, his commanding presence had been a powerful factor in the creation of the new Constitution. James Monroe, an opponent of the document, had written to Jefferson, "Be assured, his influence carried the government." After his return to Virginia, Washington wrote to his friends advocating ratification of the Constitution. He alternated between optimism and deep gloom as one state convention after another slowly and often heatedly deliberated before voting on ratification. By the end of May, 1788, eight states had ratified; only one more was needed to make the Constitution operative, and the convention in Virginia met on June 2. Washington's spirits were now up, now down, as he followed the daily exchanges in Richmond. The final vote came on June 25; one of those to whom Washington wrote in high spirits was Benjamin Lincoln.

In this engraving from the cover of a 1788 almanac, Washington and Franklin, pulled by thirteen men, escort the Constitution to ratification.

Mount Vernon June 29th. 1788.

I beg you will accept my thanks for the communications handed to me in your letter of the 3d. instant—and my congratulations on the encreasing good dispositions of the Citizens of your State of which the late elections are strongly indicative. No one *can* rejoice more than I do at every step the people of this great Country take to preserve the Union, establish good order and government—and to render the Nation happy at home and respectable abroad. No Country upon Earth ever had it more in its power to attain these blessings than United America. Wonderously strange then, and Much to be regretted indeed would it be, were we to neglect the means and to depart from the road which providence has pointed us to, so plainly—I cannot believe it will ever come to pass. The great Governor of the Universe has led us too long and too far on the road to happiness and glory to forsake us in the midst of it. By folly and improper conduct, proceeding from a variety of causes, we may now and then get bewildered; but I hope and trust that there is good sense and virtue enough left to recover the right path before we shall be entirely lost. You will, before this letter can have reached you, have heard of the Ratification of the new Government by this State. The final question without previous amendments was taken the 25th. Ayes 89—Noes 79;

but something recommendatory, or declaratory of the rights [accompanied] the ultimate decision. This account and the News of the adoption by New Hampshire arrived in Alexandria nearly about the same time on Friday evening; and, as you will suppose, was cause for great rejoicing among the Inhabitants who have not I believe an Antifederalist among them. Our Accounts from Richmond are, that the debates, through all the different Stages of the business, though [brisk] and animated, have been conducted with great dignity and temper; that the final decision exhibited [an] auful and solomn scene, and that there is every reason to expect a perfect acquiescence therein by the minority —not only from the declaration of Mr. Henry, the great Leader of it, who has signified that though he can never be reconciled to the Constitution in its present form, and shall give it every *constitutional* opposition in his power yet that he will submit to it peaceably, as he thinks every good Citizen ought to do when it is in exercise and that he will both by precept and example inculcate this doctrine to all around him.

There is little doubt entertained here *now* of the ratification of the proposed Constitution by North Carolina; and however great the opposition to it may be in New York the leaders thereof will, I should conceive, consider well the consequences before they reject it. With respect to Rhode Island, the power that governs there has so far baffled all calculation on this question that no man would chuse to hasard an opinion lest he might be suspected of participating in its phrensy.

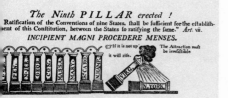

New Hampshire ratified Constitution on June 21; Virginia, a rising pillar in this drawing, four days later.

Independent Chronicle and Universal Advertiser, 1788

New York ratified in July, 1788, making eleven states. But North Carolina put off action until November of 1789, waiting for the new government to submit a proposed Bill of Rights to the states. Rhode Island, still intransigent, refused even to call a convention until 1790; then it voted to join the year-old Union. Congress—the old Congress—set March 4, 1789, as the day for the new government to go into effect. It had been pretty generally assumed that the first President could be only one man, George Washington. Although Washington was very reticent about discussing the matter, when his friend and former aide Alexander Hamilton wrote to say very candidly that the survival of the new government might well depend on his becoming President, Washington admitted that he had heard the possibility mentioned.

Mount Vernon October 3d. 1788.
In acknowledging the receipt of your candid and kind
letter by the last Post; little more is incumbent upon me,
than to thank you sincerely for the frankness with which
you communicated your sentiments, and to assure you
that the same manly tone of intercourse will always be
more than barely wellcome, Indeed it will be highly
acceptable to me. I am particularly glad, in the present
instance; you have dealt thus freely and like a friend.
Although I could not help observing from several publications and letters that my name had been sometimes
spoken of, and that it was possible the *Contingency*
which is the subject of your letter might happen; yet I
thought it best to maintain a guarded silence and to
[seek] the *counsel* of my best friends (which I certainly
hold in the highest estimation) rather than to hazard an
imputation unfriendly to the delicacy of my feelings.
For, situated as I am, I could hardly bring the question
into the slightest discussion, or ask an opinion even
in the most confidential manner; without betraying,
in my Judgment, some impropriety of conduct, or without feeling an apprehension that a premature display
of anxiety, might be construed into a vain-glorious
desire of pushing myself into notice as a Candidate.
Now, if I am not grossly deceived in myself, I should
unfeignedly rejoice, in case the Electors, by giving their
votes in favor of some other person, would save me from
the dreaded Dilemma of being forced to accept or refuse.
If that may not be—I am, in the next place, earnestly
desirous of searching out the truth, and of knowing
whether there does not exist a probability that the government would be just as happily and effectually carried
into execution, without my aid, as with it. I am *truly*
solicitous to obtain all the previous information which
the circumstances will afford, and to determine (when
the determination can with propriety be no longer postponed) according to the principles of right reason, and
the dictates of a clear conscience; without too great
a referrence to the unforeseen consequences, which
may affect my person or reputation. Untill that period,
I may fairly hold myself open to conviction—though I
allow your sentiments to have weight in them; and
I shall not pass by your arguments without giving them
as dispassionate a consideration, as I can possibly bestow

upon them.

In taking a survey of the subject in whatever point of light I have been able to place it; I will not suppress the acknowledgment, my Dr. Sir that I have always felt a kind of gloom upon my mind, as often as I have been taught to expect, I might, and perhaps must ere long be called to make a decision. You will, I am well assured, believe the assertion (though I have little expectation it would gain credit from those who are less acquainted with me) that if I should receive the appointment and if I should be prevailed upon to accept it; the acceptance would be attended with more diffidence and reluctance than ever I experienced before in my life. It would be, however, with a fixed and sole determination of lending whatever assistance might be in my power to promote the public, weal, in hopes that at a convenient and an early period, my services might be dispensed with, and that I might be permitted once more to retire — to pass an unclouded evening, after the stormy day of life, in the bosom of domestic tranquility.

But why these anticipations? If the friends to the Constitution conceive that my administering the government will be a means of its acceleration and strength, is it not probable that the adversaries of it may entertain the same ideas and of course make it an object of opposition? That many of this description will become Electors, I can have no doubt of: any more than that their opposition will extend to any character who (from whatever cause) would be likely to thwart their measures. It might be impolite in them to make this declaration *previous* to the Election, but I shall be out in my conjectures if they do not act conformably thereto — and from that the seeming moderation by which they appear to be actuated at present is neither more nor less than a finesse to lull and deceive. Their plan of opposition is systemised, and a regular intercourse, I have much reason to believe between the Leaders of it in the several States is formed to render it more effectual.

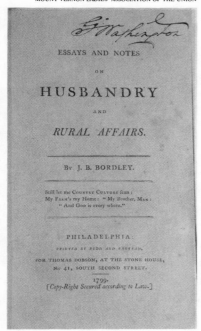

MOUNT VERNON LADIES' ASSOCIATION OF THE UNION

One of the last books Washington purchased on his favorite subject

Washington had given up his sword in 1783 and had returned to Mount Vernon with every hope and intention of spending the rest of his days there. It was becoming clear to him that once again he was going to have to say good-by to the place he loved so much.

Chapter 9

President of All the People

During the late summer and fall of 1788 George Washington was a worried man. He had already agonized — now optimistic, now gloomy — during the state-by-state ratification proceedings of the Constitution, wondering if the document would ever be approved. Now the Constitution had been ratified by eleven of the thirteen states, more than enough to make it operative; and Washington was anxiously following the elections to see if the senators, representatives, and presidential electors were Federalist or Antifederalist, supporters of the new nation envisioned in the Constitution or its enemies. Although the Antifederalists had failed to block the Constitution, it was possible that they might achieve enough power in the new government to wreck it from within. But Washington's apprehensions proved groundless. The senators-elect and representatives-elect proved to be overwhelmingly Federalist in sentiment, although the legislature of Washington's own Virginia, which was dominated by violently Antifederalist Patrick Henry, named two Antifederalist senators (senators were then chosen by state legislatures). The large majority of presidential electors were also Federalists. By the beginning of 1789 Washington was again able to view the future optimistically as he wrote to Lafayette. On the subject of himself as President-to-be, which everyone else took almost for granted, his references were modestly oblique.

> Mount Vernon Jany. 29th. 1789.
>
> My dear Marqs.:
>
> By the last Post, I was favored with the receipt of your letter, dated the 5th. of September last. Notwithstanding the distance of its date, it was peculiarly welcome to me: for I had not, in the mean time received any satisfactory advices respecting yourself or your country. By that letter, my mind was placed much more at its ease, on both those subjects, than it had been for many months.

The last letter, which I had the pleasure of writing to you, was forwarded by Mr. Gouverneur Morris. Since his departure from America, nothing very material has occurred. The minds of men, however, have not been in a stagnant State. But patriotism, instead of faction, has generally agitated them. It is not a matter of wonder, that, in proportion as we approached to the time fixed for the organization and operation of the new government, their anxiety should have been encreased, rather than diminished. The choice of Senators, Representatives and Electors, whh. (excepting in that of the last description) took place at different times, in the different States, has afforded abundant topics for domestic News, since the beginning of Autumn. I need not enumerate the several particulars, as I imagine you see most of them detailed, in the American Gazettes. I will content myself with only saying, that the elections have been hitherto vastly more favorable than we could have expected, that federal sentiments seem to be growing with uncommon rapidity, and that this encreasing unanimity is not less indicative of the good disposition than the good sense of the Americans. Did it not savour so much of partiality for my Countrymen I might add, that I cannot help flattering myself the new Congress on account of the self-created respectability and various talents of its Members, will not be inferior to any Assembly in the world. From these and some other circumstances, I really entertain greater hopes, that America will not finally disappoint the expectations of her Friends, than I have at almost any former period. Still however, in such a fickle state of existence I would not be too sanguine in indulging myself with the contemplation of scenes of uninterrupted prosperity; lest some unforeseen mischance or perverseness should occasion the greater mortification, by blasting the enjoyment in the very bud.

I can say little or nothing new, in consequence of the repetition of your opinion, on the expediency there will be, for my accepting the office to which you refer. Your sentiments, indeed, coincide much more nearly with those of my other friends, than with my own feelings. In truth my difficulties encrease and magnify as I [draw] towards the period, when, according to the common belief, it will be necessary for me to give a definitive answer, in one way or another. Should the circumstances render

Broadside announcing ratification of the Constitution by Virginia

it, in a manner inevitably necessary, to be in the affirmative: Be assured, my dear Sir, I shall assume the task with the most unfeigned reluctance, and with a real diffidence for which I shall probably receive no credit from the world. If I know my own heart, nothing short of a conviction of duty will induce me again to take an active part in public affairs—and, in that case, if I can form a plan for my own conduct, my endeavours shall be unremittingly exerted (even at the hazard of former fame or present popularity) to extricate my country from the embarrassments in which it is entangled, [through] want of credit; and to establish, a general system of policy, which, if pursued will ensure permanent felicity to the Commonwealth. I think, I see a *path*, as clear and direct as a ray of light, which leads to the attainment of that object. Nothing but harmony, honesty, industry and frugality are necessary to make us a great and happy people. Happily the present posture of affairs and the prevailing disposition of my countrymen promise to co-operate in establishing those four great and essential pillars of public felicity....

While you are quarrelling among yourselves in Europe —while one King is running mad—and others acting as if they were already so, by cutting the throats of the subjects of their neighbours: I think you need not doubt, My Dear Marquis we shall continue in tranquility here— And that population will be progressive so long as there shall continue to be so many easy means for obtaining a subsistence, and so ample a field for the exertion of talents and industry.

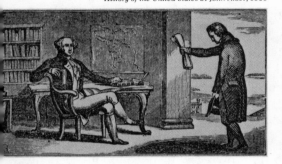

History of the United States BY JOHN FROST, 1836

As depicted in this old woodcut, Charles Thomson, secretary of the Congress and Washington's friend, comes to inform him of nomination.

Although Washington wrote of still being undecided about the Presidency, the truth was that he had already virtually decided that he would serve, thinking it possible that after the new government was running smoothly he might resign. On February 4, 1789, the electors met in their respective states and cast their ballots. The result was not to be announced officially for another month, but it was not a secret to keep: the final tally showed that the sixty-nine electors had voted unanimously for Washington for President. Among the vice-presidential choices, John Adams received the most votes, thirty-four. Under the timetable set by the old Congress, the new government was to come into being on March 4 when Congress officially convened at New York and the president pro tempore of the Senate formally opened the electors' ballots. As the date approached,

Washington's spirits once more fell at the news that Congress was showing no haste to assemble. There was no quorum on March 4, nor was there one a full month later. When Henry Knox informed him that Congress's dilatoriness had already cost the country £300,000 in spring import duties missed, Washington replied that that was not the worst part of it.

> Mount Vernon April 10th. 1789.
> The cloth & Buttons which accompanied your favor of the 30th. Ult., came safe by Colo. Hanson; and really do credit to the Manufactures of this Country. As it requires Six more of the large (engraved) button to trim the Coat in the manner I wish it to be [a coat of American-made cloth Washington was to wear at his inauguration], I would thank you, my good Sir, for procuring that number and retaining them in your hands until my arrival at New York.
>
> Not to contemplate (though it is a serious object) the loss which you say the General Government will sustain in the article of Impost, the stupor, or listlessness with which our public measures seem to be pervaded, is, to me, matter of deep regret. Indeed it has so strange an appearance that I cannot but wonder how men who sollicit public confidence or who are even prevailed upon to accept of it can reconcile such conduct with their own feelings of propriety. The delay is inauspicious to say the best of it—and the World must contemn it. With sentiments of sincerest friendship, I am etc.
>
> PS. The advices by the Mail of this Evening will, surely, inform us of a Quorum in both Houses of Congress.

Charles Thomson

At last enough senators and representatives did reach New York over the muddy spring roads to make a quorum, and the electoral votes were solemnly counted. On April 14 Charles Thomson, secretary of Congress and an old friend of Washington's, rode up to Mount Vernon. After the two men had greeted each other, Thomson made a short speech informing Washington that he had been elected and then read a letter from the president pro tempore of the Senate. Washington responded by reading his acceptance speech.

> [Mount Vernon, April 14, 1789]
> I have been accustomed to pay so much respect to the opinion of my fellow-citizens, that the knowledge of their having given their unanimous suffrages in my favour, scarcely leaves me the alternative for an option. I can not, I believe, give a greater evidence of my

293

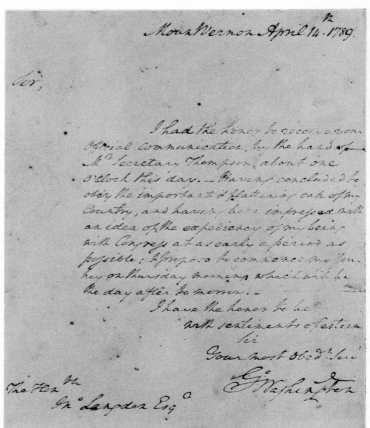

In addition to his acceptance speech, Washington wrote this letter to John Langdon, president pro tempore of the Senate, accepting the "important flattering call of my Country."

sensibility of the honor which they have done me than by accepting the appointment.

I am so much affected by this fresh proof of my Country's Esteem and Confidence that silence can best explain my gratitude. While I realize the arduous nature of the Task which is imposed upon me, and feel my own inability to perform it, I wish however that there may not be reason for regretting the Choice — for indeed all I can promise is only to accomplish that which can be done by an honest zeal.

Upon considering how long time some of the Gentlemen of both Houses of Congress have been at New-York — how anxiously desirous they must be to proceed to business — and how deeply the public mind appears to be impressed with the necessity of doing it speedily, I can not find myself at liberty to delay my journey. I shall therefore be in readiness to set out the day after tomorrow and shall be happy in the pleasure of your company; for you will permit me to say that it is a peculiar gratification to have received the communication from You.

Two days later, in midmorning of April 16, Washington's coach rolled out of the Mount Vernon drive. Washington was accompanied by Thomson and by David Humphreys, a wartime aide who had been going through Washington's papers with some intention of writing a biography. The President-elect recorded his emotions on leaving in his diary, a journal whose entries were usually quite matter-of-fact.

> April 16 [1789]. —About ten o'clock I bade adieu to Mount Vernon, to private life, and to domestic felicity; and, with a mind oppressed with more anxious and painful sensations than I have words to express, set out for New York in company with Mr. Thompson and Colonel Humphreys, with the best disposition to render service to my country in obedience to its call, but with less hope of answering its expectations.

The first leg of his journey took Washington not much more than half a dozen miles before he stopped at Alexandria for a farewell dinner with his old friends and neighbors. Only a couple of hours earlier he had felt a deep stab at leaving Mount Vernon; once again he was overcome by the poignancy of parting and the uncertainties of the future as he said his formal good-by to people he had known for many years.

> [Alexandria, April 16, 1789]

> Gentlemen:

> Although I ought not to conceal, yet I cannot describe, the painful emotions which I felt in being called upon to determine whether I would accept or refuse the Presidency of the United States.

> The unanimity in the choice, the opinion of my friends, communicated from different parts of Europe, as well as of America, the apparent wish of those, who were not altogether satisfied with the Constitution in its present form, and an ardent desire on my own part, to be instrumental in conciliating the good will of my countrymen towards each other have induced an acceptance.

> Those who have known me best (and you, my fellow citizens, are from your situation, in that number) know better than any others my love of retirement is so great, that no earthly consideration, short of a conviction of duty, could have prevailed upon me to depart from my resolution, *"never more to take any share in transactions. of a public nature"*—For, at my age, and in my circumstances, what possible advantages could I propose to

myself, from embarking again on the tempestuous and uncertain ocean of public-life?

I do not feel myself under the necessity of making public declarations, in order to convince you, Gentlemen, of my attachment to yourselves, and regard for your interests. The whole tenor of my life has been open to your inspection; and my pas[t] actions, rather than my present declarations, must be the pledge of my future conduct.

In the meantime I thank you most sincerely for the expressions of kindness contained in your valedictory address. It is true, just after having bade adieu to my domestic connections, this tender proof of your friendship is but too well calculated still farther to awaken my sensibility, and encrease my regret at parting from the enjoyments of private life.

All that now remains for me is to commit myself and you to the protection of that beneficent Being, who on a former occasion hath happily brought us together, after a long and distressing separation. Perhaps the same gracious Providence will again indulge us with the same heartfelt felicity. But words, my fellow-citizens, fail me: *Unutterable sensations must then be left to more expressive silence: while, from an aching heart, I bid you all, my affectionate friends, and kind neighbours, farewell*[!]

Washington's triumphal journey to New York was drawn by Peale (above and right, below) for a contemporary magazine. George Cruikshank drew the young ladies at Trenton (right).

The journey to New York took on the aspects of a triumphal march. Everywhere, except where the country was sparsely settled, troops of horsemen escorted him in almost unbroken relays, so that Washington often rode for hours in a cloud of dust. At Gray's Ferry near Philadelphia a floating bridge across the Schuylkill River was walled with branches of laurel and cedar and a leafy arch had been erected at each end. As Washington, astride a horse provided for the occasion, started through this floating bower, a child hidden in the greenery of the arch lowered a laurel wreath until it was suspended just above his head. First plans had been to drop the wreath on Washington's head, but it was decided that this might be a bit unnerving even to a hero. Philadelphia outdid itself in acclaiming the President-elect with roaring cannon, pealing churchbells, cheering crowds, and five addresses, to each of which Washington replied briefly. Washington was probably less than overjoyed when informed that the Philadelphia City Troop of Horse meant to escort him all the way to Princeton, for such ceremony and honor slowed his progress. Thus, when the morning turned out to be threatening, he took advantage of the situation in a way that got rid of the escort without hurting any feelings.

City-Tavern [Philadelphia]

Tuesday morning April 21 1789.

General Washington presents his compliments to the President of the State, and requests his Excellency to communicate the General's best thanks to the Officers and Gentlemen of the several Corps who did him the honor to form his escort to Philadelphia. General Washington having made his arrangements to be at the place of embarkation for New York, at a particular hour, will find himself under the necessity of leaving this City about ten o'clock — But, as the weather is likely to prove unfavorable, he must absolutely insist that the military Gentlemen of Philadelphia will not attend him in the manner they had proposed. He is so perfectly satisfied with their good intentions, that it will be impossible for them, by taking any unnecessary trouble, to make any addition to the proofs of their attachment, or the motives of his gratitude.

The bridge his army had defended against the British at Assunpink Creek near Trenton was now turned into a tunnel of green. On its face was a banner bearing the motto "The Defenders of the Mothers will also Defend the Daughters," and lining the entrance to the bridge were rows of matrons and girls of all ages. As Washington came between their ranks, a chorus of young ladies burst into a song of welcome. At the concluding lines — "Strew, ye fair, his way with flowers;/Strew your Hero's way with flowers" — small girls with baskets stepped out and spread flowers before Washington's horse. Washington, visibly moved, thanked the ladies, and that evening found time to write a note addressed to "the Ladies of Trenton who assembled at the Triumphal Arch."

David Humphreys

Trenton April 21st. 1789.

General Washington cannot leave this place without expressing his acknowledgments, to the Matrons and Young Ladies who received him in so Novel & grateful a manner at the Triumphal Arch in Trenton, for the exquisite sensation he experienced in that affecting moment. The astonishing contrast between his former and actual situation at the same spot—the elegant taste with which it was adorned for the present occasion—and the innocent appearance of the *white-robed Choir* who met him with the gratulatory song, have made such impressions on his remembrance, as, he assures them, will never be effaced.

On April 23 Washington reached Elizabeth Town Point, New Jersey, to be rowed in a barge about fifteen miles across the bay to New York, where his reception was tumultuous. He was not even given an opportunity to change his clothes before he was hauled away to a banquet and an evening of viewing the illuminated transparencies in the city's windows. For a week, while Congress fussed about arrangements for the inauguration, Washington received visits from committees, was called on by members of Congress, and was bothered from morning till night by a stream of visitors whose principal motive in wishing to see him, apparently, was curiosity. Shortly after noon on April 30 Washington was escorted to the halls of Congress at Wall and Broad streets. So that the enormous crowds might see the historic event, the oath was taken on a small balcony. Washington promised to execute faithfully the office of President and to preserve, protect, and defend the Constitution to the best of his ability, in exactly the same words that have been repeated by every President since. Then, while the cheers still rolled through the crowds, the new Chief Executive returned inside and made his inaugural speech. It was brief. Washington's recommendations to Congress went no further than to warn against such things as pettiness, "local prejudices," "party animosities," and the like. He cautiously endorsed a Bill of Rights while warning against hasty tinkering with the main substance of the Constitution, and he called frequently on the Almighty for guidance.

[New York, April 30, 1789]

Fellow Citizens of the Senate and of the House of Representatives.

Among the vicissitudes incident to Life, no event could have filled me with greater anxieties than that, of which the notification was transmitted by your order and received on the fourteenth day of the present month.

Washington's reception in New York

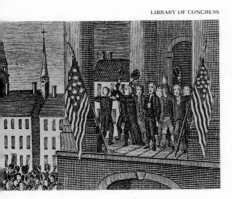

Inauguration of Washington

On the one hand, I was summon'd by my Country, whose Voice I can never hear but with veneration and love, from a retreat which I had chosen with the fondest predilection, and in my flattering hopes, with an immutable decision, as the assylum of my declining years, a retreat which was rendered every day more necessary as well as more dear to me, by the addition of habit to inclination and of frequent interruptions in my health to the gradual waste committed on it by time. On the other hand, the magnitude and difficulty of the Trust to which the voice of my country called me, being sufficient to awaken in the wisest and most experienced of her Citizens, a distrustful scrutiny into his qualifications, could not but overwhelm with despondence, one, who (inheriting inferior endowments from Nature and unpractised in the duties of civil administration) ought to be peculiarly conscious of his own deficencies. In this conflict of emotions, all I dare aver, is, that it has been my faithful study to collect my duty from a just appreciation of every circumstance by which it might be affected. All I dare hope, is, that if in executing this Task, I have been too much swayed by a grateful remembrance of former instances or by an affectionate sensibility to this transcendent proof of the confidence of my fellow Citizens; and have thence too little consulted my incapacity as well as disinclination for the weighty and untried cares before me; my error will be palliated by the motives which misled me, and its consequences be judged by my Country with some share of the partiality in which they originated.

Such being the impressions under which I have in obedience to the public summons repaired to the present station; it would be peculiarly improper to omit in this first official act my fervent supplications to that Almighty Being who rules over the Universe, who presides in the Councils of Nations and whose providential aids can supply every human defect, that his benediction may consecrate, to the Liberties and happiness of the people of the United States, a Government instituted by themselves for these essential purposes: and may enable every instrument employed in its administration, to execute with success the functions allotted to his charge.... By the article establishing the executive department, it is made the duty of the President

After his inauguration, Washington walked to St. Paul's Church (right of Brick Presbyterian Church), where prayers were offered for success.

"to recommend to your consideration such measures as he shall judge necessary and expedient." The circumstances under which I now meet you, will acquit me from entering into that subject, farther than to refer to the great consitutional Charter under which you are assembled; and which in defining your powers, designates the objects to which your attention is to be given. It will be more consistent with those circumstances and far more congenial with the feelings which actuate me to substitute in place of a recommendation of particular measures, the tribute that is due to the talents, the rectitude and the patriotism which adorn the Characters selected to devise and adopt them. In these honorable qualifications, I behold the surest pledges that as on one side, no local prejudices or attachments; no seperate views, nor party animosities, will misdirect the comprehensive and equal Eye which ought to watch over this great assemblage of communities and interests; so, on another that the foundations of our national policy will be laid in the pure and immutable principles of private morality; and the preeminence of free Government be exemplified by all the attributes, which can win the affections of its citizens and command the respect of the world....

Besides the ordinary objects submitted to your care, it will remain with your judgment to decide, how far an exercise of the occasional power delegated by the fifth article of the Constitution is rendered expedient at the present juncture, by the nature of objections which have been urged against the System, or by the degree of inquietude which has given birth to them. Instead of undertaking particular recommendations on this subject, in which I could be guided by no lights derived from official opportunities, I shall again give way to my entire confidence in your discernment and pursuit of the public good — For I assure myself that whilst you carefully avoid every alteration which might endanger the benefits of an United and effective government or which ought to await the future lessons of experience; a reverence for the characteristic rights of freemen, and a regard for the public harmony, will sufficiently influence your deliberations on the question, how far the former can be impregnably fortified or the latter be safely and advantageously promoted.

Washington also proposed that he receive no salary but only be reimbursed for his expenses, as he had been during the Revolution. Congress, however, fixed a salary of twenty-five thousand dollars a year, and although Washington drew only his expenses, over four years they amounted almost exactly to what the salary would have been. The new President was in a world without precedents, and it was important that he act carefully and wisely. He moved early to put the presidential social life in order; it was imperative that he limit the parade of visitors who called at all hours and also that he cut down on his attendance at social functions if he were to conserve his energy and get any work done. He asked Vice President Adams, Alexander Hamilton, and John Jay for their advice.

[New York, May 10, 1789]

The President of the United States wishes to avail himself of your sentiments on the following points.

1st. Whether a line of conduct, equally distant from an association with all kinds of company on the one hand and from a total seclusion from Society on the other, ought to be adopted by him? and, in that case, how is it to be done?

2d. What will be the least exceptionable method of bringing any system, which may be adopted on this subject, before the public and into use?

3d. Whether, after a little time, one day in every week will not be sufficient for receiving visits of Compliment?

4th. Whether it would tend to prompt impertinent applications & involve disagreeable consequences to have it known, that the President will, every Morning at 8 Oclock, be at leisure to give Audiences to persons who may have business with him?

5th. Whether, when it shall have been understood that the President is not to give *general entertainment* in the Manner the Presidents of Congress have formerly done, it will be practicable to draw such a line of discrimination in regard to persons, as that Six, eight or ten official characters (including in the rotation the members of both Houses of Congress) may be invited informally or otherwise to dine with him on the days fixed for receiving Company, without exciting clamours in the rest of the Community?

6th. Whether it would be satisfactory to the Public for the President to make about four great entertainmts. in a year on such great occasions as . . . the Anniversary of the Declaration of Independence . . . the Alliance with

This small mansion on the corner of Pearl and Cherry streets in New York was the first presidential abode.

France ... the Peace with Great Britain ... the Organization of the general Government: and whether arrangements of these two last kinds could be in danger of diverting too much of the Presidents time from business, or of producing the evils which it was intended to avoid by his living more recluse than the Presidts. of Congress have heretofore lived.

7th. Whether there would be any impropriety in the Presidents making informal visits—that is to say, in his calling upon his Acquaintances or public Characters for the purposes of sociability or civility—and what (as to the form of doing it) might evince these visits to have been made in his private character, so as that they might not be construed into visits from the President of the United States? and in what light would his appearance *rarely at Tea* parties be considered?

8th. Whether, during the recess of Congress, it would not be advantageous to the interests of the Union for the President to make the tour of the United States, in order to become better acquainted with their principal Characters & internal Circumstances, as well as to be more accessible to numbers of well-informed persons, who might give him useful information and advices on political subjects?

9th. If there is a probability that either of the arrangements may take place, which will eventually cause additional expences, whether it would not be proper that these ideas should come into contemplation, at the time when Congress shall make a permanent provision for the support of the Executive?

Remarks

On the one side no augmentation can be effected in the pecuniary establishment which shall be made in the first instance, for the support of the Executive. On the other, all monies destined to that purpose beyond the actual expenditures, will be left in the Treasury of the United States or sacredly applied to the promotion of some National objects.

Many things which appear of little importance in themselves and at the beginning, may have great and durable consequences from their having been established at the commencement of a new general government. It will be much easier to commence the administration, upon a well adjusted system built on tenable grounds,

Washington used this writing table in Federal Hall when the capital was still located in New York City.

The Centennial of Washington's Inauguration;
BENJAMIN FRANKLIN COLLECTION,
STERLING MEMORIAL LIBRARY, YALE UNIVERSITY

than to correct errors or alter inconveniencies after they shall have been confirmed by habit. The President in all matters of business & etiquette, can have no object but to demean himself in his public character, in such a manner as to maintain the dignity of Office, without subjecting himself to the imputation of superciliousness or unnecessary reserve. Under these impresions, he asks for your candid and undisguised Opinions.

Both Hamilton and Adams advised Washington to remain aloof. The President compromised somewhat; he set two weekly occasions: a "levee" for men and a tea for both sexes over which Martha would preside, during which, for one hour, any citizen could call and meet the President. There was also to be a weekly dinner at which the President would be host to groups of government officials. There were precedents to be set in government, too. When, for instance, a letter arrived from the King of France addressed both to the President and to Congress, Washington in informing Congress said that he would take care of the answer and left the unmistakable implication that such matters were strictly in his province.

United States September 29th. 1789.

Gentlemen of the Senate and House of Representatives:

His most Christian Majesty, by a letter dated the 7th. of June last, addressed to the President and Members of the General Congress of the United States of North America, announced the much lamented death of his son the Dauphin. The generous conduct of the French Monarch and Nation towards this Country renders every event that may affect his or their prosperity interesting to us, and I shall take care to assure him of the sensibility with which the United States participate in the affliction which a loss so much to be regretted must have occasioned both to him and them.

Louis XVI

There were hundreds of appointments for Washington to make, most of them for customs collectors and the like, but also for the high offices of the justices of the Supreme Court and the judges of the eleven district courts, as well as the members of the President's own Cabinet— although it appears that Washington himself did not use the term Cabinet. Alexander Hamilton was appointed Secretary of the Treasury; Henry Knox became Secretary of War; Thomas Jefferson, Secretary of State; and Edmund Randolph, Attorney General. John Jay, the leading diplomat of the old government, was appointed first Chief Justice of the United States. Congress

303

adjourned on September 29, and on October 15 the President set out on a tour of New England. He kept a careful record of people and places in his diary, as he had on former travels, but now there was a difference. Previously he had been mainly interested in land and soil; now he was curious about community growth, commerce, manufacturing, and other evidences of national expansion. Following are some typical excerpts from that diary.

Thursday, 15th [October, 1789]. Commenced my Journey about 9 oclock for Boston and a tour through the Eastern States. The Chief Justice, Mr. Jay—and the Secretaries of the Treasury and War Departments accompanied me some distance out of the city. About 10 Oclock it began to Rain, and continued to do so till 11, when we arrived at the house of one Hoyatt, who keeps a Tavern at Kings-bridge, where we, that is, Major Jackson, Mr. Lear and myself, with Six Servants, which composed my Retinue, dined. After dinner through frequent light showers we proceedd. to the Tavern of a Mrs. Haviland at Rye [New York]; who keeps a very neat and decent Inn....

The distance of this days travel was 31 Miles in which we passed through (after leaving the Bridge) East Chester, New Rochel & Mameroneck; but as these places (though they have houses of worship in them) are not regularly laid out, they are scarcely to be distinquished from the intermediate farms which are very close together—and separated, as one Inclosure from another also is, by fences of Stone which are indeed easily made, as the Country is immensely stony. Upon enquiry we find their Crops of Wheat & Rye have been abundant—though of the first they had sown rather sparingly on Acct. of the destruction which had of late years been made of that grain by what is called the Hessian fly.

Friday, 16th. About 7 Oclock we left the Widow Havilands, and after passing Horse Neck, six miles distant from Rye, the Road through which is hilly and immensely stoney and trying to Wheels & Carriages, we breakfasted at Stamford [Connecticut] which is 6 miles further (at one Webbs) a tolerable good house, but not equal in appearance or reality, to Mrs. Havilds. In this Town are an Episcopal Church and a Meeting house. At Norwalk which is ten miles further we made a halt to feed our Horses. To the lower end of this town

BOTH: NEW-YORK HISTORICAL SOCIETY

Washington's first Cabinet included Jefferson and Hamilton (standing to his right), and Knox reading paper.

Sea Vessels come and at the other end are Mills, Stores, and an Episcopal and Presbiterian Church. From hence to Fairfield where we dined and lodged, is 12 Miles; and part of it very rough Road, but not equal to that thro' horse Neck.... The Destructive evidences of British cruelty are yet visible both in Norwalk & Fairfield; as there are the Chimneys of many burnt houses standing in them yet. The principal export from Norwalk & Fairfield is Horses and Cattle—Salted Beef & Porke, Lumber & Indian Corn, to the West Indies—and in a small degree Wheat & Flour.

Saturday, 17th. ...[We] arrived at New haven before two Oclock; We had time to Walk through several parts of the City before Dinner. By taking the lower Road, we missed a Committee of the assembly, who had been appointed to wait upon, and escort me into town— to prepare an Address—and to conduct me when I should leave the City as far as they should judge proper. The address was presented at 7 Oclock—and at nine I received another address from the Congregational Clergy of the place. Between the rect. of the two addresses I received the Compliment of a Visit from the Govr. Mr. Huntington—the Lieut. Govr. Mr. Wolcot—and the Mayor Mr. Roger Shurman. The City of New-haven occupies a good deal of ground; but is thinly, though regularly laid out, and built. The number of Souls in it are said to be about 4000. There is an Episcopal Church and 3 Congregational Meeting Houses and a College [Yale] in which there are at this time 120 Students under the auspices of Doctr. Styles. The Harbour of this place is not good for large Vessels—abt. 16 belongs to it. The Linnen Manufacture of this place does not appear to be of so much importance as I had been led to believe—In a word I could hear but little of it. The Exports from this City are much the same as from Fairfield &ca. and flax seed (chiefly to New York). The Road from Kings bridge to this place runs as near the Sound as the Bays and Inlets will allow, but from hence to Hartford it leaves the Sound and runs more to the Northward....

Monday, 19th. Left New haven at 6 oclock, and arrived at Wallingford (13 miles) by half after 8 oclock, where we breakfasted and took a walk through the Town.... At this place (Wallingford) we see the white Mulberry

John Jay

growing, raised from the Seed to feed the Silkworm. We also saw samples of lustring (exceeding good) which had been manufactured from the Cocoon raised in this Town, and silk thread very fine. This, except the weaving, is the work of private families without interference with other business, and is likely to turn out a beneficial amusement.

Washington and his party—two secretaries and six servants—continued up the Connecticut River to Springfield, Massachusetts, then turned east toward Boston, the scene of his first victory over the British. He received a tremendous welcome but was forced to establish the supremacy of the President over the governor of a state. Washington had accepted an advance invitation to dine with Governor John Hancock, fully expecting that Hancock would call on him first. But when he arrived in Boston, Hancock was not among the welcomers and sent word that gout made it impossible for him to move from his house. Washington realized that Hancock, a strong advocate of states' rights, was trying to establish that when a President visited a state he did so only as a guest of the governor. He immediately canceled the dinner engagement. The message was not lost on Hancock, who sent emissaries and then came to call. Washington described the incident in his diary briefly and without comment.

Banner carried by Boston shoemakers during procession in honor of visit

Saturday, 24th [October, 1789]. . . . Having engaged yesterday to take an informal dinner with the Govr. today, (but under a full persuasion that he would have waited upon me so soon as I should have arrived) I excused myself upon his not doing it, and informing me thro his Secretary that he was too much indisposed to do it, being resolved to receive the visit. Dined at my Lodgings, where the Vice-President favoured me with his Company.

Sunday, 25th. Attended Divine Service at the Episcopal Church whereof Doctor Parker is the Incumbent in the forenoon, and the Congregational Church of Mr. Thatcher in the Afternoon. Dined at my Lodgings with the Vice President. Mr. Bowdoin accompanied me to both Churches. Between the two I received a visit from the Govr., who assured me that Indisposition alone had prevented his doing it yesterday, and that he was still indisposed; but as it had been suggested that he expected to *receive* the visit from the President, which he knew was improper, he was resolved at all hazds. to pay his Compliments today. The Lt. Govr. & two of the Council to wit Heath & Russel were sent here last Night to express the Govrs. Concern that he had not been in a condition to call upon me so soon as I came to Town. I informed them in explicit terms that I should not see the Govr., unless it was at my own lodgings.

Hancock had been carried, heavily swathed in bandages, into Washington's lodgings when he called on the President; but if Washington suspected that the Governor's gout was feigned, he did not confide it to his diary. The constitutional issue was settled, and the precedence of President over governor established. On his fifth day in Boston, Washington escaped from the ceremonial and social activities and began to become better acquainted with the city.

Wednesday, 28th [October, 1789]. Went after an early breakfast to visit the duck Manufacture which appeared to be carrying on with spirit, and is in a prosperous way. They have manufactured 32 pieces of Duck of 30 or 40 yds. each in a week; and expect in a short time to encrease it to [   ]. They have 28 looms at work & 14 Girls spinning with Both hands (the flax being fastened to their waste). Children (girls) turn the wheels for them, and with this assistance each spinner can turn out 14 lbs. of thread pr. day when they stick to it, but as they are pd. by the piece, or work they do, there is no other restraint upon them but to come at 8 Oclock in the Morning and return at 6 in the evening. They are the daughters of decayed families, and are girls of Character—none others are admitted. The number of hands now employed in the different parts of the work is [   ] but the Managers expect to encrease them to [   ]. This is a work of public utility & private advantage. From hence I went to the Card Manufactury where I was informed about 900 hands of one kind and for one purpose or another. All kinds of Cards are made; & there are Machines for executing every part of the work in a new and expeditious manr., especially in cutting & bending the teeth wch. is done at one stroke. They have made 63,000 pr. of Cards in a year and can under sell the Imported Cards—nay Cards of this Manufactury have been smuggled into England. . . .

Thursday, 29th. Left Boston about 8 o'clock. Passed over the Bridge at Charles Town and went to see that

John Hancock

A view of the bridge over Charles River, which President Washington described as "useful and noble"

at Malden, but proceeded to the college at Cambridge [Harvard], attended by the Vice President, Mr. Bowdoin, and a great number of Gentlemen: At this place I was shewn by Mr. Willard the President, the Philosophical Aparatus, and amongst others Popes Orary (a curious piece of Mechanism for shewing the revolutions of the Sun, Earth, and many other of the Planets,)—the library, (containing 13,000 volumes,)—and a Museum. The Bridges of Charles town and Malden are useful & noble —doing great credit to the enterprising spirit of the People of this State. From Boston, besides the number of Citizens which accompanied me to Cambridge, & many of them from hence to Lynn—the Boston Corps of Horse escorted me to the line between Middlesex and Essex County where a party of Horse with Genl. Titcomb met me, and conducted me through Marblehead (which is 4 miles out of the way, but I wanted to see it,) to Salem. The Chief employmt. of the People of Marblehead (Male) is fishing—about 110 Vessels and 800 Men and boys are engaged in this business. Their chief export is fish. About 5000 Souls are said to be in this place which has the appearance of antiquity; the Houses are old—the streets dirty—and the common people not very clean.

Washington continued his journey, through Salem, which he thought "a neat town," on to Newburyport, and into New Hampshire, where there was another rousing welcome by militia, horsemen, and dignitaries, including the president (governor) of the state, John Sullivan, his good friend and onetime general. Two days later he crossed the river from Portsmouth, New Hampshire, to Kittery in Maine, then a province of Massachusetts. He and his party went fishing for cod, "but it not being a proper time of tide, we only caught two." From this northernmost point he began his return, asking that all ceremony be avoided. There was little pomp and circumstance in his passage through farmland and hamlets; like any other mortal, he talked with farmers about crops, asked directions and sometimes got bad advice, and occasionally had trouble finding lodgings.

Friday, 6th [November, 1789]. A little after Seven oclock, under great appearances of Rain or Snow, we left Watertown [Massachusetts], and Passing through Needham (five Miles therefrom) breakfasted at Sherburn which is 14 Miles from the former. Then passing through Holliston 5 Miles, Milford 6 More, Menden 4 More, and Uxbridge 6 More, we lodged at one Tafts 1 Miles further; the whole distance of this days travel being 36 Miles. From Watertown till you get near Needham, the Road is very level—about Needham it is hilly—then level again, and the whole pleasant and well cultivated 'till you pass Sherburn; between this and Holliston is some hilly & Rocky ground as there is in places, onwards to Uxbridge; some of wch. are very bad; Upon the whole it may be called an indifferent Rd.—diversified by good & bad land—cultivated and in woods—some high and Barren—and others low, wet and Piney. Grass and Indian Corn is the chief produce of the Farms. Rye composes a part of the culture of them, but wheat is not grown on Acct. of the blight. The Roads in every part of this State are amazingly crooked, to suit the convenience of every Mans fields; & the directions you receive from the People equally blind & ignorant; for instead of going to Watertown from Lexington, if we had proceeded to Waltham, we should in 13 Miles have saved at least Six; the distance from Lexington to Waltham being only 5 Miles and the Road from Watertown to Sherburn going with in less than two miles of the latter, (i.e. Waltham). The Clouds of the Morning vanished before the Meridian Sun, and the Afternoon was bright and pleasant. The house in Uxbridge had a good external appearance (for a Tavern) but the owner of it being from home, and the wife sick, we could not gain admittance which was the reason of my coming on to Tafts; where, though the People were obliging, the entertainment was not very inviting. . . .

Sunday, 8th. It being contrary to Law & disagreeable to the People of this State (Connecticut) to travel on the Sabbath day—and my horses, after passing through such intolerable Roads, wanting rest, I stayed at Perkins's Tavern (which by the bye is not a good one,) all day—and a meeting House being with in few rod of the Door, I attended Morning & evening Service, and heard very lame discourses from a Mr. Pond.

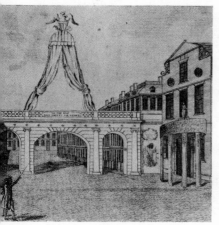

The triumphal arch and colonnade erected in Boston in front of the State House to honor the President

On his tour Washington had avoided Rhode Island, which had not yet ratified the Constitution, and Vermont, not yet a state. He arrived back in New York on Friday afternoon, November 13, just in time for Martha's weekly tea party.

Congress reconvened in early January, and Washington presented his first annual message. A week later Alexander Hamilton gave Congress a plan for strengthening national credit and reducing the public debt. It was the issue that would eventually split Washington's Administration into opposing political parties. Congress had gone deeply into debt during the Revolution. The foreign debt was almost twelve million dollars. No one knew exactly what the domestic debt was—Army quartermaster foraging parties, for instance, had given thousands of hastily written certificates to farmers for requisitioned grain or cattle—but it was fixed at something more than forty-four million dollars. Hamilton proposed that this entire debt be funded, with the almost worthless old securities exchanged at face value for new bonds, which would be gradually retired through excise taxes. Hamilton further proposed that the Government assume some $21,500,000 in debts owed by the states. The financial community approved Hamilton's plan, but elsewhere there was intense opposition. Most of the certificates given to farmers and soldiers had long since passed into the hands of speculators for a few cents on the dollar. James Madison fought hard but unsuccessfully for a plan to make at least partial payment to the original bearers of certificates. There was even greater controversy over federal assumption of state debts. The southern states, except South Carolina, had already paid their war debts and had no desire to be taxed again to help New Englanders who had let their obligations drift.

In mid-May Washington became so ill with pneumonia that his doctors believed he was dying; then he passed a crisis and a week later was able to go out in his carriage for exercise. In mid-June, Congress was still wrangling over the money bill, and Washington was well enough to write to Dr. David Stuart, husband of the widow of Jack Custis. Stuart had complained that Virginia sentiment toward the new government had been soured by the actions of Congress, by its slowness, and because the members "it is said, sit only four hours a day, and like School-boys observe every Saturday as a Holy day." In his reply Washington defended the legislature.

> New York June 15. 1790.
>
> Your description of the public mind in Virginia gives me pain—It seems to be more irritable, sour, and discontented than (from the information I receive) it is in any other State in the union, except Massachusetts, which from the same causes, but on quite different principles is tempered like it.
>
> That Congress does not proceed with all that dispatch which people at a distance expect, and which, were they to hurry business they possibly might, is not to be denied. That measures have been agitated which are not pleasing to Virginia, and others, pleasing perhaps to her, but not so to some other States is equally unquestionable.

Can it well be otherwise in a Country so extensive, so diversified in its interests? And will not these different interests naturally produce in an Assembly of Representatives, who are to legislate for, and to assimilate, and reconcile them to the *general* welfare, long, warm, and animated debates? Most assuredly they will—and if there was the same propensity in mankind for investigating the motives, as there is for censuring the conduct of public characters, it would be found that the censure so freely bestowed is oftentimes unmerited and uncharitable—for instance, the condemnation of Congress for sitting only four hours in the day. The fact is, by the established rules of the House of Representatives, no Committee can sit whilst the House is sitting; and this is and has been for a considerable time, from ten o'clock in the forenoon until three, often later, in the afternoon; before and after which the business is going on in Committees. If this application is not as much as most constitutions are equal to, I am mistaken: Many other things which undergo malignant constructions, would be found, upon a candid examination to wear better faces than are given to them. The misfortune is, that the enemies to the Government, always more active than its friends—and always upon the watch to give it a stroke—neglect no opportunity to aim one. If they tell truth, it is not the whole truth, by which means one side only of the picture is exhibited; whereas if both sides were seen, it might and probably would, assume a different form in the opinion of just and candid men, who are disposed to measure matters on a continental scale. I do not mean, however, from what I have here said, to justify the conduct of Congress in all its movements; for some of these movements, in my opinion, have been injudicious, and others unseasonable; whilst the questions of assumption, residence, and other matters, have been agitated with a warmth and intemperence—with prolixity and threats, which it is to be feared has lessened the dignity of that body, and decreased that respect which was once entertained for it—and this misfortune is increased by many Members, even among those who wish well to the Government ascribing in letters to their respective States when they are defeated in a favorite measure, the worst motives for the conduct of their Opponents; who, viewing matters through another medium, may,

Carriage built for George Washington during his first presidential term

and do, retort in their turn, by which means jealousies and distrusts are spread most impoliticly far and wide, and will it is to be feared, have a most unhappy tendency to injure our public affairs, which if wisely managed might make us (as we are now by Europeans thought to be) the happiest people upon Earth. . . .

The question of assumption has occupied a great deal of time, and no wonder; for it is certainly a very important question; and, under *proper* restrictions, and scrutiny into accounts will be found, I conceive, to be a just one. The cause, in which the expenses of the war was incurred was a common cause. The States (in Congress) declared it so at the beginning, and pledged themselves to stand by each other; If then, some States were harder pressed than others, or from particular or local circumstances contracted heavier debts, it is but reasonable when this fact is clearly ascertained, though it is a sentiment which I have not communicated here, that an allowance ought to be made them. Had the invaded and hard pressed States believed the case would have been otherwise, opposition would very soon, I believe, have changed to submission in them, and given a different termination to the war.

In a letter of last year to the best of my recollection, I informed you of the motives, which *compelled* me to allot a day for the reception of idle and ceremonious visits (for it never has prevented those of sociability and friendship in the afternoon, or at any other time) but if I am mistaken in this, the history of this business is simply and shortly as follows. Before the custom was established, which now accommodates foreign characters, Strangers, and others who from motives of curiosity, respect, to the Chief Magistrate, or any other cause, are induced to call upon me I was unable to attend to any business *whatsoever*; for Gentlemen, consulting their own convenience rather than mine, were calling from the time I rose from breakfast—often before—until I sat down to dinner. This, as I resolved not to neglect my public duties, reduced me to the choice of one of these alternatives, either to refuse them *altogether*, or to appropriate a time for the reception of them. The first would, I well knew, be disgusting to many—The latter, I *expected*, would undergo animadversion, and blazoning from those who would find fault,

The large house in New York City to which the Washingtons moved in 1790

with, or *without* cause. To please every body was impossible—I therefore adopted that line of conduct which combined public advantage with private convenience, and which in my judgment was unexceptionable in itself. That I have not been able to make bows to the taste of poor Colonel Bland, (who by the by I believe never saw one of them) is to be regretted especially too as (upon those occasions) they were indiscriminately bestowed, and the best I was master of—would it not have been better to have thrown the veil of charity over them, ascribing their stiffness to the effects of age, or to the unskillfulness of my teacher, than to pride and dignity of office, which God knows has no charms for me? for I can truly say I had rather be at Mount Vernon with a friend or two about me, than to be attended at the Seat of Government by the Officers of State and the Representatives of every Power in Europe.

By and large, things were going well for the new nation. The Bill of Rights, or first ten amendments to the Constitution, had been submitted to the states for ratification and would become part of the fundamental law on December 15, 1791. Meanwhile Rhode Island, the last hold-out, ratified the Constitution in May, 1790 (North Carolina had done so the previous November). But Hamilton's plan for funding the debt seemed doomed; federal assumption of state debts had been voted down in the House committee sessions. Hamilton, in despair, went to Jefferson for help. The issue could split the nation, he said. New England might well secede if assumption were defeated. Jefferson recognized the gravity of the situation and agreed there was probably room for compromise. At a meeting with Hamilton and James Madison an agreement was worked out: in return for the Southerners' accepting assumption of debts, there would be northern support for locating the permanent capital of the country in the South, at a site to be selected by Washington on the banks of the Potomac River. As a sop to Pennsylvania politicians, the capital was to be moved to Philadelphia until the new city on the Potomac was ready. Within a few weeks the bills to move the capital and to approve the funding measures had been passed by Congress.

After Congress adjourned in August, Washington remained in New York only long enough to make his personal arrangements for moving. On August 30 he left for Philadelphia. Although the largest house in the city, that of Robert Morris, had been placed at his disposal, he found fault with it, and wrote to his secretary, Tobias Lear, about changes in the dwelling and arrangements for making it the Executive Mansion.

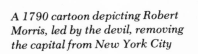

A 1790 cartoon depicting Robert Morris, led by the devil, removing the capital from New York City

Philadelphia, Septr. 5th. 1790.
After a pleasant Journey we arrived in this City about 2 Oclock on thursday last. Tomorrow we proceed (if Mrs. Washingtons health [allows?], for she has been much indisposed since she came here) towards Mount Vernon.

The House of Mr. R. Morris had, previous to my arrival, been taken by the Corporation for my residence. It is the best they could get. It is, I believe, the best *single House* in the City; yet, without additions it is inadequate to the *commodious* accomodation of my family. These, I believe, will be made.

The first floor contains only two public Rooms (except one for the *upper* Servants). The second floor will have two public (drawing) Rooms, & with the aid of one room with the partition in it in the back building will be Sufficient for the accomodation of Mrs. Washington & the Children, & their Maids—besides affording me a small place for a private Study & dressing Room. The third Story will furnish you & Mrs. Lear with a good lodging room—a public Office (for there is no place below for one) and two Rooms for the Gentlemen of the family. The Garret has four good Rooms which must serve Mr. and Mrs. Hyde (unless they should prefer the room over the wash House)—William—and such Servants as it may not be better to place in the addition (as proposed) to the Back Building. There is a room over the Stable (without a fire place, but by means of a Stove) may serve the Coachman & Postilions; and there is a Smoke House, which, possibly, may be more useful to me for the accomodation of Servants than for Smoking of meat. The intention of the addition to the Back building is to provide a Servants Hall, and one or two (as it will afford) lodging rooms for the Servants; especially those who are coupled. There is a very good Wash House adjoining to the Kitchen (under one of the rooms already mentioned). There are good Stables, but for 12 Horses only, and a Coach House which will hold all my Carriages....

PS. In a fortnight or 20 days from this time it is expected Mr. Morris will have removed out of the House. It is proposed to add Bow Windows to the two public rooms in the South front of the House—But as all the other apartments will be close & secure the sooner after that time you can be in the House with the furniture, the better, that you may be well fixed and see how matters go on during my absence.

From Philadelphia the President continued on to Mount Vernon, where he remained more than two months, conducting some official business by mail, happily writing letter after letter to Tobias Lear about arrangements for the new President's House, and thoroughly enjoying being home again. He returned to Philadelphia late in November, and on December 8, 1790, made his second annual address to Congress when that body met for the first time in the new capital. In his message the President reported that he found crops good, commerce flourishing, the national credit improving. A loan had been obtained from Holland; the Kentucky District of Virginia was applying for separate statehood; the threats of war between Europe's maritime powers should make the United States think of building up its own merchant marine. Washington also devoted a considerable part of his address to the Indians on the western frontier.

[Philadelphia, December 8, 1790]
It has been heretofore known to Congress, that frequent incursions have been made on our frontier settlemts. by certain banditti of Indians from the North West side of the Ohio. These with some of the tribes dwelling on and near the Wabash have of late been particularly active in their depridations; and being emboldened by the impunity of their crimes, and aided by such parts of the neighbouring tribes as could be seduced to join in their hostilities or afford them a retreat for their prisoners and plunder, they have, instead of listening to the

315

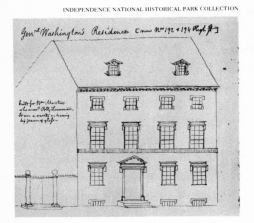

The Morris house in Philadelphia, which became home to the Washingtons after 1790

humane overtures made on the part of the United States, renewed their violences with fresh alacrity and greater effect. The lives of a number of valuable Citizens have thus been sacrificed, and some of them under circumstances peculiarily shocking; whilst others have been carried into a deplorable captivity.

These aggravated provocations rendered it essential to the safety of the Western Settlements that the aggressors should be made sensible that the Governmt. of the Union is not less capable of punishing their crimes, than it is disposed to respect their rights and reward their attachments. As this object could not be effected by defensive measures it became necessary to put in force the Act which empowers the President to call out the Militia for the protection of the frontiers. And I have accordingly authorized an expedition in which the regular troops in that quarter are combined with such drafts of Militia as were deemed sufficient. The event of the measure is yet unknown to me.

Indian matters had absorbed much of Washington's time almost from the day he took office and would do so until he retired. The frontier was always a sensitive area and the possibility of trouble ever-present. Although the Administration did what it could to protect the treaty rights of the Indians, settlers disregarded boundaries and treaties when they wanted to move onto Indian land. To aggravate the situation, both Spain and England turned the unrest of the red men to their own uses. The Spanish in Florida and Louisiana surreptitiously encouraged tribesmen in the southwestern United States to resist settlers from the southern states; in the Northwest the British at Detroit and other posts on American soil quietly aided the Indians north of the Ohio River. In his address, Washington was referring to certain tribes north of the Ohio who were warring with the encroaching settlers. The President, however, was not entirely candid in saying that he had no idea at that moment of the outcome of the military expedition sent against the Indians, for at least a week earlier he had had an unofficial report that the force, led by Brigadier General Josiah Harmar, had been defeated. When the official report arrived, it showed that 180 men had been lost. (Another expedition sent on the same mission a year later suffered much more grievously; six hundred of its nine hundred officers and men were killed or wounded.)

The subsequent session of Congress was concerned chiefly with two measures prepared by Hamilton to further strengthen the nation's credit. One was a revenue bill to place higher taxes on imported liquors and to levy excise taxes on those distilled in the United States. The excise tax bill would have eventful consequences before Washington left the Presidency. The other measure was a bill to create a national bank modeled after the Bank of England. Both bills were passed despite strong opposition, and Washington was then faced with deciding whether the bank bill was constitutional. Among his advisers, Randolph and Jefferson, both Republicans and literal interpreters of the Constitution, argued that the Constitution did not give Congress authority to create such a corporation as the bank. Hamilton, of course, had no doubts. Washington, convinced that the young nation must have a strong central government if it was to survive, accepted Hamilton's arguments and signed the bill into law. Congress adjourned on March 3, 1791, and later in the month Washington set out to tour the South, as he had New England a year and a half earlier.

Monday, 21st [March, 1791]. Left Philadelphia about 11 O'clock to make a tour through the Southern States. Reached Chester about 3 oclock—dined & lodged at Mr. Wythes. Roads exceedingly deep, heavy & cut in places by the Carriages which used them.

In this tour I was accompanied by Majr. Jackson. My equipage & attendance consisted of a Chariet & four horses drove in hand—a light baggage Waggon & two horses—four saddle horses besides a led one for myself—and five Servants—to wit—my Valet de Chambre, two footmen, Coachman & Postilion.

Tuesday, 22d. At half past 6 Oclock we left Chester, & breakfasted at Wilmington. Finding the Roads very heavy—and receiving unfavourable Accts. of those between this place and Baltimore I determined to cross the Bay by the way of Rockhall and crossing Christiana Creek proceeded through Newcastle & by the Red Lyon to the Buck tavern 13 Miles from Newcastle and 19 from Wilmington where we dined and lodged. At the Red Lyon we gave the horses a bite of Hay—during their eating of which I discovered that one of those wch. drew the Baggage Waggon was lame and appd. otherwise much indisposed—had him bled and afterwards led to the Buck tavern.

This is a better house than the appearances indicate.

Wednesday, 23d. ... The lame horse was brought on, and while on the Road appd. to move tolerably well, but as soon as he stopped, discovered a stiffness in all his limbs which indicated some painful disorder. I fear a Chest founder. My riding horse also appeared to be very

Christ Church in Philadelphia, where Washington had a pew

unwell, his appetite havg. entirely failed him.

The Winter grain along the Road appeared promising and abundant.

Thursday, 24th.   Left Chester town about 6 Oclock. Before nine I arrived at Rock-Hall where we breakfasted and immediately; after which we began to embark — The doing of which employed us (for want of contrivance) until near 3 Oclock — and then one of my Servants (Paris) & two horses were left, notwithstanding two Boats in aid of the two Ferry Boats were procured. Unluckily, embarking on board of a borrowed Boat because She was the largest, I was in imminent danger, from the unskillfulness of the hands, and the dulness of her sailing, added to the darkness and storminess of the night. For two hours after we hoisted Sail the Wind was light and a head — the next hour was a stark calm — after which the wind sprung up at So. Et. and encreased until it blew a gale — about which time, and after 8 Oclock P.M. we made the Mouth of Severn River (leading up to Annapolis) but the ignorance of the People on board, with respect to the navigation of it run us aground first on Greenbury point from whence with much exertion and difficulty we got off; & then, having no knowledge of the Channel and the Night being immensely dark with heavy and variable squals of wind — constant lightning & tremendous thunder. We soon grounded again on what is called Hornes point — where finding all efforts in vain, & not knowing where we were we remained, not knowing what might happen, 'till morning.

Friday, 25th.   Having lain all night in my Great Coat & Boots, in a birth not long enough for me by the head, & much cramped; we found ourselves in the Morning within about one mile of Annapolis & still fast aground. Whilst we were preparing our small Boat in order to land in it, a sailing Boat came of to our assistance in wch. with the Baggage I had on board I landed, & requested Mr. Man at whose Inn I intended lodging, to send off a Boat to take off two of my Horses & Chariet which I had left on board and with it my Coachman to see that it was properly done — but by mistake the latter not having notice of this order & attempting to get on board afterwards in a small Sailing Boat was overset and narrowly escaped drowning.

It is possible Washington overestimated the peril of crossing Chesapeake Bay; although brave in battle, he never had cared much for the water. He received a heartfelt welcome from the worried officials at Annapolis, the Maryland state capital, who had been waiting for hours for his overdue boat. Then he proceeded to Georgetown, on the site of the permanent national capital, where he met with the commissioners, discussed plans, examined the sketches of Pierre Charles L'Enfant, who was designing the city, and looked over the grounds. A paragraph from a later entry in his diary throws a very human and revealing light on Washington, whose innate courtesy so often made him suffer fools. Tired of having ridden all day in the midst of clouds of dust raised by escorts of local horsemen in southern Virginia, he resorted to a stratagem to obtain some relief the next morning.

> *Friday,* 15th [April, 1791]. Having suffered very much by the dust yesterday—and finding that parties of Horse, & a number of other Gentlemen were intendg. to attend me part of the way to day, I caused their enquiries respecting the time of my setting out, to be answered that, I should endeavor to do it before eight O'clock; but I did it a little after five, by which means I avoided the inconveniences above-mentioned.

L'Enfant's plan for Federal City

Washington found the South poorer, less populous, and much less developed than New England, with very little industry. His welcomes, however, were just as warm. Some typical excerpts from his diary follow.

Saturday, 16th [April, 1791]. Got into my Carriage a little after 5 Oclock, and travelled thro' a cloud of dust until I came within two or three miles of Hix' ford when it began to rain. Breakfasted at one Andrews' a small but decent House about a mile after passing the ford (or rather the bridge) over Meherrin River. Although raining moderately, but with appearances of breaking up, I continued my journey — induced to it by the crouds which were coming into a general Muster at the Court House of Greensville [Virginia], who would I presumed soon have made the Ho. I was in too noizy to be agreeable. I had not however rode two miles before it began to be stormy, & to rain violently which, with some intervals, it contind. to do the whole afternoon. The uncomfortableness of it, for Men & Horses, would have induced me to put up; but the only Inn short of Hallifax having no stables in wch. the horses could be comfortable, & no Rooms or beds which appeared tolerable, & every thing else having a dirty appearance, I was compelled to keep on to Hallifax [North Carolina]; 27 miles from Andrews — 48 from Olivers — and 75 from Petersburgh. At this place (i.e. Hallifax) I arrived about Six Oclock, after crossing the Roanoke; on the South bank of which it stands....

Wednesday, 20*th*. Left Allans before breakfast, & under a misapprehension went to a Colo. Allans, supposing it to be a public house; where we were very kindly & well entertained without knowing it was at his expence, until it was too late to rectify the mistake. After breakfasting, & feeding our horses here, we proceeded on & crossing the River Nuse 11 miles further, arrived in Newbern [North Carolina] to dinner....

Thursday, 21st. Dined with the Citizens [of Newbern] at a public dinner given by them; & went to a dancing assembly in the evening — both of which was at what they call the Pallace — formerly the government House & a good brick building but now hastening to ruins. The Company at both was numerous — at the latter there were abt. 70 ladies....

Sunday, 24th. Breakfasted at an indifferent House about 13 miles from Sages—and three Miles further met a party of Light Horse from Wilmington [North Carolina]; and after them a Commee. & other Gentlemen of the Town; who came out to escort me into it, and at which I arrived under a federal salute at very good lodgings prepared for me, about two Oclock. At these I dined with the Commee. whose company I asked. . . .

Charleston, South Carolina, in 1780

Wilmington is situated on the Cape Fear River, about 30 Miles *by water* from its mouth, but much less by land. It has some good houses pretty compactly built. The whole undr. a hill; which is formed entirely of Sand. The number of Souls in it amount by the enumeration to about 1000, but it is agreed on all hands that the Census in this State has been very inaccurately & shamefully taken by the Marshall's deputies; who, instead of going to Peoples houses, & there, on the spot, ascertaining the Nos.; have advertised a meeting of them at certain places, by which means those who did not attend (and it seems many purposely avoided doing it, some from an apprehension of its being introductory of a tax, & others from religious scruples) have gone, with their families, unnumbered. In other instances, it is said these deputies have taken their information from the Captains of Militia companies; not only as to the Men on their Muster Rolls, but of the souls in their respective families; which at best, must in a variety of cases, be mere conjecture whilst all those who are not on their lists—Widows and their families—&ca. pass unnoticed.

His years and the cares of office had not diminished Washington's lively interest in the ladies who turned out to meet him.

Tuesday, 3d [May, 1791]. Breakfasted with Mrs. Rutledge (the Lady of the Chief justice of the State who was on the Circuits) and dined with the Citizens at a public dinr. given by them at the Exchange.

Was visited about 2 Oclock, by a great number of the most respectable ladies of Charleston [South Carolina]—the first honor of the kind I had ever experienced and it was as flattering as it was singular.

Wednesday, 4th. Dined with the Members of the Cin-

321

Washington visited Sullivans Island (above) and Cowpens (below), scene of one of the battles of the Revolution. When he returned, he heard of the "Bloody Indian Battle" in Ohio, which the broadside opposite describes.

Pictorial Field-Book of the Revolution, LOSSING

cinnati, and in the evening went to a very elegant dancing Assembly at the Exchange — at which were 256 elegantly dressed and handsome ladies.

In the forenoon (indeed before breakfast to day) I visited and examined the lines of attack & defence of the City and was satisfied that the defence was noble & honorable altho the measure was undertaken upon wrong principles and impolitic.

Thursday, 5th. Visited the works of Fort Johnson on James's Island, and Fort Moultree on Sullivans Island; both of which are in ruins, and scarcely a trace of the latter left — the former quite fallen.

Dined with a very large Company at the Governors, & in the evening went to a Concert at the Exchange at wch. there were at least 400 lad[ie]s the number & appearance of wch. exceeded any thing of the kind I had ever seen.

Friday, 6th. Viewed the town on horseback by riding through most of the principal Streets.

Dined at Majr. Butlers, and went to a Ball in the evening at the Governors where there was a select company of ladies.

There were "about 100 well dressed and handsome ladies" at a "dancing Assembly" at Purysburg, South Carolina; "between 60 and 70 well dressed ladies" at an assembly in Augusta; at Columbia, South Carolina, there were "a number of Gentlemen and Ladies...to the amount of 150, of which 50 or 60 were of the latter." Washington also visited the scenes of most of the important Revolutionary battles that had been fought in the South. This was his first view of these battlefields; he inspected them with interest, occasionally giving a terse criticism.

The President stopped at Mount Vernon and was back in Philadelphia in early July after a trip he reckoned at 1,887 miles. Old problems waited. The British still refused to give up frontier posts within the northern United States, arguing, with some merit, that the United States had not honored some parts of the peace treaty. Spain controlled the mouth of the Mississippi, an essential outlet for the commerce of western settlers. In August, the ominous news came that the French King had been virtually imprisoned; the uprising that had produced constitutional government in 1789 was turning into revolution. And as 1791 drew to a close, word came that an expedition sent against the Indians north of the Ohio River had been disastrously routed, leaving some six hundred dead or wounded.

What distressed the President most was the increasing division of the Government and of the country into political parties. The terms Federalist and Antifederalist, which only recently had denoted those for and those against the Constitution, had come to mean something quite different. The Federalists, whose chief spokesman was Alexander Hamilton, now were those who supported a strong central government, favored encouragement of industry, commerce, and finance, and believed that government should be by an elite of the propertied class and that the mass of the people could not be trusted to govern themselves. In the Cabinet, Secretary of War Knox sided with Hamilton.

Thomas Jefferson dominated the Antifederalist, or Republican, faction. The Republican point of view was that the people should govern themselves democratically, that government should be decentralized, that the best nation was one of small farmers with few cities, little industry, and a minimum of bankers. There were among the Republicans many who ac-

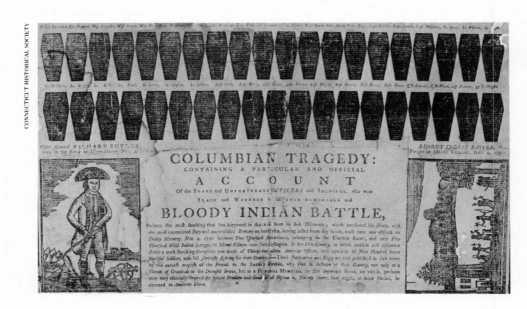

cused Washington of an overfondness for pomp and circumstance and even a secret ambition to become a monarch. The criticism was muted at first because of Washington's tremendous popularity, but it would grow, and in time would produce a tide of hate and invective. Possibly the growing division into antagonistic parties was what caused Washington to hedge slightly when he asked James Madison to help him prepare a farewell address as election time neared.

Mount Vernon May 20th. 1792.

As there is a possibility if not a probability, that I shall not see you on your return home; or, if I should see you, that it may be on the road and under circumstances which will prevent my speaking to you on the subject we last conversed upon; I take the liberty of committing to paper the following thoughts, & requests.

I have not been unmindful of the sentiments expressed by you in the conversations just alluded to: on the contrary I have again, and again revolved them, with thoughtful anxiety; but without being able to dispose my mind to a longer continuation in the Office I have now the honor to hold. I therefore still look forward to the fulfilment of my fondest and most ardent wishes to spend the remainder of my days (which I can not expect will be many) in ease & tranquility.

Nothing short of conviction that my deriliction of the Chair of Government (if it should be the desire of the people to continue me in it) would involve the Country in serious disputes respecting the chief Magestrate, & the disagreeable consequences which might result therefrom in the floating, & divided opinions which seem to prevail at present, could, in any wise, induce me to relinquish the determination I have formed: and of this I do not see how any evidence can be obtained previous to the Election. My vanity, I am sure, is not of that cast as to allow me to view the subject in this light.

Under these impressions then, permit me to reiterate the request I made to you at our last meeting—namely—to think of the proper time, and the best mode of anouncing the intention; and that you would prepare the latter. In revolving this subject myself, my judgment has always been embarrassed. On the one hand, a previous declaration to retire, not only carries with it the appearance of vanity & self importance, but it may be construed into a manoeuvre to be invited to remain. And on the other hand, to say nothing, implys consent; or, at any rate,

GEORGE WASHINGTON
PRESIDENT
1792

A commemorative medal shows an Indian chief with a peace pipe after the signing of a peace treaty in 1792.

Washington's letter to Hamilton, trying to heal the split between him and Jefferson, admits "differences in political opinions are as unavoidable as, to a certain point they may, perhaps, be necessary."

would leave the matter in doubt, and to decline afterwards might be deemed as bad, & uncandid.

I would fain carry my request to you farther than is asked above, although I am sensible that your compliance with it must add to your trouble; but as the recess may afford you leizure, and I flatter myself you have dispositions to oblige me, I will, with out apology desire (if the measure in itself should strike you as proper, & likely to produce public good, or private honor) that you would turn your thoughts to a Valadictory address from me to the public; expressing in plain & modest terms—that having been honored with the Presidential Chair, and to the best of my abilities contributed to the Organization & Administration of the government—that having arrived at a period of life when the private Walks of it, in the shade of retirement, becomes necessary, and will be most pleasing to me; and the spirit of the government may render a rotation in the Elective Officers of it more congenial with their ideas of liberty & safety, that I take my leave of them as a public man; and in bidding them adieu (retaining no other concern than such as will arise from fervent wishes for the prosperity of my Country) I take the liberty at my departure from civil, as I formerly did at my military exit, to invoke a continuation of the blessings of Providence upon it— and upon all those who are the supporters of its interests, and the promoters of harmony, order & good government.

During the next months the feud between Hamilton and Jefferson turned from one of political philosophy to a bitter personal antagonism. Washington, deeply perturbed by the split between his close friends and advisers, cautiously wrote of the schism to his Secretary of State in a letter that otherwise dealt with Spanish Florida and western Indians.

Mount Vernon, August 23, 1792.
How unfortunate, & how much is it to be regretted then, that whilst we are encompassed on all sides with avowed enemies & insidious friends, that internal dissensions should be harrowing & tearing our vitals. The last, to me, is the most serious, the most alarming & the most afflicting of the two; and without more charity for the opinions & acts of one another in governmental matters; or some more infallible criterion by which the truth of speculative opinions, before they have undergone the

test of experience, are to be forejudged, than has yet fallen to the lot of fallibility, I believe it will be difficult, if not impracticable to manage the reins of Government, or to keep the parts of it together; for if, instead of laying our shoulders to the machine after measures are decided on, one pulls this way & another that, before the utility of the thing is fairly tried, it must inevitably be torn asunder: and, in my opinion, the fairest prospect of happiness & prosperity that ever was presented to man will be lost—perhaps, forever!

My earnest wish & my fondest hope, therefore is, that, instead of wounding suspicions & irritable charges, there may be liberal allowances, mutual forbearances & temporizing yieldings on *all sides.* Under the exercise of these, matters will go smoothly, and, if possible, more prosperously. Without them every thing must rub; the wheels of Government will clogg; our enemies will triumph, & by throwing their weight into the disaffected scale may accomplish the ruin of the goodly fabrick we have been erecting.

I do not mean to apply this advice, or these observations to any particular person or character. I have given them in the same general terms to other Officers of the Government; because the disagreements which have arisen from difference of opinions—and the attacks which have been made upon almost all the measures of Government, & most of its Executive Officers, have, for a long time past, filled me with painful sensations; and cannot fail, I think, of producing unhappy consequences at home and abroad.

A similar letter went to Hamilton three days later. Each man answered by defending his own position and claiming to be the injured party. Both gave rather unconvincing promises that they would try to compromise their differences. Hamilton and Jefferson did agree in one thing; they were both among the chorus of Washington's friends who urged the President to run for another term, as the only man who could hold the infant nation together in a time of troubles. The farewell address Washington had asked Madison to prepare went undelivered—for the time being, at least. When the electors met early in 1793, the only contest was between John Adams, who received seventy-seven votes for Vice President, and George Clinton, an avowed Republican, who got fifty. Washington once again was the unanimous choice for President.

A Picture Portfolio

First in Peace

A DISPLAY of the UNITED STATES of AMERICA

"NO FASCINATING ALLUREMENTS FOR ME"

George Washington was unanimously elected the nation's first President on February 4, 1789, by members of the Electoral College from ten of the thirteen states whose seals ring the engraved portrait at left. On the probability that this honor might be bestowed on him, he had written earlier to his old friend and confidant the Marquis de Lafayette that "it has no enticing charms, and no fascinating allurements for me." His reluctance was very real. But he also knew all too well that "the first transactions of a nation, like those of an individual upon his first entrance into life, make the deepest impression, and . . . form the leading traits in its character. . . ." After so many years of service to the infant country, he could never have refused the new call to leadership. He set off on horseback from Mount Vernon for the triumphal journey to his inauguration in New York, greeted everywhere by joyous throngs in gaily bedecked cities such as Trenton (below), the scene of one of his greatest military victories.

FIRST CAPITALS

"Long live George Washington, President of the United States!" cried Chancellor Robert Livingston of New York, after he administered the oath on the balcony of Federal Hall (below); and the crowds in the streets took up the cheer. Washington never lived in the elegant house in New York City (right) provided for him by a grateful citizenry, since the capital was soon moved to Philadelphia. There the Washingtons moved into the Robert Morris house (right, below).

331

SOCIETY LEADERS

The portraits of George and Martha Washington below were painted in 1790 by Edward Savage for Vice President John Adams, and they still hang, as they always have, above the sideboard in the Adams house in Quincy, Massachusetts. During the first year of his Presidency, the Washingtons rented a large house on Broadway in New York, and four days later held their first reception, like the one portrayed in the nineteenth-century painting at right. Mrs. Washington stands serenely on a dais (left), with Chief Justice John Jay, Vice President John Adams, and Secretary of the Treasury Alexander Hamilton on her right. Behind them are Mrs. Adams and Mrs. Hamilton. In describing these levees, Abigail Adams wrote that she was received with "great ease and politeness" by her hostess, and she waxed enthusiastic about Washington, in a black velvet suit (center), whom she found "affable without familiarity, distant without haughtiness, grave without austerity, modest, wise and good." Her acerbic husband, on the other hand, was not always as enchanted and once referred to Washington as "an old mutton head."

333

BURDENS OF OFFICE

During his terms as President, two of Washington's most crucial tests of leadership were in putting down the Whisky Rebellion of 1794 and in keeping peace between his Federalist Secretary of the Treasury Alexander Hamilton (below, far left) and his Antifederalist Secretary of State Thomas Jefferson (below, near left). When the federal excise tax on whiskey enraged western Pennsylvanians, Washington donned his old uniform, raised a force of twelve thousand men, rode to Fort Cumberland (left), and by so doing stopped the rebellion cold. He was not so lucky with Hamilton and Jefferson, who remained bitterly opposed to each other's policies. As he neared the end of his Presidency in 1796, Washington was again painted in uniform, this time with his family (below), as they gathered around a large map of the projected Federal City, the plan for a new national capital he had put into effect but did not live to see completed.

The Washington Family BY EDWARD SAVAGE, NATIONAL GALLERY OF ART, WASHINGTON, D.C., ANDREW MELLON COLLECTION

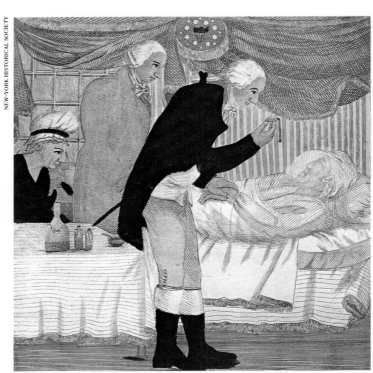

LADY
WASHINGTON'S
LAMENTATION FOR THE
DEATH OF HER HUSBAND.

WHEN Columbia's brave sons sought my hero to
   lead them,
To vanquish their foes and establish their freedom,
I rejoic'd at his honors, my fears I dissembled,
At the thought of his dangers my heart how it
   trembled,
     Oh, my Washington ! O my Washington !
      Oh, my washington ! all was hazardous.

The contest decided, with foes to the nation,
My hero return'd 'midst loud acclamation,
Of men without number and praise without measure,
And my own heart exulted in transports or pleasure,
    Oh my Washington. Oh, &c. all was hazardous.

Our freedom with order by faction rejected,
A new constitution our country elected,
My hero was rais'd to preside our the union,
And his cares interrupted our bliss and communion.
    Oh, my happiness ! &c. &c. how precarious.

Declining the trust of his dignified station,
With joy to the seat of his dear estimation,
Surrounded with honors he humbly retreated,
Sweet hope softly whisper'd my bliss was completed.
    Oh, my happiness ! &c. &c. how precarious.

When the pangs of disease, had, ah ! fatally seiz'd
   him,
My heart would have yielded its life to have eas'd
   him,
And I pray'd the Most High if for death he design'd
   him,
That he would not permit me to loiter behind him.
    Oh, my Washington ! &c. &c. all was dubious.

When my hopes had all fled, and I saw him resigning
His soul to his God without fear or repining,

What, my heart, were thy feelings ? lamenting, ad-
   miring,
To behold him so calmly, so nobly expiring.
    Oh, my Washington ! &c. &c. has forsaken us.

When I follow'd his corpse with grief unconfined,
And saw to the tomb his dear relics consigned,
When I left him in darkness and silence surround-
   ed,
With what pangs of fresh anguish my bosom was
   wounded !
    Oh, my Washington ! &c. &c. has forsaken us.

An aspect so noble pale grave clothes disfigure,
His conquering arm is despoil'd of its vigour,
On those limbs which dropt wisdom is silence im-
   posed,
And those kind beaming eyes now forever are
   closed,
    Oh, my Washington ? &c. &c. has forsaken us.

When with tears of sweet musing I ponder the
   story,
Of his wars, of his labours, his virtues and glory,
I breathe out a pray'r with sad order of spirit,
Soon to join him in bliss and united inherit
    Endless Blessedness ! &c. &c. oh, how glorious.

But why with my own single grief so confounded,
When my country's sad millions in sorrows are
   drowned,
Let me mingle the current that flows from my bosom,
With my country' vast ocean of tears while they
   lose them,
    Tho' my Washington, &c. &c. has forsaken us.

PRINTED AND SOLD BY NATHANIEL COVERLY, JR
   CORNER THEATRE-ALLEY, *Milk-Street*—BOSTON.

"WHY DOTH AMERICA WEEP!"

Washington did not intend "to quitt the theatre of this world until
the new century had been rung in," Martha later wrote. But a ride
on a chill and wet December day in 1799 brought his doctors to his
bedside (above, near left), and he died on December 14, at the age
of sixty-seven, just short of that joyous celebration. "Why doth
America weep!" mourned the verses on the print above, far left,
as the tributes and elegies poured forth from the presses of the
grief-stricken nation. Thomas Birch drew one of the somber pro-
cessions in commemoration of Washington's death as it passed the
country marketplace on High Street in Philadelphia (left). Martha
Washington survived her beloved husband by only three years. The
poignant cry attributed to her in the lamentation on the broadside above was really the cry from millions of American hearts:
"Oh, my Washington! Oh, my Washington! Oh, my Washington! has
forsaken us."

Chapter 10

The Discords of Party

Washington had won another splendid victory. For a second time he had been elected President without a single dissenting vote, in an outpouring of confidence and affection such as is granted to very few men. He would not have been human if he had not been pleased, but at the same time he faced his second term with the reluctance he always felt about giving up his cherished private life at Mount Vernon to take on a public duty. He wrote of his feelings in a letter to his old and close friend Governor Henry Lee of Virginia.

> Philadelphia Jany. 20th. 1793.
> I have been favored with your letter of the 6th. instant congratulatory on my re-election to the Chair of Government. A mind must be insensible indeed, not to be gratefully impressed by so distinguished, & honorable a testimony of public approbation & confidence: and, as I suffered my name to be contemplated on this occasion, it is more than probable that I should, for a moment, have experienced chagreen if my re-election had not been by a pretty respectable vote. But to say I feel pleasure from the prospect of *commencing* another tour of duty, would be a departure from truth; for however it might savour of affectation in the opinion of the world (who by the bye can only guess at my sentimts. as it never has been troubled with them) my particular, & confidential friends well know, that it was after a long and painful conflict in my own breast, that I was withheld (by considerations which are not necessary to mention) from requesting, *in time,* that no vote might be thrown away upon me; it being my fixed determination to return to the walks of private life, at the end of my term.

Washington's averseness to a second term would have been greater could he have foreseen the troubles that would beset him during the next four years. Some of them were already taking form even as he wrote to Governor Lee. Congress had increasingly taken sides in the Hamilton-Jefferson dispute, until the split between Federalists and Republicans was so wide that no serious business was being conducted during the first months of 1793, and the legislators were engaged in purely partisan wrangles. Washington remained outside the conflict and did what he could to reconcile the warring factions.

The feud was carried on in the press as well. Although his Administration was violently attacked, especially by the fanatically Republican *National Gazette* edited by Philip Freneau, Washington himself had been spared. That period of grace ended when the nation observed the President's sixty-first birthday on February 22, 1793, and Freneau took advantage of the occasion to accuse Washington of ambitions to be a king: "The monarchical farce of the birthday was as usual kept. . . . Hitherto [the American people] have passed over the absurdities of *levees, & every species of royal pomp and parade*, because they were associated with the man of their affections, and perhaps, in hopes that they might serve as a new rattle, which would amuse during its novelty, and be thrown aside, when it was worn off. . . ."

Political problems had not freed Washington from personal ones. His nephew, George Augustine Washington, who had managed Mount Vernon since the time of the Constitutional Convention, had been in steadily failing health for many months. A month before Freneau's attack, the President had sat down to that most difficult of tasks, writing a letter to someone very close who is dying, and who knows he is dying. George Augustine died a week after his uncle penned the following letter.

Rare British caricature of George Washington, which was done in 1796

Philada. January 27. 1793.

I do not write to you often, because I have no business to write upon—because all the News I could communicate is contained in the papers which I forward every week—because I conceive it unnecessary to repeat the assurances of sincere regard & friendship I have always professed for you or the disposition I feel to render every service in my power to you & yours; and lastly, because I conceive the more undisturbed you are, the better it is for you.

It has given your friends much pain to find that change of air has not been productive of that favorable change in your health which was the wishes of them all. But the will of Heaven is not to be controverted or scrutinized by the children of this world. It therefore [becomes] the creatures of it to submit [with patience and resignation] to the will of the Creator, whether it be to prolong or to

Washington's unanimous election to a second term was recorded (above) in the Senate Journal; broadside at right lists names and addresses of both Senators and Representatives.

shorten the number of our days—to bless them with health, or afflict them with pain.

My fervent wishes attend you, in which I am heartily joined by your Aunt, & these are extended with equal sincerity to Fanny & the Children. I am always Your affectionate Uncle.

The President had hired a new manager, Anthony Whiting, for Mount Vernon. Although Whiting was hard-working and capable, the affairs of the plantation were so complex and Washington was so exacting that long and detailed letters left the President's desk almost weekly. They advised, commanded, questioned, explained, sometimes scolded. The following letter is typical of scores of such dispatches he found time to write in the midst of his official duties.

Philadelphia Feby. 3d. 1793.

Mr. Whiting:

Your letter of the 25th. of Jany. came duly to hand; but the usual one, containing the Reports, is not yet arrived; detained, as is supposed with the Mail, by Ice in the Susquehanna.

Under cover with this letter you will receive some Lima Beans which Mrs. Washington desires may be given to the Gardener; also Panicum or Guinea Corn, from the Island of Jamaica, which may be planted merely to see the uses it can be applied to; & the white bent grass with the description of it by Mr. Hawkins (one of the Senators, who had it from Mr. Bassett of Delaware State, another of the Senate). If the acct. of it be just, it must be a valuable grass; I therefore desire it may be sowed in drills, & to the best advantage for the purpose of seed. *These things* which are intended for experiments, or to raise as much seed from, as can be; shd. never be put in fields, or meadows; for there, (if not forgot) they are neglected; or swallowed up in the fate of all things within the Inclosures that contain them. This has been the case of the Chicorium (from Mr. Young) & a grass which sold for two Guineas a quart in England and presented to me—and the same, or some other fate equally as bad has attended a great many curious seeds which have been given to, & sent home by me at different times but of which I have heard nothing more; either from the inattention which was given to them in the first instance; neglect in the cultivation; or not watching the period of their seeding, and gathering them without waste....

I will enquire if Orchard grass seed is to be had here & will send some; but I must entreat you to save me, as much as possible from the necessity of purchasing seeds; for the doing it is an intolerable expence. I once was in the habit of saving a great deal of this & other seeds annually; and this habit might easily have been continued, if measures had been taken in time for it.

I am sorry to hear that you have so sick a family. In all cases that require it, let the Doctor be sent for in time. As I do not know what boy (before I get home) would be best to send to the Mill, the measure may be suspended until I arrive. If the Miller would be attentive (in time) to the wants of the Mill, there is certainly intercourse enough between the Mansion house and it, to obtain supplies without special messengers; & I know no right he has to be sending my people on any other business.

I have no doubt, at all, of wheat and flours bearing a good price this Spring; the causes that occasioned the rise in these articles still exist, & in a greater degree; but, that

Fanny Bassett Washington, wife of George Augustine, Washington's favorite nephew and manager of Mount Vernon until his death in 1793

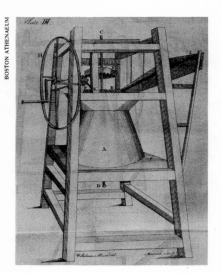

Washington's lifelong interest in all things agricultural is most in evidence among the many books on the subject in his personal library. The engraving above is from a book on farm implements. At right is the handsome certificate admitting him as a Foreign Honorary Member of the Board of Agriculture in London.

I may know when the price offered, comes up to my ideas, keep me regularly advised of the Alexandria rates; the prices here of Superfine flour is 42/. [42 shillings] & that of fine 39/. pr. Barrl. of 196 lbs.—wheat 8/6 [8 shillings, 6 pence] pr. Bushl.

It appears to me, that it is scarcely necessary to put Tom Davis to the saw so late in the season; the time is not far off when Brick laying—preparing the foundation—&ca. must necessarily take him from it. Therefore, as he is better acquainted with the business than any of my people I should conceive he had better employ the interval in finishing the painting, unless you think (house) Frank could do it equally well. In that case, as it will probably be the last of March before I shall be at home —for a few days—he might be as advantageously occupied in that business as in any other.

Speaking of laying bricks (by which I mean the foundation for the Barn at Dogue run) it reminds me of asking again if the Bricks at that place have been assorted & counted; that the deficiency of the wanted number, if any, might have had the earth thrown up, from the foundation of the building, in time to be ameliorated by the frosts of the winter. Directions will forever escape you, unless you keep a pocket Memorandum book to refresh the memory; and questions asked (in my letters) will often go unanswered unless, when you are about to

write, the letter *is then,* not only read over, but all the parts, as you read on, is noted, either on a piece of waste paper, or a Slate which require to be touched upon in your answr.

I hope the delivery to and the application of Nails, by the Carpenters, will undergo a pretty strict comparative scrutiny, without expressing any suspicion, unless cause shall be given for it. I cannot conceive how it is possible that 6000 twelve penny Nails could be used in the Corn house at River Plantn. but of one thing I have no great doubt and that is—if they can be applied to other uses—or converted into cash, rum, or other things, there will be no scruple in doing it.

I can conceive no latch (sufficient to answer the purpose, & not always out of sorts) more simple or cheaper than those to the white gates, unornimented, which is unnecessary. A thin plate of Iron, kept in place by an old Iron hoop (of which I presume hundreds could be got in Alexandria for a mere song) & staple for it to catch in, is, in my opinion, as cheap as anything that (will not always be a plague) can be devised. The advantage of this latch is, that let the Gate swag as it may, it always catches. . . .

It would be proper, I conceive, as the house people are under the care of Mr. Butler, to entrust Will (Overseer as he is called) in preference to Davis, with the Command of the Boat, & such other out of sight jobs, as may occur, and require confidence; and, as they do not agree, to let them interfere as little as can be avoided, with each other. The latter is high spirited, and in the instance you mention was disobedient to the other whom he ought to have respected on two accts.—namely—being his uncle, & having been an Overseer. The former (Will) unless he feels hurt on being superseded in his Overseership, is entitled to more confidence; though, I believe, both of them will drink.

Sarah Flatfoot (you call her Lightfoot) has been accustomed to receive a pair of Shoes, Stockings, a Country cloth Petticoat, & an Oznabrig shift, all ready made, annually, & it is not meant to discontinue them: you will therefore furnish them to her.

As the matter has been mentioned to Mr. Chichester, I now wish you would see him yourself on the subject of Major Harrisons land; and find out, if you can from him,

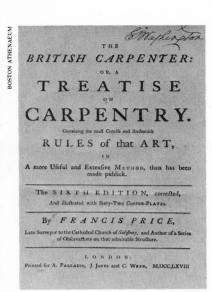

THE
BRITISH CARPENTER:
OR A
TREATISE
ON
CARPENTRY.
Containing the moſt Conciſe and Authentick
RULES of that ART,
IN
A more Uſeful and Extenſive METHOD, than has been
made publick.

The SIXTH EDITION, corrected,
And illuſtrated with Sixty-Two Copper-Plates.

By *FRANCIS PRICE,*
Late Surveyor to the Cathedral Church of *Saliſbury,* and Author of a Series
of Obſervations on that admirable Structure.

LONDON:
Printed for A. PALLADIO, J. JONES and C. WREN. M,DCC,LXVIII.

Book on carpentry, published in England, from Washington's library

the circumstances under which it is—whether he seems to have any inclination to become the purchaser of it—At what price pr. Acre, or otherwise, it was offered to him; and for what he thinks it could be bought; Intimating what you conceive to be my motives for making it—if made at all by me.

If the Mail should arrive before this letter is closed, and I have time, I will acknowledge the receipt of it; if not, and nothing requires to be noticed sooner, I shall delay writing until this day week as usual.

There were no precedents for the time or manner of a change in presidential terms, so after discussion with his Cabinet, Washington directed that the ceremony be held on March 4 in the Senate chamber, with a justice of the Supreme Court administering the oath. The inaugural was a simple ceremony. Washington arrived at the Senate chamber about noon, was ushered inside, and after John Adams announced in a sentence that a justice of the Supreme Court was ready to administer the prescribed oath, Washington stood and read what probably remains the shortest inaugural address on record.

[Philadelphia,] March 4th. 1793.

Fellow-Citizens:

I am again called upon by the voice of my Country to execute the functions of its Chief Magistrate. When the occasion proper for it shall arrive, I shall endeavour to express the high sense I entertain of this distinguished honor, and of the confidence which has been reposed in me by the people of United America.

Previous to the execution of any official act of the President, the Constitution requires an Oath of Office. This Oath I am now about to take—and in your presence—that if it shall be found during my administration of the Government, I have in any instance violated willingly, or knowingly, the injunctions thereof, I may (besides incurring Constitutional punishmt.) be subject to the upbraidings of all who are now witnesses of the present solemn Ceremony.

Washington then repeated the oath, walked from the room, and returned to work. Soon news from abroad, always many weeks behind the event, brought increasingly ominous dispatches from France. That country was at war with Austria and Prussia, and Washington's close

George Washington painted during second term by Adolph Wertmuller

friend Lafayette, commanding a French army, had been outlawed by the radical government in Paris, had fled, and had been imprisoned in Austria. The President, already working for the release of Lafayette, responded to a direct appeal for help from Lafayette's wife, couching his letter in cautious terms in case it was intercepted.

Philada. 16 March 1793.

Dear Madam:

I addressed a few lines to you on the 31st. of January, in a state of entire uncertainty in what country or condition they might find you: as we had been sometimes told you were in England, sometimes in Holland, & at sometimes in France. Your Letter of Octob: 8 — 1792, first relieved me from doubt, & gave me a hope that, being in France: and on your own Estate, you are not as destitute as I had feared, of the resources which that could furnish. But I have still to sympathize with you on the deprivation of the dearest of all your resources of happiness, in comparison with which, others vanish. I do it in all the sincerity of my friendship for him, & with ardent desires for his relief; in which sentiment I know that my fellow-citizens participate. The measures you were pleased to intimate in your letter, are perhaps not exactly those which I could pursue — perhaps indeed not the most likely, un-

345

der actual circumstances to obtain our object. But be assured, that I am not inattentive to his condition, nor contenting myself with inactive wishes for his liberation. My affection to his nation & to himself are unabated, & notwithstanding the line of separation which has been unfortunately drawn between them I am confident that both have been led on by a pure love of Liberty, & a desire to secure public happiness; and I shall deem that among the most consoling moments of my life which shall see them reunited in the end, as they were in the beginning, of their virtuous enterprise. Accept I pray you the same lively sentiments of interest & attachment to yourself & your dear children, from Dr. madm. Your most obt. & devoted servt.

Lafayette would eventually be released unharmed, but not for another four years. In mid-March came news that King Louis XVI had been guillotined and a Republic of France proclaimed. Despite rumors of general war in Europe, Washington went to Mount Vernon at the beginning of April. He had much to do at home. There was the burial of his nephew George Augustine Washington, a simple and private ceremony. He wanted to try to sell his land holdings in the Dismal Swamp and on the Kanawha River. There were long-overdue debts he hoped to try to collect. And many plantation problems demanded his attention. But he had been at Mount Vernon only a brief while when a letter from Alexander Hamilton confirmed that France, already at war with Austria, Prussia, and Sardinia, had declared war on England, Spain, and Holland.

The President cut his stay short and returned to Philadelphia. He was worried about the wild enthusiasm many Americans were showing for the new revolutionary government in France, and he was uncertain what course the United States should take toward the new republic. When France had recognized the independence of the Colonies in 1778 during the Revolution, the two nations signed a pair of treaties. One was simply a treaty of amity and commerce, to put trade on a mutually advantageous basis. The other was a treaty of alliance, to become operative in case recognition caused Britain to make war on France, as it did. It stipulated that neither country would make a separate peace, and that after the United States had become a free nation, France would guarantee American independence and boundaries, and the United States in its turn would guarantee France in possession of her islands in the West Indies.

Now, with France and England at war, the United States could be drawn into the conflict if France insisted that her ally adhere to the terms of the treaty. Many questions were raised. The treaty of alliance had been made with a French monarchy but now a revolutionary government was in power; was the treaty then any longer in effect? Republicans said an emphatic Yes, Federalists, No. And what of the envoy being sent by the revolutionary government, in what manner should he be received — or should he be received at all? Washington sent to each of his Cabinet members a list of questions to study before a meeting the next day.

Philada. 18 April 1793.

Question I.   Shall a proclamation issue for the purpose of preventing interferences of the Citizens of the United States in the War between France and Great Britain &ca.? Shall it contain a declaration of neutrality, or not? What shall it contain?

Quest. II.   Shall a Minister from the Republic of France be received?

Quest. III.   If received, shall it be absolutely, or with qualifications; & if with qualifications — of what kind?

Quest. IV.   Are the U.S. obliged, by good faith, to consider the treaties, heretofore made with France, as applying to the present situation of the parties? May they either renounce them, or hold them suspended 'till the Government of France shall be *established*?

Questn. V.   If they have the right, is it expedient to do either, and which?

Questn. VI.   If they have an option, would it be a breach of neutrality, to consider the treaties still in operation?

Quest. VII.   If the treaties are to be considered as now in operation, is the Guarantee in the treaty of alliance applicable to a defensive war only, or to war either offensive or defensive?

VIII.   Does the war, in which France is engaged, appear to be offensive, or defensive, on her part? or of a mixed & equivocal character?

IX.   If of a mixed & equivocal character, does the Guarantee in any event apply to such a war?

X.   What is the effect of a Guarantee, such as that to be found in the treaty of Alliance between the U.S. & France?

XI.   Does any article, in either of the treaties, prevent Ships of war, other than privateers, of the Powers opposed to France, from coming into the Ports of the United States, to act as convoys to their own Merchantment? or does it lay any other restraints upon them more than would apply to the Ships of war of France?

Contemporary engraving of the execution of King Louis XVI from La Revolution Française *by Berthault*

Quest. XII. Should the future Regent of France send a Minister to the United States, ought he to be received?

XIII. Is it necessary, or adviseable, to call together the two Houses of Congress, with a view to the present posture of European affairs? If it is, what should be the particular objects of such a call?

At its meeting the next day the Cabinet agreed to proclaim American neutrality. Jefferson, the one Nay vote, argued that a declaration of neutrality was nothing more than "a declaration that there should be no war," and that Congress alone had the power to decide a question of war or peace. It was agreed, then, that the word "neutrality" would not be contained in the proclamation. All four members were in accord that the minister of the French Republic, Edmond Genêt (Citizen Genêt), should be received, but there was intense disagreement on whether he should be received with or without qualification. Hamilton argued that to receive Genêt without qualification would be tantamount to announcing that the United States was continuing the treaties of alliance and commerce made with the French monarchy in 1778. We should wait, said Hamilton, until we see what form the French Republic finally takes before committing ourselves. Jefferson, the champion of republican France, violently disagreed, and the matter was temporarily resolved only by putting it aside for further study. Three days later Washington issued the Proclamation of Neutrality.

[Philadelphia, April 22, 1793]

Whereas it appears that a state of war exists between Austria, Prussia, Sardinia, Great-Britain, and the United Netherlands of the one part and France on the other, and the duty and interest of the United States require that they should with sincerity and good faith adopt and pursue a conduct friendly and impartial towards the belligerent powers:

I have therefore thought fit by these presents to declare the disposition of the United States to observe the conduct aforesaid towards those powers respectively, and to exhort and warn the citizens of the United States carefully to avoid all acts and proceedings whatsoever which may in any manner tend to contravene such disposition.

And I do hereby also make known that whosoever of the citizens of the United States shall render himself liable to punishment or forfeiture under the law of nations by committing, aiding, or abetting hostilities against any of the said powers, or by carrying to any of them those articles which are deemed contraband by the *modern* usage of nations, will not receive the protection of the United States against such punishment or forfeiture; and further, that I have given instructions to those officers to whom it belongs to cause prosecutions to be instituted against all persons who shall, within the cognizance of the courts of the United States, violate the law of nations with respect to the powers at war, or any of them.

Citizen Genêt had already landed in Charleston, South Carolina, where he remained long enough to commission four privateers to prey on British shipping. Then—already a hero to Republicans but a villain to Federalists—he journeyed to Philadelphia, being greeted with ovations along the way. On May 18, almost six weeks after his arrival in the United States, he presented his credentials to Washington, who received him with cool formality. On June 5 the President had Jefferson inform Genêt that his granting of commissions on American soil was an infringement of American sovereignty; furthermore, that the privateers already commissioned would have to leave American waters. Genêt promised to comply but before long blandly ordered the arming of a British ship, the *Little Sarah*, which had been captured by a French vessel. Told not to send the vessel—refitted and renamed *La Petite Démocrate*—to sea, Genêt threatened to appeal to the American people over Washington's head. Washington, angered, asked his Secretary of State what action should be taken.

> Philadelphia 11 July 1793
>
> After I had read the papers (which were put into my hands by you) requiring "instant attention," & before a messenger could reach your Office, you had left town.
>
> What is to be done in the case of the Little Sarah, now at Chester? Is the Minister of the French Republic to set the Acts of this Government at defiance, *with impunity*? and then threaten the Executive with an appeal to the people? What must the world think of such conduct & of the Government of the U. States in submitting to it?
>
> These are serious questions. Circumstances press for decision and as you have had time to consider them (upon me they come unexpectedly) I wish to know your opinion upon them—even before tomorrow—for the Vessel may then be gone.

Two or three days after Washington wrote his note to Jefferson, Genêt did give the word that sent *Little Sarah* to sea. Even Jefferson felt that the French ambassador had gone too far. The President's

Proclamation of Neutrality came increasingly under intemperate attack both in the pro-French Republican press and by many private citizens. Washington usually bore such attacks stoically, but occasionally he unburdened himself in private to good friends, as in the following letter to Governor Henry Lee of Virginia.

Philadelphia July 21st. 1793.

I should have thanked you at an earlier period for your obliging letter of the 14th. ulto., had it not come to my hands a day or two only before I set out for Mount Vernon; and at a time when I was much hurried, and indeed very much perplexed with the disputes, Memorials and what not, with which the Government were pestered by one or other of the petulant representatives of the Powers at War—and because, since my return to this City (nine days ago) I have been more than ever overwhelmed with their complaints. In a word, the trouble they give is hardly to be described.

My journey to and from Mt. Vernon was sudden & rapid, and as short as I could make it. It was occasioned by the unexpected death of Mr. Whitting (my Manager) at a critical season for the business with which he was entrusted. Where to supply his place, I know not; of course my concerns at Mt. Vernon are left as a body without a head—but this bye the by.

The communications in your letter were pleasing and grateful. For, although I have done no public act with which my Mind upbraids me, yet, it is highly satisfactory to learn that the things which I do (of an interesting tendency to the peace & happiness of this Country) are generally approved by my fellow Citizens. But were the case otherwise, I should not be less inclined to know the sense of the People upon every matter of great public concern; for as I have no wish superior to that of promoting the happiness & welfare of this Country, so, consequently, it is only for me to know the means to accomplish the end, if it is within the compass of my Powers.

That there are in this, as in all other Countries, discontented characters, I well know; as also that these characters are actuated by very different views—Some good, from an opinion that the measures of the general Government are impure—Some bad, and (if I might be allowed to use so harsh an epithet) diabolical; inasmuch as they are not only meant to impede the measures of that Government generally, but more especially (as a great mean towards the accomplishment of it) to destroy the confidence, which it is necessary for the People to place (until they have unequivocal proof of demerit) in their public Servants; for in this light I consider myself, whilst I am an occupant of Office; and, if they were to go farther & call me there Slave, (during this period) I would not dispute the point. But in what will this abuse terminate? The result, as it respects myself, I care not; for I have a consolation within that no earthly efforts can deprive me of—and that is, that neither ambitious nor interested motives have influenced my conduct. The arrows of Malevolence therefore, however barbed & well pointed, never can reach the most valuable part of me; though, whilst I am *up* as a *mark*, they will be continually aimed. The publications in Freneau's and Beache's [Benjamin Franklin Bache, editor of the *Aurora* of Philadelphia] Papers are outrages on common decency; and they progress in that style in proportion as their pieces are treated with contempt, and are passed by in silence by those at whom they are aimed. The tendency of them, however, is too obvious to be mistaken by men of cool & dispassionate minds, and, in my opinion, ought to alarm them; because it is difficult to prescribe bounds to the effect.

CULVER PICTURES

Edmond Charles Genêt

The light in which you endeavored to place the views and conduct of this Country to Mr. G---t [Genêt]; and the sound policy thereof as it respected his own; was, unquestionably the true one, and such as a man of penetration, left to himself, would most certainly have viewed them in—but mum on this head. Time may unfold more, than prudence ought to disclose at present.

As we are told that you have exchanged the rugged & dangerous field of Mars, for the soft and pleasurable bed of Venus, I do in this as I shall in every thing you may pursue, like unto it good & laudable, wish you all imaginable success and happiness....

The mischief-making of Genêt continued. He had spent much of his time in America with radical Republicans and became president of the pro-French "Friends of Liberty and Equality" in Philadelphia. Such societies, patterned after the Jacobin clubs of Paris, were set up in other cities, notably Charleston and New York, and became anathema to the Federalists—and to Washington, who was more and more taking the advice of Hamilton. But whatever his support among hotheads, Genêt had gone too far. When the story of his machinations sifted through to the public, a small flood of messages came to Washington, expressions of support for their President, who had been insulted by the man from France. Genêt went into an eclipse, although he quietly continued to stir up trouble, including an intrigue to recruit Americans on the southwestern frontier to attack Spanish Louisiana. But at last the slow sailing ships brought word that the French Government had acted, and Washington was able to give a brief but unmistakably satisfied report to Congress.

United States, Jany. 20 1794.

Gentlemen of the Senate, and of the House of Representatives:

Having already laid before you a letter of the 16. of August 1793. from the Secretary of State to our Minister at Paris; stating the conduct, and urging the recall of the Minister plenipotentiary of the Republic of France; I now communicate to you, that his conduct has been unequivocally disapproved; and that the strongest assurances have been given, that his recal should be expedited without delay.

When the new French minister, Joseph Fauchet, arrived in late February of 1794, he bore a request for the arrest and return to France of Genêt. The Girondist faction, which had sent Genêt, had been ousted by the even more radical Jacobins. Washington, knowing that return would mean death on the guillotine for Genêt, permitted the man who had acted so cavalierly toward him to remain in the United States. Genêt moved to Albany, eventually married the daughter of Governor George Clinton, and lived out his days as an obscure American citizen. Thus, one crisis had been survived; but others were ahead. The British still held the northwest frontier forts on American soil, had been confiscating American cargoes at sea, and were otherwise acting in ways that appalled even Federalists. War seemed probable. Washington sent a brief message to the Senate.

United States 16 April 1794.

Gentlemen of the Senate:

The communications, which I have made to you during your present session, from the dispatches of our Minister in London, contain a serious aspect of our affairs with Great Britain. But as peace ought to be pursued with unremitted zeal, before the last resource, which has so often been the scourge of nations, and cannot fail to check the advanced prosperity of the United States, is contemplated; I have thought proper to nomi-

History of Philadelphia, BY SCHARF AND WESTCOTT, 1884

Both Genêt and Fauchet lived in this house, one of Philadelphia's finest.

nate, and do hereby nominate

John Jay, as Envoy extraordinary of the United States to his britannic majesty.

My confidence in our Minister plenipotentiary in London continues undiminished. But a mission, like this, while it corresponds with the solemnity of the occasion, will announce to the world a solicitude for a friendly adjustment of our complaints, and a reluctance to hostility. Going immediately from the United States, such an envoy will carry with him a full knowledge of the existing temper and sensibility of our Country; and will thus be taught to vindicate our rights with firmness, and to cultivate peace with sincerity.

Washington was sending John Jay, Chief Justice of the United States, on a delicate mission that involved more than frontier forts. The financial security of the country depended in large part on tariff revenues, and most of those revenues came from trade with Great Britain. If trade with Britain were cut off in retaliation for English acts, as the Republicans were clamoring that it be, it would wreck the American economy. Jay was to put things right, but instead his actions would, in coming months, bring down a torrent of abuse on Washington.

Changes had taken place in the tight circle around Washington. Tobias Lear, his secretary since 1786, had left him the previous June, first to go to Europe and then to set himself up in business in the Federal City, which was taking shape on the Potomac. Anthony Whiting, his manager at Mount Vernon, had died the same June, and Washington was now sending his letters about seeding, harvest, and the management of lazy slaves to a new manager, William Pearce. Of much greater import, not only to Washington but to the nation, was the loss of Thomas Jefferson, whose resignation as Secretary of State became effective at the end of 1793. He was replaced by Attorney General Edmund Randolph, whose office in turn was filled by William Bradford, a little-known lawyer and a veteran of the Revolution. Although the President had been veering away from Jefferson's philosophy and turning more and more toward Hamilton's Federalism, he did not forget old friends. Jefferson was no longer one of his official family, but he was nevertheless a fellow farmer. A personal letter went to him on a matter of mutual interest.

Phila. 24th. April 1794

The letter herewith enclosed, came under cover to me in a packet from Mr. Lear, accompanied with the following extract of a letter, dated—London February 12th. 1794.

"A Mr. Bartrand, a famous Agriculturalist belonging to Flanders, put into my hands a few days ago several papers for Mr. Jefferson on the Subject of Manuring & vegitation, requesting that I would forward them to him by some vessel going to America; being uncertain whether Mr. Jefferson is in Philada. or Virginia, I have taken the liberty of putting them under cover to you."

Nothing, is more wanting in this Country, than a thorough knowledge of the first; by which the usual, and inadequate modes practiced by us may be aided. Let me hope then, if any striking improvements are communicated by Mr. Bartrand on the above important Subjects that you will suffer your friends to participate in the knowledge which is to be derived from his instructions.

We are going on in the old way "Slow." I hope events will justify me in adding "and sure" that the proverb may be fulfilled—"Slow and Sure." With very great esteem etc.

One feature of Hamilton's controversial fiscal plan had been an excise tax on whiskey. It was a tax opposed by back-country Americans ever since it was passed in 1791, for the only way a western farmer could possibly take his grain to market across the mountains and make any profit was by first reducing it to whiskey. The democratic Westerners bitterly resented Hamilton's entire program as putting power in the hands of the upper classes, and the tax on whiskey was the most obvious target on which to vent their accumulated resentment. In July of 1794 a federal marshal was attacked while serving papers on a distiller in western Pennsylvania, and the home of the excise inspector in the same area was burned. There were other acts against authority, in what came to be known as the Whisky Rebellion. Washington, groping for a course of action, called on his Cabinet for advice. Hamilton held that the insurgents were in a state of treason, and that the insurrection should be quelled by force. There was cooler counsel. Secretary of State Randolph believed that force would only harden the resolve of the rebels to resist. It was decided to send federal commissioners to western Pennsylvania to offer amnesty to the rebels, while at the same time the recruiting of some thirteen thousand militia was to begin in case force became necessary. A proclamation of warning was issued by Washington the next day.

[Philadelphia, August 7, 1794]

Whereas combinations to defeat the execution of the

laws laying duties upon spirits distilled within the United States, and upon stills, have from the time of the commencement of those laws existed in some of the Western parts of Pennsylvania:

[Here follows a long series of whereases, detailing the unlawful acts of the Westerners, after which the point of the proclamation is reached.]

Wherefore, and in pursuance of the proviso above recited, I, GEORGE WASHINGTON, President of the United States, do hereby command all persons, being insurgents as aforesaid, and all others whom it may concern, on or before the first day of September next, to disperse and retire peaceably to their respective abodes. And I do moreover warn all persons whomsoever against aiding, abetting, or comforting the perpetrators of the aforesaid treasonable acts; and do require all officers and citizens, according to their respective duties and the laws of the land, to exert their utmost endeavors to prevent and suppress such dangerous proceedings.

While he waited for word from the peace commissioners, Washington wrote of the insurrection and what he considered its causes to his friend Governor Henry Lee of Virginia.

German Town Augt. 26th. 1794.

As the Insurgents in the western Counties of this State are resolved (as far as we have yet been able to learn from the Commissioners, who have been sent among them) to persevere in their rebellious conduct until what they call the excise Law is repealed, and acts of oblivion and amnesty are passed; it gives me sincere consolation amidst the regret with which I am filled, by such lawless & outrageous conduct, to find by your Letter above mentioned, that it is held in general detestation by the good people of Virginia; and that you are disposed to lend your *personal* aid to subdue this spirit, & to bring those people to a proper sense of their duty.

On this latter point I shall refer you to letters from the War office; and to a private one from Colo. Hamilton (who in the absence of the secretary of war, superintends the *military* duties of that Department) for my sentiments on this occasion.

It is with equal pride and satisfaction I add, that as far as my information extends, this insurrection is viewed with universal indignation; and abhorrence; except by those who have never missed an opportunity by side blows, or otherwise, to aim their shafts at the General Government; and even among these there is not a spirit hard enough, yet, *openly* to justify the daring infractions of Law and order; but by palliatives are attempting to suspend all proceedings against the insurgents until Congress shall have decided on the case, thereby intending to gain time, and if possible to make the evil more extensive—more formidable—and of course more difficult to counteract and subdue.

I consider this insurrection as the first *formidable* fruit of the Democratic Societies; brought forth I believe too prematurely for their own views, which may contribute to the annihilation of them.

That these Societies were instituted by the *artful* & *designing* members (many of their body I have no doubt mean well but know little of the real plan) primarily to sow the seeds of jealousy & distrust among the people, of the government, by destroying all Confidence in the administration of it; and that these doctrines have been budding & blowing ever since, is not new to any one who is acquainted with the characters of their leaders, and have been attentive to their manoeuvres. I early gave it as my opinion to the confidential characters around me, that if these Societies were not counteracted (not by prosecutions, the ready way to make them grow stronger) or did not fall into disesteem from the knowledge of their origin, and the views with which they had been instituted by their father, Genet, for purposes well known to the Government; that they would shake the government to its foundation. Time and circumstances have confirmed me in this opinion, and I deeply regret the probable consequences, not as they will affect me personally—(for I have not long to act on this theatre, and sure I am that not a man amongst them can be more anxious to put me aside, than I am to sink into the profoundest retirement) but because I see, under a display of popular and fascinating guises, the most diabolical attempts to destroy the best fabric of human government & happiness, that has ever been presented, for the acceptance of mankind.

During these weeks of marking time, the President received from Martha Washington's granddaughter Elizabeth Parke Custis a letter asking for his picture. It was one of the few softer and lighter moments of many months; he responded partly playfully, partly with a shower of the maxims he could not resist when writing to someone young.

German Town, Septr. 14th. 1794.

My dear Betcy:

Shall I, in answer to your letter of the 7th. instant say —when you are as near the *Pinnacle* of happiness as your sister Patcy conceives herself to be; or when your candour shines more conspicuously than it does in *that* letter, that I will *then,* comply with the request you have made, for my Picture?

No—I will grant it without either: for if the latter was to be a preliminary, it would be sometime I apprehend before *that* Picture would be found pendant *at* your breast; it not being within the bounds of probability that the contemplation of an inanimate thing, whatever might be the reflections arising from the possession of it, can be the *only* wish of your heart.

Respect may place it among the desirable objects of it, but there are emotions of a softer kind, to wch. the heart of a girl turned of eighteen, is susceptible, that must have generated much warmer ideas, although the fruition of them may, apparently, be more distant than those of your Sister's.

Having (by way of a hint) delivered a sentiment to Patty [Elizabeth's sister Martha Parke Custis, then engaged to be married], which may be useful to her (if it be remembered after the change that is contemplated, is consummated) I will suggest another, more applicable to yourself.

Do not then in your contemplation of the marriage state, look for perfect felicity before you consent to wed. Nor conceive, from the fine tales the Poets & lovers of old have told us, of the transports of mutual love, that heaven has taken its abode on earth: Nor do not deceive yourself in supposing, that the only mean by which these are to be obtained, is to drink deep of the cup, & revel in an ocean of love. Love is a mighty pretty thing; but like all other delicious things, it is cloying; and when the first transports of the passion begins to subside, which it assuredly will do, and yield —oftentimes too late—to more sober reflections, it

Elizabeth Parke Custis, a portrait by Robert Edge Pine painted in 1785

Our First Century BY R. M. DEVENS, 1894

During the Whisky Rebellion, a federal tax collector was tarred and feathered by a Pennsylvania mob.

serves to evince, that love is too dainty a food to live upon *alone,* and ought not to be considered farther than as a necessary ingredient for that matrimonial happiness which results from a combination of causes; none of which are of greater importance, than that the object on whom it is placed, should possess good sense—good dispositions—and the means of supporting you in the way you have been brought up. Such qualifications cannot fail to attract (after marriage) your esteem & regard, into wch. or into disgust, sooner or later, love naturally resolves itself; and who at the sametime, has a claim to the respect, & esteem of the circle he moves in. Without these, whatever may be your first impressions of the man, they will end in disappointment; for be assured, and experience will convince you, that there is no truth more certain, than that all our enjoyments fall short of our expectations; and to none does it apply with more force, than to the gratification of the passions.

On September 24 word came from the commissioners that all attempts to reach an agreement with the insurgents had met with dead ends. The next day Washington issued a second proclamation, saying that he was calling out the militia of four states to suppress the Whisky Rebellion. In those simple, early days of the nation, Washington felt that as Commander in Chief he should accompany the militia, at least until the action was well launched. On the last day of September he left Philadelphia with his private secretary and Hamilton, who, in the temporary absence of Henry Knox, was acting Secretary of War as well as Treasury Secretary. Washington in his diary described the journey westward.

> Tuesday, 30th [September, 1794]. Having determined from the Report of the Commissioners, who were appointed to meet the Insurgents in the Western Counties in the State of Pennsylvania, and from other circumstances—to repair to the places appointed for the Rendezvous, of the Militia of New Jersey Pennsylvania Maryland & Virginia; I left the City of Philadelphia about half past ten oclock this forenoon accompanied by Colo. Hamilton (Secretary of the Treasury) & my private Secretary. Dined at Norris Town and lodged at a place called the Trap—the first 17, and the latter 25 Miles from Philadelphia.
>
> At Norris Town we passed a detachment of Militia who were preparing to March for the rendezvous at

Carlisle—and at the Trap, late in the evening, we were overtaken by Major Stagg principal Clerk in the Department of War with letters from Genl. Wayne & the Western Army containing official & pleasing accounts of his engagement with the Indians near the British Post at the Rapids of the Miami of the Lake and of his having destroyed all the Indian Settlements on that River in the vicinity of the said Post quite up to the grand Glaize —the quantity not less than 5000 acres—and the Stores &c. of Colo. McGee the British Agent of Indian Affairs a mile or two from the Garrison.

The news of Anthony Wayne's victory was welcome indeed. Twice during Washington's first Administration, expeditions sent against the same Indians had been badly defeated; now the area would be safe for settlers, and as a result of the treaty concessions that would inevitably be wrung from the natives, large tracts of land would be opened to settlement. It was not, however, the end of all Indian problems. During the months and years still left of his Presidency, Washington would often be turning his attention to the endless futility of treaty making or would be impotently railing at the invasion of Indian lands by white frontiersmen. After having spent the first part of October organizing various units of militia, the President—as his diary relates—met with two members of a committee from the rebellious Pennsylvania counties.

[October, 1794]. ...On the 9th. William Findley and David Redick—deputed by the Committee of safety (as it is disignated) which met on the 2d. of this month at Parkinson Ferry arrived in Camp with the Resolutions of the said Committee; and to give information of the State of things in the four Western Counties of Pennsylvania to wit—Washington Fayette Westd. [Westmoreland] & Alligany in order to see if it would prevent the March of the Army into them.

At 10 oclock I had a meeting with these persons in presence of Govr. Howell (of New Jersey) the Secretary of the Treasury, Colo. Hamilton, & Mr. Dandridge: Govr. Mifflin [of Pennsylvania] was invited to be present, but excused himself on acct. of business.

I told the Deputies that by one of the Resolutions it would appear that they were empowered to give information of the disposition & of the existing state of matters in the four Counties above men.; that I was ready to hear & would listen patiently, and with candour

Dramatic depiction of Wayne's fight with the Indians, from John Frost's Pictorial Life of Washington, *1853*

to what they had to say.

Mr. Findley began. He confined his information to such parts of the four Counties as he was best acquainted with; referring to Mr. Reddick for a recital of what fell within his knowledge, in the other parts of these Counties.

The substance of Mr. Findleys communications were as follows—viz.—That the People in the parts where he was best acquainted, had seen there folly; and he believed were disposed to submit to the Laws; that he thought, but could not undertake to be responsible, for the re-establishment of the public Offices for the Collection of the Taxes on distilled Spirits & Stills—intimating however, that it might be best *for the present,* & until the peoples minds were a little more tranquilized, to hold the Office of Inspection at Pitsburgh under the protection—or at least under the influence of the Garrison; That he thought the Distillers would either enter their stills or would put them down; That the Civilian authority was beginning to recover its tone; & enumerated some instances of it; That the ignorance, & general want of information among the people far exceeded any thing he had any conception of; That it was not merely the excise law their opposition was aimed at, but to *all* law, & Government; and to the Officers of Government; and that the situation in which he had been, & the life he had led for sometime, was such, that rather than go through it again, he would prefer quitting this scene altogether....

[Mr. Redick] added, that for a long time after the riots commenced, and until lately, the distrust of one another was such, that even friends were affraid to communicate their sentiments to each other; That by whispers this was brought about; and growing bolder as they became more communicative they found their strength, and that there was a general disposition not only to acquiesce under, but to support the Laws—and he gave some instances also of Magistrates enforcing them.

He said the People of those Counties believed that the opposition to the Excise law—or at least that their dereliction to it, in every other part of the U. States was similar to their own, and that no Troops could be got to march against them for the purpose of coercion; that every acct. until very lately, of Troops marching

William Findley, by Rembrandt Peale

George Washington's own copy of a book describing the Whisky Rebellion

against them was disbelieved; & supposed to be the fabricated tales of governmental men; That now they had got alarmed; That many were disposing of their property at an under rate, in order to leave the Country, and added (I think) that they wd. go to Detroit....

After hearing what both had to say, I briefly told them—That it had been the earnest wish of governmt. to bring the people of those counties to a sense of their duty, by mild, & lenient means; That for the purpose of representing to their sober reflection the fatal consequences of such conduct Commissioners had been sent amongst them that they might be warned, in time, of what must follow, if they persevered in their opposition to the laws; but that coercion wou'd not be resorted to except in the dernier resort: but, that the season of the year made it indispensible that preparation for it should keep pace with the propositions that had been made; That it was unnecessary for me to enumerate the transactions of those people (as they related to the proceedings of government) forasmuch as they knew them as well as I did; That the measure which they were now witness to the adoption of was not less painful than expensive— Was inconvenient, & distressing—in every point of view; but as I considered the support of the Laws as an object of the first magnitude, and the greatest part of the expence had already been incurred, that nothing Short of the most unequivocal *proofs* of absolute Submission should retard the March of the army into the Western counties, in order to convince them that the government could, & would enforce obedience to the laws—not suffering them to be insulted with impunity. Being asked again what proofs would be required, I answered, they knew as well as I did, what was due to justice & example. They understood my meaning—and asked if they might have another interview. I appointed five oclock in the Afternoon for it.

Washington talked with the two men the next day, but nothing further was accomplished. He could only promise that if the Westerners met the troops peaceably, there would be no bloodshed. Then, after he had put Governor Henry Lee of Virginia in command of the militia, Washington started back to Philadelphia to be there for the convening of Congress on November 3. During the following weeks Hamilton sent frequent reports of mass arrests and seizures of stills. By late November the Whisky Rebellion had been quelled without bloodshed. The military action had decisively established the ascendancy of the Federal Government and strengthened the power of Hamilton and the Federalists. In fact, there is some evidence that Hamilton had quietly caused the peacemaking efforts of the federal commissioners to fail so that there could be a military confrontation. Of the few dozen insurrectionists arrested, only two were convicted in trials, and Washington would pardon both.

Hamilton and Knox resigned from the Cabinet, leaving only Edmund Randolph of the original four. Knox was replaced by Postmaster General Timothy Pickering, a capable negotiator with the Indians, which was then probably the main qualification of a War Secretary. At the end of January, 1795, Comptroller of the Treasury Oliver Wolcott succeeded Hamilton.

No important matters were calling for the President's instant attention those first weeks of the new year, but the relative calm was broken on March 7 when there arrived a copy of the "Treaty of Amity, Commerce, and Navigation," the result of John Jay's long negotiations in England. Jay had written, "It must speak for itself.... To do more was not possible." Washington read the text of the treaty with some consternation. Jay had failed to achieve most of his objectives, although Britain did promise to move out of the frontier posts by June 1, 1796. Article XII opened the important British West Indies trade to American vessels, but only to those of seventy tons or less, and they could not carry cotton, sugar, or molasses, the main source of profit for American traders. Mixed commissions were to be set up to settle such things as disputed boundaries. The treaty ignored such matters as payment by the British for slaves removed during the war and impressment of American seamen. What Jay had not known was that his power to negotiate had been undermined from the beginning; Hamilton, fearful that something might happen to the British trade so important to his fiscal plans, had quietly let the British know in advance the limits of Jay's bargaining power.

The President continued, as always, to be plagued by cadgers and special pleaders. Charles Carter, a friend from Fredericksburg, Virginia, wrote to ask the President for a loan of one thousand pounds for his son's business and got a report on the state of Washington's finances instead.

> Philadelphia 10th. March 1795.
> Your favor of the 23d. Ulto. came duly to hand. I wish, sincerely it was in my power to comply with your request in behalf of your son, but it really is not, to the extent of it.
> My friends entertain a very erroneous idea of my pecuniary resources, when they set me down for a money lender, or one who (now) has a Command of it. You may believe me, when I assert that the bonds which were due to me before the Revolution, were

John Jay was hanged in effigy when the terms of his treaty became known.

discharged during the progress of it—with a few exceptions in depreciated paper (in some instances as low as a shilling in the pound). That such has been the management of my Estate, for many years past, especially since my absence from home, now six years, as scarcely to support itself. That my public allowance (whatever the world may think of it) is inadequate to the expence of living in this City; to such an extravagant height has the necessaries as well as the conveniencies of life arisen. And moreover, that to keep myself out of debt, I have found it expedient, now and then to sell Lands, or some thing else to effect this purpose.

These are facts I have no inclination to publish to the World, nor should I have disclosed them on this occasion, had it not been due to friendship, to give you some explanation of my inability to comply with your request. If, however by joining with nine others, the sum required can be obtained—notwithstanding my being under these circumstances—and notwithstanding the money will be to be withdrawn from another purpose—I will contribute one hundred pounds towards the accommodation of your sons wants, without any view to the receipt of interest therefrom.

In the meantime, Washington and Secretary of State Randolph kept the terms of Jay's Treaty a tight secret until the Senate returned on June 8 and was given the treaty to consider. Even then secrecy was preserved, for the bitter debate was carried on behind closed doors. Washington's own attitude toward the treaty was that if it accomplished nothing else, it would prevent war with England, which would have been disastrous to the United States. The Republicans, opposed to any treaty that did not favor France, were outmaneuvered on all points except Article XII, the West Indies trade section, which even many Federalists found too bitter to swallow. On June 24 the Senate approved the treaty, except Article XII, for which Washington was to prepare a substitute; when the substitute was approved by the Senate, he could ratify the treaty and return it to Britain. Even while the Senate was still debating, a copy of the treaty had leaked out to the Republican press. John Jay was hanged in effigy. Mass meetings were held, some for, most against, the treaty. Addresses from a score of cities protesting the treaty came to the President. In New York City, when Alexander Hamilton tried to speak in defense of the treaty, he was stoned. Washington, in a letter to Hamilton, unburdened himself of some of his anger and frustration.

The American copy (above) of Jay's "Treaty of Amity, Commerce, and Navigation" and the version issued in Great Britain (opposite)

Mount Vernon, July 29, 1795.

As the measures of the government, respecting the treaty, were taken before I left Philadelphia, something more imperious than has yet appeared, must turn up to occasion a change. Still, it is very desirable to ascertain, if possible, after the paroxysm of the fever is a little abated, what the real temper of the people is, concerning it; for at present the cry against the Treaty is like that against a mad-dog; and every one, in a manner, seems engaged in running it down.

That it has received the most tortured interpretation, and that the writings agt. it (which are very industriously circulated) are pregnant of the most abominable misrepresentations, admits of no doubt; yet, there are to be found, so far as my information extends, many well disposed men who conceive, that in the settlement of *old* disputes, a proper regard to reciprocal justice does not appear in the Treaty; whilst others, also well enough affected to the government, are of opinion that to have had *no* commercial treaty would have been better, for this country, than the restricted one, agreed to; inasmuch, say they, the nature of our Exports, and imports (without any extra: or violent measures) would have forced, or led to a more adequate intercourse between the two nations; without any of those shackles which the treaty has imposed. In a word, that as our *exports* consist chiefly of *provisions* and *raw materials,* which to the manufacturers in G. Britain, and to their Islands in the West Indies, affords employment and food; they must have had them on *our* terms, if they were not to be obtained on their *own*; whilst the *imports* of this country, offers the best mart for their fabricks; and, of course, is the principal support of their manufacturers: But the string which is most played on, because it strikes with most force the popular ear, is the violation, as they term it, of our engagements with France; or in other words, the predilection shown by that instrument to G. Britain at the expence of the French nation.

The consequences of which are more to be apprehended than any, which are likely to flow from other causes, as ground of opposition; because, whether the fact is, in *any* degree true, or not, it is the interest of the French (whilst the animosity, or jealousies betwn. the two nations exist) to avail themselves of such a spirit, to keep *us* and *G. Britain* at variance; and they will, in my opinion, accordingly do it. To what *length* their policy may induce them to carry matters, is too much in embryo at this moment to decide: but I predict much embarrassment to the government therefrom, and in my opinion, too much pains cannot be taken by those who speak, or write, in favor of the treaty, to place this matter in its true light.

I have seen with pleasure, that a writer in one of the New York papers under the Signature of Camillus, has promised to answer, or rather to defend the treaty, which has been made with G. Britain. To judge of this work from the first number, which I have seen, I auger well of the performance; and shall expect to see the subject handled in a clear, distinct and satisfactory manner: but if measures are not adopted for its dissimination a few only will derive lights from the knowledge, or labour of the author; whilst the opposition pieces will spread their poison in all directions; and Congress, more than probable, will assemble with the unfavorable impressions of their constituents. The difference of conduct between the friends, and foes of order, and good government, is in nothg. more striking than that, the latter are always working, like bees, to distil their poison; whilst the former, depending, often times *too much,* and *too long,* upon the sense, and good dispositions of the people to work conviction, neglect the means of effecting it.

Washington had gone to Mount Vernon for a brief rest, but his stay there was cut short by a mysterious note from Secretary of War Timothy Pickering, saying there was a "special reason" for the President to hurry back, "which can be communicated to you only in person." On his return Washington was shocked to be told by Pickering that during his absence the British had delivered an intercepted letter, written a year earlier by French Ambassador Joseph Fauchet to his superiors in Paris. In it Fauchet implied that Randolph had come to him proposing that for a suitable bribe he, Randolph, could bring about a peaceable end to the Whisky Rebellion and so prevent the crushing of the pro-French Westerners. Washington said nothing for eight days, until Randolph had readied Jay's Treaty and an accompanying memorial to the British ambassador. Then, on the morning of August 19, in the presence of Pickering and Secretary of the Treasury Wolcott, Washington handed a translation of the incriminating letter to Randolph. After trying to explain the apparently damning evidence against him, Randolph, Washington's friend of twenty years, his closest adviser, resigned in a letter expressing his resentment over the humiliating way he had been treated. He asked for a copy of the original of the letter and of dispatch No. 6, referred to in Fauchet's letter. Washington replied with chilly formality.

Philadelphia 20 Aug. 1795.

Sir:

Your resignation of the office of State, is received.

Candor induces me to give you in a few words, the following narrative of facts.

The Letter from Mr. Fauchet, with the contents of which you were made acquainted yesterday, was, as you supposed, an intercepted one. It was sent by lord Grenville to Mr. Hammond — by him put into the hands of the secretary of the Treasury; by him shewn to the Secy. of War & the Attorney General; and a translation thereof was made by the former for me.

At the time Mr. Hammond delivered the letter, he requested of Mr. Wolcott an attested copy; which was accordingly made by Mr. Thornton his late secretary, and which is understood to remain at present with Mr. Bond. Whether it is known to others I am unable to decide. Whilst you are in pursuit of means to remove the strong suspicions arising from this letter, no disclosure of its contents will be made by me; and I will enjoin the same on the public officers (who are acquainted with the purport of it) unless something shall appear to render an explanation necessary on the part of Government — & of which I will be the Judge.

A Copy of Mr. Fauchets' letter shall be sent to you — No. 6 referred to therein, I have never seen.

Oliver Wolcott, by Trumbull

It has appeared with the passage of time that Randolph was probably innocent. Ambassador Fauchet denied that Randolph had proposed a bribe; when dispatch No. 6 appeared, it further weakened the case against Randolph. The culprits were apparently Wolcott and Pickering, who, even if they believed Randolph guilty, connived to convict him without a trial. As staunch Federalists, the two men must have feared that Randolph might be standing in the way of swift ratification of the treaty and wished to discredit him with Washington. But if Washington ever felt he had made a mistake, there is no evidence of it. There was a continuing torrent of abuse over Jay's Treaty in the Republican press during the following months, and protests came to the President from a number of cities. Except for one or two that he considered too abusive to deserve a reply, he answered the protests formally but politely.

Edmund Randolph

> Philada. 31st. Augt. 1795.
>
> I have received your Letter of the 6th. inst. inclosing the proceedings of the meeting at Norfolk on the 5th. relative to the Treaty lately negociated between the United States and Great Britain.
>
> On subjects of so complex *and relative* a nature as those embraced by the Treaty a diversity of opinion was to have been expected. My determination which is known to have been in affirmance of the Treaty as advised and consented to by the Senate, was formed after the most mature deliberation and with a sincere regard to the public good.
>
> Though it cannot be uninteresting to me to know that the wishes of a part of my fellow Citizens have been contravened by this decision, yet if the purity of my intentions will entitle me to their approbation, it has not been forfeited on the present important occasion.

The national political climate was such that the President trod gingerly in whatever he did. When in late September he received a letter from George Washington Lafayette, son of the Marquis de Lafayette and newly arrived in Boston from France, his instinct must have been to invite the youth to Philadelphia at once. Instead, he had to stop and consider what effect taking him into his home might have on relations with republican France, and even more so, how it could exacerbate the antagonisms between Federalists and Republicans at home. As a result, he wrote to George Cabot, Federalist Senator from Massachusetts, asking Cabot to act in his stead for a time. As a matter of fact, Washington did not see young Lafayette in Philadelphia until the following April, after Congress had formally taken note of the youth's presence in the United States.

> Philadelphia, September 7, 1795.
>
> The enclosed letters (which after reading, be so good as to return to me) will be the best appology I can offer for the liberty I am about to take and for the trouble, if you comply with my request, it must necessarily give.
>
> To express all the sensibility wch. has been excited in my breast by the receipt of young Fayettes letter, from the recollection of his fathers merits, services and sufferings, from my friendship for him, and from my wishes to become a *friend* and *father* to his Son; are unnecessary.

Mount Vernon, LOSSING

Washington's namesake, George Washington Lafayette, son of the General's wartime friend and ally

Let me in a few words, declare that I *will be his friend*; but the manner of becomg. so considering the obnoxious light in which his father is viewed by the French government, and my own situation, as the Executive of the U. States, requires more time to consider in all its relations, than I can bestow on it at present; the letters not having been in my hands more than an hour, and I myself on the point of setting out for Virginia to fetch my family back whom I left there about the first of August.

The mode which, at the first view strikes me as the most eligable to answer his purposes and to save appears. is, I. to administer all the consolation to young Gentleman that he can derive from the most unequivocal assurances of my standing in the place of and becoming to him, a *Father, friend, protector,* and *supporter.* but 2dly. for prudential motives, as they may relate to himself; his mother and friends, whom he has left behind; and to my *official* character it would be best not to make these sentiments public; of course, that it would be ineligable, that he should come to the Seat of the genl. government where all the foreign characters (particularly that of his own nation) are residents, until it is seen what opinions will be excited by his arrival; especially too as I shall be necessarily absent five or Six weeks from it, on business, in several places. 3. considering how important it is to avoid idleness and dissipation; to improve his mind; and to give him all the advantages which education can bestow; my opinion, and my advice to him is, (if he is qualified for admission) that he should enter as a student at the University in Cambridge [Harvard] altho' it shd. be for a short time *only.* The expence of which, as also of every other mean for his support, I will pay; and now do authorise you, my dear Sir, to draw upon me accordingly; and if it is in any degree *necessary,* or *desired,* that Mr. Frestel his Tutor should accompany him to the University in that character; any arrangements which you shall make for the purpose, and any expence thereby incurred for the same, shall be borne by me in like manner.

One thing more, and I will conclude: Let me pray you my dear Sir to impress upon young Fayette's mind, and indeed upon that of his tutors that the reasons why I do not urge him to come to me, have been frankly related, and that their prudence must appreciate them with caution. My friendship for his father so far from being diminshd. has encreased in the ratio of his misfortunes; and my inclination to serve the son will be evidenced by my conduct; reasons wch. will readily occur to *you*, and wch. can easily be explained to him, will acct. for my not acknowledging the receipt of his, or Mr. Frestal's Letter. With sincere esteem &c.

PS. You will perceive that young Lafayette has taken the name of Motier. Whether it is best he should retain it and aim at perfect concealment, or not, depends upon a better knowledge of circumstances than I am possessed of, and therefore I leave this matter to your own judgment after a consultation with the parties.

As 1795 drew to a close, Alexander Hamilton had become the constant though unofficial adviser to the President; Washington wrote to his former Secretary of the Treasury for counsel frequently and on a wide variety of matters. Letters to James Madison, his most trusted adviser of his first years as President, and to Jefferson, on whom he had also once leaned so heavily, were now few and far between and never on matters of national policy; his infrequent correspondence with the two Republicans was on such subjects as crops and fertilizers and plans for a national university. At year's end the Cabinet was solidly Federalist, four good disciples of Hamilton. Although Washington spoke often about the evils of party division, he found the conservatism of Federalism much more congenial than the tenets of the Republican party. The concerns of government, however, did not distract Washington from his long-time preoccupation with the affairs of Mount Vernon. Early in 1796 an advertisement appeared in a number of American newspapers and in England as well.

Philadelphia, February 1, 1796.

TO BE LET

AND POSSESSION GIVEN IN AUTUMN

The Farms appertaining to the Mount Vernon Estate, in Virginia; four in number; adjoining the Mansion House Farm. Leases will be given for the term of fourteen years to *real* farmers of *good* reputation, and none others need apply.

The largest of these, called River Farm, contains 1207 acres of ploughable land; 879 of which, are in seven fields, nearly of a size, and under good fences; 212 acres (in one enclosure) are, generally in a common grass pasture; and 116 acres more, are in *five* grass lots, and an orchard (of the best grafted fruit) all of them contiguous to the dwelling house and barn. On the premises, are a comfortable dwelling house (in which the Overlooker resides) having three rooms below, and one or two above; an old barn (now in use) and a brick one building 60 by 30 feet; besides ends and wings, sufficient for stabling 20 working horses, and as many oxen; and an excellent brick dairy, with a fine

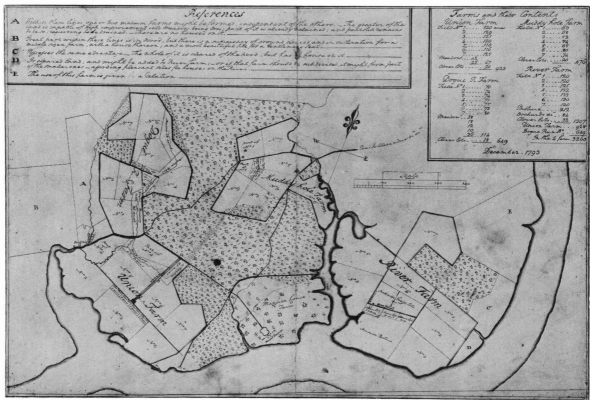

Drawn from field notes, this map by Washington, made in December, 1793, shows the four farms surrounding the Mount Vernon mansion house and estate.

spring in the middle of it. Thirty black labourers (men and women) being the usual number which have been employed on this farm, are, with their children, warmly lodged chiefly in houses of their own building. The soil is a loam, more inclined to clay than sand, and with slight dressings yields grain well, particularly wheat. Encompassed on two sides by the river Potomack, and on a third by a navigable creek, the inlet therefrom, in a variety of places, afford an inexhaustible fund of rich mud for manure or compost. The water abounds in a variety of fish and wild fowl; and one or more shad and herring fisheries might be established thereon.

The advertisement described in similar fashion the other three dependent farms of Mount Vernon, with the terms on which they could be rented. Washington, after he had assembled over the years, often field by field, thousands of Mount Vernon's acres, looked down the short road of his remaining years and decided that there was too much plantation for an aging man. He did not mean to give any of it up, only to rent it, but for a man who knew and loved every foot of its great expanse, even the thought of familiar fields in the hands of tenant farmers must have been a wrench. None of it, though, would ever be farmed by a tenant while Washington lived, for he would never find a prospective renter who satisfied him. Near the end of February, Washington sent a brief but important message to the Senate.

United States Feby. 26th. 1796

Gentlemen of the Senate:

I send herewith the Treaty concluded on the 27th. of October last between the United States and Spain by their respective Plenipotentiaries.

The Communications to the Senate referred to in my message of the 16th. of December 1793 contain the instructions to the Commissioners of the United States, Messrs. Carmichael and Short, and various details relative to the negociations with Spain. Herewith I transmit Copies of the documents authorizing Mr. Pinckney the Envoy extraordinary from the United States to the Court of Spain, to conclude the negociation, agreeably to the original instructions above mentioned; and to adjust the Claims of the United States for the Spoliations committed by the Armed Vessels of his Catholic Majesty on the Commerce of our Citizens.

The numerous papers exhibiting the progress of the negociation under the conduct of Mr. Pinckney, being in the French and Spanish languages, will be communicated to the Senate as soon as the translations which appear necessary shall be completed.

Stripped of its eighteenth-century official phraseology, Washington's message to the Senate meant that after a dozen years of frustrating negotiations, agreement had at last been reached with Spain on navigation of the Mississippi River and on the southern boundary of the United States. The pact, signed in October of 1795, was the Treaty of San Lorenzo, or more familiarly, Pinckney's Treaty—for Thomas Pinckney, who, as special envoy, had helped conclude the negotiations. By the agreement, Spain granted American citizens free use of the Mississippi, whose

371

lower reaches ran through Spanish territory. Also granted was the right of deposit at New Orleans of American freight brought down the river for transshipment by sea. Spain accepted the thirty-first parallel of latitude as the southwestern boundary of the United States (previously she had claimed a line about ninety miles farther north), and she promised to curb Indian incursions into American territory. And finally, the Spanish agreed to settle claims arising from their seizure of American ships. These sweeping concessions very probably were the result of Spanish fear that Jay's Treaty secretly provided for an Anglo-American alliance that could be a threat to Spain. In any event, the effect of the treaty was to ease the difficulties of western settlers and to remove the possibility that in frustration they might attempt to form a separate nation. For Washington, the agreement removed several problems that had vexed him from the beginning of his Presidency.

As the months of 1796 passed away, the President prepared a farewell address with Hamilton's help. The lengthy document was never actually delivered but was published widely, first in Philadelphia in the *American Daily Advertiser* of September 19, 1796. The Address was a notable message. In four basic sections, it gave Washington's reasons for refusing a third term; it inveighed against party divisions, especially along sectional lines; it counseled that the nation's credit must always be cherished and protected; and it warned against permanent foreign alliances. The caution against permanent alliances remained a keystone of American foreign policy until less than a generation ago; a thousand spread-eagle orators since have misquoted Washington as warning against "entangling alliances"—that phrase was to be Jefferson's. The core of what George Washington wrote follows.

> The great rule of conduct for us, in regard to foreign Nations, is in extending our commercial relations, to have with them as little *political* connection as possible. So far as we have already formed engagements let them be fulfilled with perfect good faith. Here let us stop.
>
> Europe has a set of primary interests, which to us have none, or a very remote relation. Hence she must be engaged in frequent controversies, the causes of which are essentially foreign to our concerns. Hence, therefore, it must be unwise in us to implicate ourselves, by artificial ties, in the ordinary vicissitudes of her politicks, or the ordinary combinations and collisions of her friendships, or enmities.
>
> Our detached and distant situation invites and enables us to pursue a different course. If we remain one People, under an efficient government, the period is not far off, when we may defy material injury from external annoyance; when we may take such an attitude as will cause

the neutrality, we may at any time resolve upon, to be scrupulously respected; when belligerent nations, under the impossibility of making acquisitions upon us, will not lightly hazard the giving us provocation; when we may choose peace or war, as our interest, guided by justice, shall counsel.

Why forego the advantages of so peculiar a situation? Why quit our own to stand upon foreign ground? Why, by interweaving our destiny with that of any part of Europe, entangle our peace and prosperity in the toils of European ambition, rivalship, interest, humour or caprice?

'Tis our true policy to steer clear of permanent alliances, with any portion of the foreign world; so far, I mean, as we are now at liberty to do it; for let me not be understood as capable of patronising infidility to existing engagements. I hold the maxim, no less applicable to public than to private affairs, that honesty is always the best policy. I repeat it, therefore, let those engagements be observed in their genuine sense. But in my opinion, it is unnecessary and would be unwise to extend them.

Taking care always to keep ourselves, by suitable establishments, on a respectable defensive posture,

The first page of Hamilton's draft of Washington's farewell address

we may safely trust to temporary alliances for extraordinary emergencies.

[The President closed with a typical Washingtonian note of apology for his inadequacies, and of his pleasure at anticipating the joys of retirement.]

Though in reviewing the incidents of my administration, I am unconscious of intentional error: I am nevertheless too sensible of my defects not to think it probable that I may have committed many errors. Whatever they may be I fervently beseech the Almighty to avert or mitigate the evils to which they may tend. I shall also carry with me the hope that my Country will never cease to view them with indulgence; and that after forty five years of my life dedicated to its service, with an upright zeal, the faults of incompetent abilities will be consigned to oblivion, as myself must soon be to the mansions of rest.

Relying on its kindness in this as in other things, and actuated by that fervent love towards it, which is so natural to a man, who views in it the native soil of himself, and his progenitors for several generations; I anticipate with pleasing expectation that retreat, in which I promise myself to realize, without alloy, the sweet enjoyment of partaking, in the midst of my fellow Citizens, the benign influence of good laws under a free government—the ever favourite object of my heart, and the happy reward, as I trust, of our mutual cares, labours and dangers.

A COLLECTION
OF THE
SPEECHES
OF THE
President of the United States
TO BOTH
HOUSES OF CONGRESS,
At the OPENING of every SESSION,
WITH THEIR
ANSWERS.
ALSO, THE
ADDRESSES to the PRESIDENT,
WITH HIS
ANSWERS,
FROM THE TIME OF HIS ELECTION:
WITH AN *APPENDIX,*
CONTAINING
The CIRCULAR LETTER of GENERAL
WASHINGTON to the GOVERNORS of the
several STATES, and his FAREWELL ORDERS,
to the ARMIES of AMERICA, and the ANSWER.
DEDICATED TO THE
Citizens of the United States of America.
Published according to Act of Congress.

PRINTED AT BOSTON,
By MANNING AND LORING,
For *SOLOMON COTTON,* jun.
BOOKSELLER AND STATIONER,
Sold by him, at his Bookstore, No. 51, Marlborough-Street.
JULY, 1796.

In July, 1796, a book was published in Boston containing Washington's speeches to Congress and other of his official pronouncements. This is the title page from his own copy.

By January, 1797, the results of the presidential election were known, and the growing strength of the Republicans was obvious. Although Federalist John Adams won, he barely edged out—71 votes to 68—Thomas Jefferson, who thereby became Vice President. Thomas Pinckney, Federalist, received 59 votes; Aaron Burr, Republican, 30.

The last three months of Washington's Administration spun to an end. He would not leave a secure and tranquil nation; both British and French warships were stopping American merchant vessels and removing goods bound for the other country; American citizens were bitterly divided as they took sides in the European conflict. But for the moment the United States appeared safe from war; Washington had started the country on its way and had given it a breathing spell. On March 3, 1797, he signed a pardon for ten men convicted of treason in connection with the Whisky Rebellion and remitted a fine imposed on a smuggler. These appear to be his last two official acts as President. That same day he gave a farewell dinner "to take my leave of the President elect, of the foreign characters, the heads of departments, &c." The next day he went alone to Congress Hall to witness the swearing in of John Adams as second President of the United States. The ceremony was brief, and in a few minutes Washington walked forth a private citizen. Of his two last days in office he left little record in his diary.

> 3 [March, 1797]. Mercury at 34. Morning very lowering & threatning but clear & pleasant afterwards— Wind fresh from the So. Wt.
>
> 4. Much such a day as yesterday in all respects— Mercury at 41.

When Washington was inaugurated in 1789, the Presidency of the United States was no more than a concept, words in the untried Constitution. In eight years he had created an office that was established and workable, flesh and blood. It is safe to say that no other man of his time could have done the same thing, such were his unique talents and the great trust the people reposed in him.

His Administration was not a flamboyant one, but like the man himself it was marked by caution, sober assessment of the prevailing situation, and careful planning. Perhaps the greatest of his achievements was to hold a number of self-willed states together until their people had acquired a sense of themselves as a nation. He kept the country at peace, divorcing America from the quarrels of Europe in spite of clamor around him for involvement, for he knew that war then could wreck the infant republic. He assumed the Presidency of a country submerged in debt and left it well on its way to fiscal soundness, a tribute not to his financial acumen but to his ability to choose able advisers and then to support the programs they recommended. He gave to the Presidency not only dignity but established it as a coequal arm with Congress; a lesser man might well have let the office become ceremonial and subservient to the legislature.

In one thing he failed. He had wanted to keep the new nation free of the divisiveness of party politics. It was a vain hope, for party divisions, Federalists against Republicans, were only the surface indications of deep economic and philosophical rifts, of bankers and merchants against farmers, of the wealthy few against the many poor. Washington for a long time attempted a nonpartisan stance, dividing his Cabinet equally between Federalists and Republicans, but his own instincts were conservative, and during his last years in office his Cabinet was composed entirely of Federalists, who shared his belief in a strong central government. It detracts little from Washington's greatness as a President to observe that he was basically a Federalist when he turned the Presidency over to John Adams.

Chapter **11**

To Rest by the Potomac

Washington tarried a few days in Philadelphia, paying his respects to the new President, being honored at a dinner by the people of Philadelphia, breaking up his household. Happily, his dependable secretary of former years, Tobias Lear, was in the capital and could take over a big part of the chore of moving, including the packing of some two hundred boxes, trunks, casks, and other items belonging to Washington for shipment by water to Mount Vernon, and then cleaning and making the President's House ready for John Adams. Washington left for home the morning of March 9, 1797. In his party, besides Martha, were Martha's eighteen-year-old granddaughter Eleanor (Nelly), George Washington Lafayette, and Lafayette's tutor. As always, cities along the way paid honor to Washington as he passed through, not only Baltimore, Georgetown, and Alexandria, but also the still unfinished city of Washington—which the former President still modestly referred to as the Federal City. There an artillery escort turned out and gave him a sixteen-gun salute.

There was much to be done at Mount Vernon. As of the first of the year, still another manager, James Anderson, had taken over from rheumatic William Pearce, and although he was proving diligent and capable, he had much to learn that only Washington could teach him. Washington put painters to work freshening up the mansion house, only to discover that other things should have been taken care of first: a marble mantel was almost falling out, the main beam under one room was so badly decayed that it would have collapsed if the room had been filled with people, there was other deterioration in the outer buildings as well as in the mansion house. The owner spoke of his problems in a letter to Tobias Lear.

> Mount Vernon 25th. March 1797.
> Your letter of the 20th. instt., with the Bill of lading for the Goods in the Sloop Salem, and another letter of the 15th. are both received; and I hope this will find you

safely arrived in the Federal City.

I have got Painters at work in order to prepare my rooms for the furniture which is expected; but I find I have begun at the wrong end, for some joiners work (of the deficiency of which I was ignorant before it was examined) ought to have preceeded theirs, as the fixing of the chimney pieces ought also to do. The first I have engaged, but cannot, on enquiry, find that a skilful hand is to be had in Alexandria to execute the latter. I would thank you therefore for engaging one, if to be had in the Federal City or George town, to be here on Monday or tuesday at farthest as my work will be at a stand without. To prevent imposition, and to avoid disputes, I would prefer employing the artisan by the day. The work *immediately* foreseen, and which must be done without delay, is, to refix the Marble chimney piece in the Parlour which is almost falling out; to fix the New one (expected from Philadelphia) in the small dining room; to remove the one *now* there into what is called the School room; to fix the Grate which is coming round in the large dining room; and to give some repairs to the steps; which (like most things else I have looked into since I have been at home) are sadly out of repair.

The summer house at Mount Vernon

Washington received news of the death of his only sister, Betty Washington Lewis, in a letter from her son, George Lewis. The squire of Mount Vernon replied with a letter of condolence that reads very strangely, since it seems less concerned with their loss than with his building problems.

Mount Vernon, April 9, 1797.
Your letter of the 31st. Ult. from Culpeper County, came to my hands late at night on the 5th. inst., and the enclosure for your brother Fielding was sent to him early next morning.

The melancholy of your writing has filled me with inexpressable concern. The debt of nature however sooner or later, must be paid by us all, and although the separation from our nearest relatives is a heart rending circumstance, reason, religeon and philosophy, teach us to bear it with resignation, while time alone can ameliorate, and soften the pangs we experience at parting.

Washington's sister, Betty Lewis

It must have been a consoling circumstance to my deceased Sister, that so many of her friends were about her. I find myself almost in the Situation of a new beginner, so much does my houses, and every thing about them, stand in need of repairs. What with Joiners, Painters, Glasiers, etc. etc. I have scarcely a room to go into at present, that is free from one, or other of them. But the inside will soon be done, tho' it will require a good deal of time to make good the decays which I am every day discerning in the out buildings and Inclosures.

This leads me to ask if you know of a good House Joiner (white or black) that could be hired by the year, or month, and on what terms. I want one who is capable of making a rich finished pannel Door, Sash, and wainscot; and who could be relied on for his sobriety and diligence.

At any time, and at all times, we should be very glad to see you and Mrs. Lewis at this place; and with best regard to you both, in which your Aunt joins, I am, etc.

Washington was soon back in the familiar rhythm of a farmer's life, one regulated by the sun and the seasons. He also found himself caught up again in the demands of Virginia hospitality, as he had been before he became President; there was always someone eating at his table, asking to stay overnight, or begging other favors of him. He wrote to Secretary of War James McHenry, describing his life in retirement.

Mount Vernon 29th. May 1797.

I am indebted to you for several unacknowledged letters, but n'er mind that—go on as if you had them. You are at the source of information & can find many things to relate, while I have nothing to say that could either inform, or amuse a Secretary of War in Philadelphia.

To tell him that I begin my diurnal Course with the sun,—that if my Hirelings are not in their places at that time; I send them messages expressive of my sorrow for their indisposition, then having put these wheels in motion, I examine the state of things further; and the more they are probed the deeper I find the wounds are which my buildings have sustained by an absence & neglect of Eight Years. By the time I have accomplished these matters breakfast (a little after seven O'clock about the time I presume you are taking leave of Mrs. McHenry) is ready. This over I mount my horse and ride round my farms, which employs me until it is time to dress for dinner at which I rarely miss seeing strange faces, come as they say out of respect for me—Pray would not the word curiosity answer as Well? And how different this from having a few social friends at a chearful board? The usual time of Sitting at Table—a walk—and Tea, brings me within the dawn of candle light; previous to which if not prevented by company, I resolve that as soon as the glimmering taper supplies the place of the great luminary, I will retire to my writing table, & acknowledge the letters I have received but when the lights are brought I feel tired & disinclined to engage in this work, conceiving that the next night will do as well: the next comes & with it the same causes for postponement & effect & so on.

This will account for *your* letters remaining so long unacknowledged—and having given you the History of a day, it will serve for a year; and I am persuaded you will not require a second edition of it: but it may strike you that in this detail no mention is made of any portion of time allotted for reading; The remark would be just—for I have not looked into a Book since I came home, nor shall I be able to do it until I have discharged my Workmen, probably not before the nights grow longer, when possibly I may be looking in doomsday book.

China bearing motif of Society of the Cincinnati, purchased by Washington

Mount Vernon, LOSSING

Washington's complaint about visitors who came to Mount Vernon out of mere curiosity went back many years, but his innate hospitality made it impossible for him to close his gates to strangers. He sent a brief note on July 1 to Tobias Lear, who was still in business in the city of Washington: "I am alone *at present*, and shall be glad to see you this evening. Unless someone pops in, unexpectedly—Mrs. Washington and myself will do what I believe has not been done within the last twenty years by us—that is to set down to dinner by ourselves."

Despite what Washington had told McHenry about his simple daily routine, the truth was that much of his heart and mind remained with the affairs of the nation. He was kept informed of developments by the Secretaries of War and State, and the information was not always cheerful. Before he retired, Washington had appointed Charles Cotesworth Pinckney Minister to France to replace James Monroe. Previously Washington had offered Pinckney, at one time or another, command of the Army, a seat on the Supreme Court, and the secretaryships of War and State, and as a result he considered it not only an insult to the United States but a personal affront when the French Government—the Directory—refused to accept Pinckney's credentials. It sent relations with France from bad to worse. The United States was no more prepared for war with France than it had been to fight with England at the time of Jay's Treaty. President Adams sent John Marshall (later Chief Justice) and Elbridge Gerry (a Republican, to give the group a bipartisan image) to join Pinckney in dealing with the Government in Paris. About the first of December, Washington received letters from Pinckney and Marshall, written from Holland in September. His responses to both men were similar in tone; following is his letter to Pinckney.

Mount Vernon 4 Decr. 1797.

With much pleasure I received your letter of the 19th. of Septr. from Rotterdam; and that pleasure proceeded in a great measure from the congeniality of sentiments which prevail between you and Genl. Marshall, as I had taken the liberty of introducing him to you, as a Gentleman in whom you might place entire confidence.

What has been the reception of the embassy by the French Directory, is, to me, unknown; and what will be the result of it, is not for me to predict. The change however which took place at Paris on the 4th. of Septr. [a coup d'état against the Directory] adds nothing to my hope of a favorable issue. In this I *may* be mistaken; but of another thing I am certain I shall not and that is, that the failure (if such be the case) cannot be attributed to the want of justice on the part of the United States or from the want of an able representation of it, on the part of their Negociators. Of course the issue must be favorable, or conviction will be produced in all Except those who do not want to be convinced, that we have nothing to expect from the [justice of the] Nation with whom we are treating. In either case we shall ascertain our ground.

That the Government of France views us as a divided people I have little doubt, and that they have been led to entertain that opinion, from representations and the conduct of many of our own citizens, is still less doubtful, but I shall be very much mistaken in deed in the Mass of the people of the United States, if an occasion should call for an unequivocal expression of the public voice, if the first would not find themselves very much deceived—and the latter (their leaders excepted) to change their notes. I pray devoutly that the Directory may not bring the matter to trial....

...The enclosed for young Lafayette I must request

your care of. Having received premature advice (from some of his correspondants in Hamburg) of the liberation of his father and friends his eagerness to embrace them in the first moments of it could not be restrained, although I endeavoured to convince him that it would be more prudent to await the confirmation from *themselves,* and among other things observed to him, that although it was not *probable,* still it was *possible* that his parents might be on their voyage to America whilst he was seeking them in Europe. Should this prove to be the case (as appears not unlikely from the injunction of the Emperor) it will be a matter of sore regret to both. The confidence however which he placed in his information; the advancement of the Season & fear of a Winters passage; gave the preponderancy to his inclination over my opinion. He is a sensible & well disposed young man, full of filial affection & every sentiment to render him estimable.

Information with respect to public matters will go to you from a more direct and purer fountain than mine— (I mean the Department of State)—and things which more immediately concerns myself is too unimportant to trouble you with, further than to assure you, which I can do with much truth that in your public [mission] and in your private capacity—I wish you all the success and prosperity that your heart can desire; . . .

Silhouettes of George and Martha Washington in their later years

It was the last chance Washington would have to give either Pinckney or Marshall news and advice; there would be no further reports from any of the three envoys for many weeks. Meanwhile, Washington was facing problems with his grandson George Washington Parke Custis very reminiscent of those he had had a generation earlier with his stepson, the boy's father, Jack Custis. Like his father, young Custis was lazy, without ambition, had the same predilection for sporting companions, and possessed the same ability to soft-talk the squire of Mount Vernon into believing that no matter what transgressions or failures there had been in the past, a new leaf had just been turned. As Jack had dropped out of King's College after a desultory try, so had his son left the College of New Jersey (later Princeton) after a poor showing and returned to Mount Vernon. Washington, ever hopeful, sent the young man a memorandum outlining what was expected of him at Mount Vernon.

[Mount Vernon, January 7, 1798]

System in all things should be aimed at; for in execution, it renders every thing more easy.

If now and then, of a morning before breakfast, you are inclined, by way of change, to go out with a Gun, I shall not object to it; provided you return by the hour we usually set down to that meal.

From breakfast, until about an hour before Dinner (allowed for dressing, & preparing for it, that you may appear decent) I shall expect you will confine yourself to your studies; and diligently attend to them; endeavouring to make yourself master of whatever is recommended to, or required of you.

While the afternoons are short, and but little interval between rising from dinner and assembling for Tea, you may employ that time in walking, or any other recreation.

After Tea, if the Studies you are engaged in require it, you will, no doubt perceive the propriety & advantage of returning to them, until the hour of rest.

Rise early, that by habit it may become familiar — agreeable — healthy — and profitable. It may for a while, be irksome to do this; but that will wear off; and the practise will produce a rich harvest forever thereafter; whether in public, or private walks of Life.

Make it an invariable rule to be in place (unless extraordinary circumstances prevent it) at usual breakfasting, dining, and tea hours. It is [not] only disagreeable, but it is also very inconvenient, for servants to be running here, & there, and they know not where, to summon you to them, when their duties, and attendance, on the company who are seated, render it improper.

Saturday may be appropriated to riding to your Gun, or other proper amusements.

Time disposed of in this manner, makes ample provision for exercise & every useful, or necessary recreation; at the sametime that the hours allotted for study, *if really applied to it,* instead of running up & down stairs, & wasted in conversation with any one who will talk with you, will enable you to make considerable progress in whatsoever line is marked out for you: and that you may do it, is my sincere wish.

Washington realized that advice and rules of conduct were not going to be enough for the youth. Two weeks after having sent the letter above to young Custis, he wrote to the boy's stepfather, David Stuart, for advice. There was a note almost of resignation in his letter, as though he knew that the youth's character was already set, and that little could be done to change it.

Mount Vernon, January 22, 1798. Washington leaves this today, on a visit to Hope Park, which will afford you an opportunity to examine the progress he has made in the studies he was directed to pursue.

I can, and I believe do, keep him in his room a certain portion of the 24 hours, but it will be impossible for me to make him attend to his Books, if inclination, on his part, is wanting; nor while I am out, if he chuses to be so too, is it in my power to prevent it. I will not say this is the case, nor will I run the hazard of doing him injustice by saying he does not apply, as he ought, to what has been prescribed; but no risk will be run, and candour requires I declare it as my opinion, that he will not derive much benefit in any course which can be marked out for him at this place, without an *able* Preceptor always with him, nor then, for reasons, which do not require to be detailed.

What is best to be done with him, I know not. My opinion always has been that the University in Massachusetts [Harvard] would have been the most eligable Seminary to have sent him to, 1st., because it is on a larger Scale than any other; and 2nd., because I believe that the habits of the youth there, whether from the

Saint-Memin in Virginia: Portraits and Biographies
BY FILLMORE NORFLEET, 1942

George Washington Parke Custis

discipline of the School or from the greater attention of the People, generally, to morals and a more regular course of life, are less prone to dissipation and debauchery than they are at the Colleges South of it. It may be asked, if this was my opinion, why did I not send him there? The answer is as short, as to me it was weighty; being the only male of his family and knowing (although it would have been submitted to) that it would have proved a heart rending stroke to have him at that distance I was disposed to try a nearer Seminary, of good repute; which from some cause, or combinations of causes, has not, after the experiment of a year, been found to answer the end that was contemplated. Whether to send him there *now*, or indeed to any other public School, is at least problematical, and to suffer him to mispend his time at this place, will be disgraceful to himself and me.

If I was to propose to him, to go to the University at Cambridge (in Massachusetts) he might, as has been usual for him on like occasions, say he would go wherever I chose to send him; but if he should go contrary to his inclination, and without a disposition to apply his time properly, an expense without any benefit would result from the measure. Knowing how much I have been disappointed, and my mind disturbed by his conduct, he would not, I am sure, make a candid disclosure of his sentiments to me on this or any other plan I might propose for the completion of his education; for which reason I would pray that you (or perhaps Mrs. Stuart cd. succeed better than any other) would draw [mutilated] and explicit disclosure [mutilated] wishes and views are: for if they are absolutely fixed, an attempt to counteract them by absolute controul would be as idle as the endeavour to stop a rivulet that is constantly running. Its progress while mound upon mound is erected, may be arrested; but this must have an end, and everything would be swept with the torrent.

The more I think of his entering at William and Mary, (unless he could be placed in the Bishop's family) the more doubtful I am of its utility, on many accounts; which had better be the subject of oral communications than by letter. I shall wish to hear from you on the subject of this letter. On occasion of severe reprimand, I found it necessary to give Washington sometime ago, I received the enclosed from him. I have little doubt of his meaning well, but he has not resolution, or exertion enough to act well.

Consultations with Stuart brought a decision to send young Custis to St. John's College at Annapolis, Maryland, and the youth was sent off at the beginning of March. For a period he wrote his usual letters promising to work hard, and Washington responded with advice and encouragement. But when at the end of the school year the youth asked whether it might not be a good idea for him to leave St. John's, he drew a short and indignant reply from Washington.

French Foreign Minister Talleyrand

Mount Vernon, 24th. July, 1798.
Your letter of the 21st. was received last night. The question, "I would thank you to inform me whether I leave it entirely, or not, so that I may pack up accordingly," really astonishes me! for it would seem as if *nothing* I could say to you made more than a *momentary* impression. Did I not, before you went to that seminary, and since by letter, endeavor to fix indelibly on your mind, that the object for which you were sent there was to finish a course of education which you yourself were to derive the benefit of hereafter, and for pressing which upon you, you would be the first to thank your friends so soon as reason has its proper sway in the direction of your thoughts?

As there is a regular stage between Annapolis and the federal city, embrace that as the easiest and most convenient way of getting to the latter, from whence Mr. Law or Mr. Peter will, I have no doubt, send you hither; or a horse might meet you there, or at Alexandria, at an appointed time.

Long before Washington had written the last of the foregoing letters to his grandson, affairs with France had worsened. In early March of 1798 a report from the three envoys in France arrived at last. It detailed a long list of indignities. The ambassadors had been received only coldly and informally by French Foreign Minister Talleyrand, who thereafter declined to see them. Instead they were visited in turn by his underlings, who suggested that a bribe of $250,000 to Talleyrand, a loan of ten million dollars to France, and the withdrawal by President Adams of some "insults" to France made in a speech to Congress, would open the way to fruitful negotiations. All attempts by the Americans to get at the basic issues were met with veiled threats of French military strength and a constant return to the theme of money, until the exasperated Pinckney exclaimed, "No, no! Not a sixpence," a remark that was later transmuted and has gone down in history as "Millions for defense but not one cent for tribute." Pinckney and Marshall, considering any further attempts to negotiate useless, came home; Gerry naïvely believed that his continued presence in Paris would prevent war and remained a while longer. The envoys, in their report, referred to the French agents as X, Y, and Z, and after the report was made public the episode became popularly known as the XYZ Affair. When Talleyrand's duplicity became known, France's popularity in the United States plummeted. Washington's reaction was remarkably restrained. To Senator James Lloyd of Maryland, who sent him a copy of the XYZ papers, he replied with only a few sentences.

> Mount Vernon 15th. April 1798.
> For your kindness in forwarding a copy of the dispatches from our Envoys in France to the Government here, I pray you to accept my best thanks.
>
> What a scene of corruption and profligacy has these communications disclosed in the Directors of a People with whom the United States have endeavoured to Treat upon fair just & honorable ground.
>
> If they should be attended with the effect of "Speedily uniting our fellow Citizens with a firm determination to support our Government & preserve our Independence" as you seem to expect, it would indeed be cause for much congratulation, and no one wd. rejoice more at such an event than I should—But I wish it may be so.

A letter to Secretary of State Pickering a day later was equally brief. Washington was pessimistic that the experience of the three envoys would change the views of the most rabidly Francophile Republicans.

> Mount Vernon 16th. April 1798.
> Your obliging favor of the 11th. Inst. enclosing copies of the instructions to, & Dispatches from the Envoys of the United States at Paris was received with thankfulness by the last Post.
>
> One would think that the measure of infamy was filled, and the profligacy of, and corruption in the System pursued by the French Directory required no further disclosure of the principles by which it is actuated, than what is contained in the above Dispatches; to open the Eyes of the blindest; and yet, I am persuaded

that those Communications will produce no change in the *leaders* of the Opposition, unless there shoud appear a manifest desertion of the followers. There is a sufficient evidence already, in the *Aurora* of the turn they intend to give the business, and of the ground they mean to occupy — but I do not believe they will be able to maintain *that* — or any *other* much longer.

Then for well over a month, Washington's correspondence did not mention war or foreign affairs, except for a letter to the Secretary of War urging that the arsenal at the mouth of the Shenandoah (Harpers Ferry) be finished and activated as a piece of urgent business. Possibly so many years of contending with the problems of the nation, as well as advancing age, had wearied him to such a point that he was willing to let others cope with some of the affairs of the day. And very possibly, in such a mood of disenchantment with the present he had let his mind run back to a more carefree day, for he sat down to write a letter to Sally Fairfax, the love of his youth. He had not seen Sally since she and her husband had left for England in 1773, twenty-five years before, and he had never corresponded with her, although he had exchanged a few letters with her husband. Sally was long since a widow. Washington's letter was largely a catching up on the news of many years, but the fact that he wrote at all strongly suggests that he had never quite gotten over his first real love.

Mount Vernon May 16, 1798.

My dear madam:

Five and twenty Years have nearly passed away since I have considered myself as the permanent resident of this place; or have been in a situation to indulge myself in familiar intercourse with my friends by letter or otherwise.

During this period so many important events have occurred & such changes in man & things have taken place, as the compass of a letter wou'd give you but an inadequate idea of. None of which events however nor all of them together have been able to eradicate from my mind the recollection of those happy moments, the happiest of my life which I have enjoyed in your company.

Worn out in a manner by the toils of my past labour, I am again seated under my vine and Fig Tree, and wish I could add that there were none to make us affraid; but those whom we have been accustomed to call our good friends and allies are endeavouring if not to make

*Engraving of Mount Vernon made in
1798 by John Stockdale of London*

us affraid, yet to dispoil us of our property; and are
provoking us to act of self defence which may lead
to war. What will be the result of such measures, time
that faithful expositor of all things must disclose. My
wish is to spend the remainder of my days (which cannot
be many) in rural amusements—free from the cares
[from] which public responsibility is never exempt.

Before the war and even while it existed although
I was eight years from home at one stretch (except
the *en passant visits* made to it on my marchs to and
from the siege of York Town) I made considerable
additions to my dwelling houses and alterations in my
Offices & Gardens, but the dilapidation occasioned by
time & those neglects which are coextensive with the
absence of proprietors have occupied as much of my
time within the last twelve months in repairing them,
as at any former period in the same space—and it is
matter of sore regret when I cast my eyes towards Belvoir wch. I often do to reflect the former Inhabitants
of it, with whom we lived in such harmony and friendship—no longer reside there—and that the ruins can
only be viewed as the memento of former pleasures;
permit me to add that I have wondered often (your nearest relations being in this country) that you should not
prefer spending the Evening of your life among them

rather than close the sublunary [scene] in a foreign Country, numerous as your acquaintances may be and sincere the friendships you may have formed.

A Century hence if this Country keeps United (& It is surely its policy and Interest to do so) will produce a City, though not as large as London yet of a magnitude inferior to few others in Europe, on the Banks of the Potomack; where one is now establishing for the permanent seat of the Government of the United States (between Alexandria and George Town, on the Maryland side of the River). A situation not excelled for commanding prospect, good water, salubrious air, and safe harbour, by any in the world; and where elegant buildings are erecting & in forwardness for the reception of Congress in the year 1800.

Alexandria within the last seven Years, since the establishment of the Genl. Government has increased in buildings, in population, in the improvement of its Streets, by well executed pavements, and in the extension of its wharves in a manner of which you can have very little idea. This shew of prosperity you will readily conceive is owing to its commerce. The extension of that Trade is occasioned in a great degree by opening of the Inland navigation of Potomack River now cleared to Fort Cumberland upwards of 200 miles and by a similar attempt to accomplish the like up the Shannandoah 150 miles more—in a word if this Country can stear clear of European Politics, stand firm on its bottom & be wise and temperate in its government, it bids fair to be one of the greatest & happiest nations in the world.

In the latter part of May a letter from Alexander Hamilton contained a disturbing thought: "In the event of an open rupture with France, the public voice will again call you to command the armies of your Country." Hamilton was also dubious that the XYZ Affair had united the country as much as was commonly believed. He felt that Washington could oppose French sympathizers in Virginia and North Carolina by making a tour of those states "under some pretence of health &c. This would call forth addresses public dinners &c. which would give you an opportunity of expressing sentiments in Answering Toasts &c. which would throw the weight of your character into the scale of Government and revive an enthusiasm for your person that may be turned into the right channel." Only a little more than a year out of the Presidency, Washington must have

389

read with misgivings this first suggestion that he might be called upon to serve his country yet another time. He threw cold water on Hamilton's idea that he should make a tour, and also minimized the probability that there would be a war in which his leadership would be needed.

Mount Vernon 27th. May 1798.

Yesterday brought me your letter of the 19th. Instant.

You may be assured that my mind is deeply impressed with the present situation of our public affairs and not a little agitated by the outrageous conduct of France towards the United States and at the [inimical] conduct of its partisans who aid and abet their measures: You may believe further from assurances equally sincere that if there was any thing in my power which could be done with consistency to avert or lessen the danger of the crisis, it should be rendered with hand and heart.

The expedient however which has been suggested by you, would not in my Opinion answer the end which is proposed. The object of such a tour could not be vailed by the [ostensible] cover to be given to it; because it would not apply to the State of my health which never was better: and as the measure would be susceptible of two interpretations the enemies to it — always more active and industrious than friends wou'd endeavour, as much as in them lay, to turn it to their own advantage by malicious insinuations; unless that they should discover that the current against themselves was setting too strong, and of too serious a nature for them to stem — in which case the journey would be unnecessary, and in either case the reception might not be such as you have Supposed.

But my dear Sir dark as matters appear at present, and expedient as it is to be prepared at *all* points for the worst that can happen; (and no one is more disposed to this measure than I am) I can not make up my mind *yet*, for the expectation of *open War* or in other words for a formidable Invasion by France. I cannot believe although I think them capable [of] *any thing bad* that they will attempt to do more than they have done, that when they perceive the spirit & policy of this Country rising into resistance and that they have falsely calculated upon support from a large part of the *people* thereof — to promote their views and influence in it, that they will desist, *even from those practices;* unless unexpected events in Europe, or their possession of

Louisiana & the Floridas should induce them to continue the measure. And I believe further that although the *leaders* of their party, in this country will not change their sentiments, that they will be obliged nevertheless to change their plan, or the mode of carrying it on; from the effervescenc[e] which is appearing in all quarters & from the desertion of their followers, which must frown them into silence—at least for awhile.

If I did not view things in this light, my mind would be infinitely more disquieted than it is; for if a crisis should arrive when a sense of duty, or a call from my Country should become so imperious as to leave me no Choice I should prepare for the relinquishment & go with as much reluctance from my present peaceful abode, as I should do to the tombs of my ancestors.

The call to put on uniform again was not as remote a possibility as Washington liked to think. In early July he received two letters on the same day. One, from Secretary of War McHenry, asked, "May we flatter ourselves, that, in a crisis so awful and important, you will accept the command of all our armies?" The other, from President Adams, asked much the same thing, but in less specific terms. To McHenry, Washington replied at great length, opening his letter with an admission that he could not ignore a call to serve his country if he were really needed.

Mount Vernon 4 July 1798.
Your letter of the 26th. Ulto. propounds a very serious, interesting & important question to me; a question that might have been answered with less delay if I had been as much in the habit since, as before I became a private Citizen, of sending regularly to the Post Office on Post days for letters.

The sentiments which I mean to express to you in this letter on the subject of yours, shall be frank, undisguised & explicit; for I see, as you do, that clouds are gathering and that a Storm may ensue. And I find too, from a variety of hints, that my quiet under these circumstances does not promise to be of long continuance.

It cannot be necessary for me to premise to you, or to others who know my Sentiments as well, that to quit the tranquil walks of retirement, and enter the boundless field of responsibility and trouble, would be productive of sensations which a better pen than I possess would find it difficult to describe. Nevertheless, the principle

Secretary of War James McHenry in a portrait attributed to Sharples

by which my conduct has been actuated through life, would not suffer me, in any great emergency, to withhold any services I could render, required by my Country—especially in a case where its dearest rights are assailed by lawless ambition, and intoxicated power, contrary to every principle of justice & in violation of solemn compact, and Laws which govern all Civilized Nations. And this too with obvious intent to sow thick the Seeds of disunion for the purpose of subjugating the Government and destroying our Independence & happiness.

Under circumstances like these accompanied by an actual Invasion of our territorial rights, it would be difficult for me, at any time, to remain an idle spectator under the plea of Age or Retirement. With sorrow, it is true, I should quit the shades of my peaceful abode and the ease & happiness I now enjoy to encounter a new the turmoils of War to which, possibly, my strength

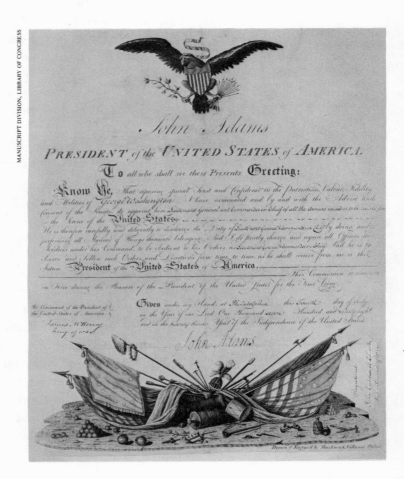

Washington's commission of July 4, 1798, appointing him "Lieutenant General and Commander in Chief of all the Armies," signed by Adams

and powers might be found incompetent. These, however, should not be stumbling blocks in my *own* way;
but there are other things highly important for me to
ascertain, and settle, before I could give a decided answer
to your question.

In the rest of his letter, Washington went on to discuss
such things as the qualifications of officers, his need to have people he
could trust about him if he were to command, and how important it was that
his age not be held against him. To the President he was briefer: if worse
came to worst he could not refuse the call of his country. But Adams, even
before he received Washington's letter, sent McHenry to Mount Vernon to
personally deliver a message. Two days later Washington gave his reply to
the President. He would, of course, serve.

Mount Vernon July 13th. 1798.
I had the honor on the evening of the 11th. instant, to
receive, by the hands of the Secretary of War, your favour
of the 7th., announcing, that you had, with the advice
and consent of the Senate, appointed me "Lieutenant
General and Commander in Chief of all the Armies
raised, or to be raised for the Service of the U.S."

I cannot express how greatly affected I am at this new
proof of public confidence, and the highly flattering
manner in which you have been pleased to make the
communication; at the same time I must not conceal
from you my earnest wish, that the Choice had fallen
upon a man less declined in years, and better qualified
to encounter the usual vicissitudes of War.

You know, Sir, what calculations I had made relative
to the probable [course] of events, on my retireing from
Office, and the determination I had consoled myself
with, of closing the remnant of my days in my present
peaceful abode; You will, therefore, be at no loss to
conceive and appreciate, the sensations I must have
experienced, to bring my mind to any conclusion, that
would pledge me, at so late a period of life, to leave
Scenes I sincerely love, to enter again upon the boundless field of public action — incessant trouble — and high
responsibility.

It was not possible for me to remain ignorant of,
or indifferent to recent transactions. The conduct of
the Directory of France towards our Country; their
insiduous hostility to its Government; their various

practices to withdraw the affection of the people from it; the evident tendency of their Arts, and those of their Agents to countenance and invigorate opposition; their disregard of solemn Treaties and the laws of Nations; their war upon our defenceless commerce; their treatment of our Ministers of Peace, and their demands, amounting to Tribute, could not fail to excite in me corresponding Sentiments with those my Countrymen have so generally expressed in their affectionate addresses to you. Believe me, Sir, no one can more cordially approve of the wise and prudent measures of your Administration. They ought to inspire universal confidence, and will, no doubt, combined with the state of things, call from Congress such laws and means as will enable you to meet the full force and extent of the Crisis.

Satisfied, therefore, that you have sincerely wished and endeavoured to avert war, and exhausted to the last drop the cup of reconciliation, we can with pure hearts appeal to Heaven for the justice of our Cause, and may confidently trust the final result to that kind Providence who has heretofore, and so often, signally favoured the people of the United States.

Thinking in this manner, and feeling how incumbent it is upon every person, of every description, to contribute at all times to his Country's welfare, and especially in a moment like the present, when everything we hold dear and sacred so seriously threatned, I have finally determined to accept the Commission of Commander in Chief of the Armies of the United States, with the reserve only, that I shall not be called into the field until the Army is in a situation to require my presence, or it becomes indispensable by the urgency of circumstances.

In making this reservation, I beg to be understood that I do not mean to withhold any assistance to arrange or organize the Army, which you may think I can afford. I take the liberty also to mention, that I must decline having my acceptance considered as drawing after it any immediate charge upon the Public, or that I can receive any emoluments annexed to the appointment, before entering into a situation to incur expence.

The Secretary of War being anxious to return to the Seat of Government, I have detained him no longer than is necessary to a full communication on the several points he had in charge.

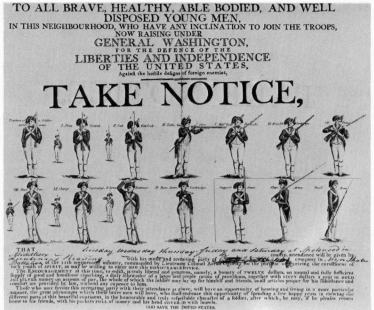

*A 1798 recruiting poster used
during the quasi war with France*

Congress authorized increasing the size of the Army, which had shrunk to thirty-five hundred men, by another ten thousand. In addition, a "Provisional Army" of fifty thousand men and officers was to be recruited for the duration of the emergency. Washington's first problem was to select the three men who, as major generals, would be his immediate subordinates. For the senior of the three he wanted Alexander Hamilton. In that position Hamilton would rank second only to Washington and would ordinarily be in actual command, for Washington had stipulated that he should not be called to active duty until French invasion or other emergency required his presence in the field. Next, Washington nominated Charles Cotesworth Pinckney, although Pinckney's wartime rank of brigadier general outranked the lieutenant colonelcy of Hamilton. And third, Washington placed Henry Knox, a major general during the war, his dependable chief of artillery, his close friend, and his Secretary of War when he was President. Washington wrote to his old friend to explain his decision.

Mount Vernon 16th. July 1798.

Little did I imagine when I retired from the theatre of public life, that it was probable, or even possible, that any event would arise *in my day,* that could induce me to entertain, *for a moment*, an idea of relinquishing the tranquil walks, and refreshing shades, with which I am surrounded. But it is in vain, I perceive, to look for ease & happiness in a world of troubles.

The call of my Country, and the urgency of my friends to comply with it, have produced a letter from me to the

Ice house at Mount Vernon
BOTH: *Mount Vernon*, LOSSING

President of the United States, which, probably, will be given to the public; but if it should not, the principal feature thereof, is, that with the reservation of not being called into the Field until the Army is in a situation to require my presence, or it becomes indispensable by the urgency of circumstances, that I will accept the Commission with which the Secretary of War came charged. Desiring, however, that it might be understood, that my Coadjutors, in the first grades, and principal staff of the Army, must be men in whom I could place entire confidence; for that, it was not to be expected, at my time of life, that I would forsake the ease & comforts which are essential in old age—encounter the toils & vicissitudes of War, with all its concomitants—and jeopardize the reputation which the partiality of the World has been pleased to bestow on me (when the hazard of diminishing, is at least equal to the prospect of increasing it,) without securing such assistance as would enable me to go with confidence into such a field of responsibility.

After this exordium, it is almost unnecessary to add, that I have placed you among those characters on whom I wish to lean, for support. But my dear Sir, as you always have found, and I trust ever will find, candour a prominent trait of my character, I must add, that causes—which would exceed the limits of an ordinary letter to explain, are in the way of such an arrangement as might render your situation perfectly agreeable; but I fondly hope that, the difficulty will not be insurmountable, in your decision.

For the present, and augmented force, three Major Generals, and four Brigadiers are allowed by the Act establishing the latter; and in a consultation with the Secretary of War, the characters proposed for the former are Colo. Hamilton, Genl. Chas. Cotesworth Pinckney and yourself. The first of these, in the public estimation, as declared to me, is designated to be second in command; with some fears, I confess, of the consequences; although I must acknowledge at the sametime that I know not where a more competent choice could be made. General Pinckney's character as an active, spirited and intelligent Officer you are acquainted with, and know that it stands very high in the Southern Hemisphere—it being understood *there*, that he made Tactics as much, if not more his study, than any Officer in the American army during the last War. His character in other respects, in that quarter before his late Embassy, was also high; and throughout the Union it has acquired celebrity by his conduct as Minister & Envoy. His connexions are numerous—their influence extensive; but most of all, with me, when to these considerations I add, as my *decided* opinion (for reasons unnecessary to enumerate) that if the French intend an Invasion of this Country *in force*, their operations will commence South of Maryland; & probably of Virginia; you will see at once the importance of embarking this Gentleman and all his connexions *heartily* in the active scenes that would follow, instead of damping their ardour, and thereby giving more activity to the leaven that is working in others, where unity of sentiment would be most desirable.

Viewing things in this light, I would fain hope, as we are forming an Army *A New*, which Army, if needful *at all*, is to fight for every thing that ought to be dear and sacred to freemen, that former rank will be forgot; and among the fit & chosen characters, the only contention will be, who shall be foremost in zeal, at this crisis, to serve his Country in whatever situation circumstances may place him. Most of those, who are best qualified to oppose the enemy, will have Sacrifices of ease—Interest—or Inclination to make; but what are these, when put in competition with the loss of our Independence or the Subjugation of our Government? both of which are evidently struck at, by an intoxicated, ambitious and domineering Foe.

The arrangement made with the Secretary of War is on a seperate Sheet of paper, and meant for your perusal *only*, until the decision of the President relative to it, is announced.

With that esteem & regard which you know I feel for you, I remain your sincere friend and Affectionate Servant.

P.S. From the best recollection I have of them, the Secretary of War is furnished with a list of Field & other Officers of the late Army of most celebrity, from whence to draw the Field Officers for the Corps to be raised. If you would afford your aid also it wd. be obliging.

Century plant sent to Washington from Puerto Rico (left) and a large lemon tree imported from West Indies

Knox's response was bitter and expressed his hurt at having his long devotion to Washington answered by seeing others "greatly my juniors in rank . . . preferred before me." Even more humiliating, said Knox, was that he had not been consulted in advance. Washington, deeply disturbed, tried to mollify Knox, and succeeded so well that Knox asked to serve as Washington's aide-de-camp if there was any fighting. Knox, however, refused the commission as Major General. Although he failed to gain the services of Knox, Washington did enlist another valuable associate of earlier days, his former secretary Tobias Lear. Lear had served him so well from 1785 until the end of his first Administration that he had become Washington's valued confidant and virtually a member of the family. Lear agreed to give up his business in the city of Washington and to take up his old duties as secretary once more. He would serve Washington for what remained of the latter's life.

> [Mount Vernon]
> Thursday night, August 30, 1798.
> I have, at length, received the President's answer (through the Secretary of War) to my request to be allowed a Secretary, who gives it as his opinion that I have an undoubted right to one, or all of my military family, if I find it convenient, and that their pay &c. will be allowed.
>
> And the Secretary having thrown a *mass* of Papers upon me which I have not looked into (being this moment arrived) I should be glad if you would now come & take your station.

Washington went to Philadelphia on November 10, to spend more than a month with Major Generals Hamilton and Pinckney discussing the Provisional Army, drawing up tables of organization, making plans for recruitment, compiling lists of prospective officers for the proposed twelve regiments, taking care of the countless other details involved. In addition, there were numerous dinners and receptions to consume Washington's time and energy. And there was at least one personal item to take care of. Washington had all his life been cursed with bad teeth and had lost them one by one, until after middle age they were all false. While in Philadelphia, Washington wrote to John Greenwood of New York, who had been his dentist for some time and in whom he had much confidence.

> Philadelphia 12th. Decr. 1798.
> Your letter of the 8th. came safe—and as I am hurrying, in order to leave this City tomorrow, I must be short.
>
> The principal thing you will have to attend to, in the alteration you are about to make, is to let the upper bar fall back from the lower one thus ❱ ; whether the teeth are quite straight, or inclining a little in thus, ❱ or a little rounding outwards thus ❱ is immaterial, for I find

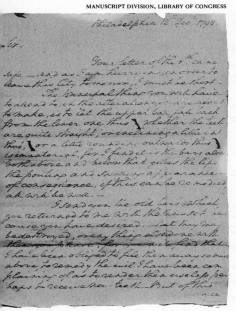

Washington's letter to his dentist

it is the bars alone both above and below that gives the lips the pouting and swelling appearance—of consequence, if this can be remedied, all will be well.

I send you the old bars, which you returned to me with the new set, because you have desired. But they may be destroyed, or any thing else done with them you please, for you will find that I have been obliged to file them away so much above, to remedy the evil I have been complaining of as to render them useless perhaps to receive new teeth. But of this you are better able to judge than I am. If you can fix the teeth (now on the new bars which you have) on the old bars which you will receive with this letter I should prefer it, because the latter are easy in the Mouth. And you will perceive moreover that when the edges of the upper and lower teeth are put together that the upper falls back into the mouth, which they ought to do, or it will have the effect of forcing the lip out just under the nose.

I shall only repeat again, that I feel much obliged by your extreme willingness, and readiness to accomodate me and that I am, etc.

On returning home, Washington became the Virginia farmer again, but never quite completely, for there was always a stream of letters about Army business passing to and fro. Occasionally personal and military business became intermixed, as in the matter of his grandson George Washington Parke Custis. The previous September Washington had decided that it would be a waste of time to send the young man off to college; now he wrote to David Stuart, young Custis's stepfather, to propose the Army as a place where the lackadaisical youth might find some purpose in life.

Mount Vernon 30th. Decr. 1798.
Company, ever since my return home, has prevented my mentioning a matter before, which will be the subject of this letter now.

When the applications for Military appointments come to be examined at Philadelphia, it was pleasing to find among them, so many Gentlemen of family, fortune & high expectations, soliciting Commissions; & not in the high grades.

This, and a thorough conviction that it was a vain attempt to keep Washington Custis to any literary pursuits, either in a public Siminary, or at home under the direction of any one, gave me the first idea of bringing him

Washington's watch, seal, and key,
with close-up impression of the seal

forward as a Cornet of Horse. To this measure too I was induced by a conviction paramount in my breast, that if real danger threatened the Country, no young Man ought to be an idle Spectator of its defence; and that, if a state of preparation would avert the evil of an Invasion, he would be entitled to the merit of proffered service, without encountering the dangers of War: and besides, that it might divert his attention from a matrimonial pursuit (for a while at least) to which his constitution seems to be too prone.

But, though actuated by these ideas, I intended to proceed no farther in the business than to provide a vacancy in one of the Troops of light Dragoons, & to consult Mrs. Stuart & his Grandmother as to their inclinations respecting his filling it, before any intimation of it should be given to him: But, Mr. Lear hearing the matter talked of, and not knowing that this was the ground on which I meant to place the appointment (if the arrangement met the Presidents approbation) wrote to Washington on the Subject, in order to know if it would be agreeable to him, or not, to receive it.

Under these circumstances (and his appearing highly delighted) concealment—I mean an attempt at it—would have proved nugatory. He stands arranged therefore a Cornet in the Troop to be Commanded by Lawrence Lewis [Washington's nephew] (who I intended as his Mentor)—Lawrence Washington junr. (of Chotanck) is the Lieutenant of the Troop. But all this it will be remembered is to be approved—first by the President, & consented to by the Senate to make it a valid act; & therefore, the less it is *publicly* talked of the better.

Mrs. Washington does not seem to have the least objection to his acceptance of the Commission; but it rests with Mrs. Stuart to express her Sentiments thereon, and soon; as I requested the Secretary of War to forward the Commissions for *this* Troop of Light Dragoons, under cover to me.

The only hesitation I had, to induce the caution before mentioned, arose from his being an only Son; indeed the only male of his Great great Grandfathers family; but the same Providence that wd. watch over & protect him in domestic walks, can extend the same protection to him in a Camp, or the field of battle, if he should ever be in one.

Although Washington was in constant correspondence with Hamilton and Secretary of War James McHenry about organizing the Provisional Army, weeks and months passed, and the patriotic zeal of Americans dwindled when there was no actual recruitment. Washington and Hamilton decided between them that the fault lay with McHenry, who fussed endlessly with details, was unable to delegate authority, and never made a firm decision. At last Washington took the problem to McHenry himself.

Mount Vernon 25th. March 1799.

You will not only consider this letter as a *private one*, but as a *friendly one*, from G.W. to J.M. And if the sentiments which you will find in it, are delivered with more freedom and candour than are agreeable, say so; not by implication only, but in explicit language; and I will promise to offend no more by such conduct; but confine myself (if occasion should require it) to an Official Correspondence.

Thus premising, let me, in the name and behalf of the Officers who have been appointed, and of the army intended to be raiséd, ask what keeps back the Commissions; and arrests the Recruiting Service?

Be assured that *both*, among the friends of Government, excite astonishment and discontent. Blame is in every Mind, but it is not known where to fix it. Some attach it to the P. [President]—some to the S. of W. [Secretary of War]—and some, *fertile in invention*, seek for other causes. Many of the appointed Officers have quitd. their former occupations, that they might be in perfect readiness to proceed in their Military duties the moment they should receive their Commissions & Recruiting Instructions. Others, who were about to enter into business, and plans of future life, stand suspended. Many are highly disgusted; some talk of giving up the idea of becoming Officers, unable to remain longer in the aukward situation they are involved; and *all* are complaining. Applications are made by numbers to me, to know what the cause of the delay is, what they are to expect, and what they ought to do. What could I say? Am I not kept in as much ignorance as they are themselves? Am I advised of any new appointments? any changes which have taken place? any of the views or designs of Government relatively to the Army? It is not unreasonable to suppose, that if there be reasons of State, operating the policy of these delays, that I was entitled to sufficient confidence to be let into the secret; or, if they proceeded from uncontroulable causes, *I*, still more than

Inkstand used by Washington for his always voluminous correspondence
BOTH: *Mount Vernon*, LOSSING, 1883

the *Public*, ought not to have been left in the field of Conjecture, without a guide to direct me to the knowledge of them....

... The zeal, enthusiasm, and indeed resentments, which warmed the breasts of the American youth, and would have induced the sons of the respectable Yeomanry (in all parts of the United States) to have enlisted as noncommissioned officers & Privates, is now no more; they are evaporated, & a listlessness has supplied its place. The next, most favourable opportunity—namely—the idle, & dreary scenes of winter which bring on dissipation & want, from the cessation of labour, has also passed away! The enlivening prospect of Spring, the calls of the Husbandman, indeed of every avocation, for labourers in the approaching busy season, hath supplanted all thoughts of becoming Soldiers; and *now*, many young Gentlemen who had (conditionally) last Summer & Autumn, engaged their Companies, will find it difficult to enlist a *single man* of those so engaged—The latter Pretending, that having waited a considerable time to see if their services would be wanted in the Field, and no overtures for them made it became necessary for them to seek some other employment.

What is the natural consequence of all this? Why, that we must take the Rif-raf of the populous Cities; Convicts; & foreigners: or, have Officers without men. But even this is not the worst of it. The Augmented Corps (if I have conceived the matter rightly) must have been intended as a well organized, and well disciplined body of Men, for others (in case of need) to resort to, & take example from. Will this be the case if the enemy should invade this Country? Far from it! What better, in the first instance, are Regiments so composed than Militia? And what prospect have those who Command them, of rendering Service to their Country, or doing honor to themselves in the Field, opposed to Veteran Troops, practiced in Tactics, and unaccustomed to defeat? These, my dear McHenry, are serious considerations to a Man who has nothing to gain, and is putting every thing to a hazard....

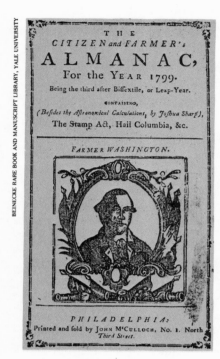

In the year of Washington's death he was labeled "Farmer Washington" on the cover of a farmer's almanac

Washington continued at length. He complained of the unfairness of the system of appointing officers, citing the case of one man strongly recommended by four generals and with a record of excellent service throughout the Revolution whose application for a commission was denied by "the Veto of a Member of Congress." Conversely, he told of an officer scarcely more than a boy who had been promoted over men older and better qualified. Washington's stance of objectivity and his indignation over outside influences in officer selection were forgotten briefly as he inquired, "... may I ask if there would be any impropriety in letting Mr. Custis step from a Cornetcy into the rank of Lieutenant? ... If ample fortune, good Education, more than common abilities, and good dispositions, free from Vice of any kind, give him a title, in the 19th. year of age, his pretensions thereto (though not to the injury of another) are good." Could this young paragon be the same grandson of whose indolence and lack of purpose Washington had often complained, the same who was taken out of college because he was learning nothing? But at last Washington reached the most delicate part of his letter. Although he tried to be gentle, it was not easy to tell a man that he was badly mishandling his job.

> ... There is one matter more, which I was in doubt whether to mention to you, or not, because it is of a more delicate nature than any I have touched upon; but finally, friendship have got the better of my scruples.
>
> It respects yourself *personally*. Whilst I was in Philadelphia — and after the Members of Congress had begun to Assemble, it was hinted to me, in pretty *strong terms* by more than one of them, that the Department of War would not — nay could not — be conducted to advantage (if War should ensue) under your auspices; for instead of attending to the *great* out lines, and *principles* of your office, & keeping the subordinate Officers of the Department rigidly to their respective duties, *they*, were inattentive, while *you*, were bewildered with trifles. You will recollect, I dare say, that more than once, I expressed to you my opinion of the expediency of committing the *Details* of the Department to the execution of others; and to bestow your thoughts and attention to the more important Duties of it; which, in the scenes we were contemplating, were alone sufficient to occupy the time, and all the consideration of the Secretary. I went no farther *then*, nor should I have renewed the subject *now*, had not the delay in issuing of the Commissions, and commencing the Recruiting service, excited general reprobation, and blame, though, as I have observed before, no one knows where, with precision, to fix it. Generally however, it is attributed to the want of System, & exertion in the Department of War. To apprise you of this, is my motive for this communication.

I prefaced the sentiments of this letter with a request, that they might be considered as proceeding from a private man to his friend. No one would be struck more forcibly than myself, with the impropriety of such a letter from the Commander in Chief of the Army of the U. States to the Secretary of War. If they are received in good part, the end is obtained. If otherwise, my motives, & the purity of my intentions, is the best apology I can offer for the liberty I have taken. In either case however, be assured of this truth, that with very great esteem and regard, I remain &c.

Washington's letter infused no new energy into McHenry. Recruiting continued to lag; the public had lost most of its patriotic ardor—and besides, the superiority of the British fleet made it extremely unlikely that any French armies would invade the United States. Only three thousand men were enlisted in the Regular Army, and the fifty-thousand-man Provisional Army never got beyond the paper stage. At sea the picture was considerably different. In the spring and early summer of 1798, Congress had created a Navy Department, authorized enlargement of the tiny three-frigate Navy, commissioned privateers, and ordered the Navy to capture all armed French vessels—virtually all merchant ships were armed. In the quasi war that followed, most action was by privateers, for the French navy was too busy in Europe to spare more than a few warships for American waters. American vessels were overwhelmingly successful, both in privateering enterprises and in the few encounters between naval vessels. American ships captured some ninety French vessels, the French took one American. The undeclared war ended somewhat inconclusively in the autumn of 1800.

Much of that, however, still lay in the future. At Mount Vernon, Washington continued to spend hours in the saddle checking on the affairs of the several farms of the plantation. His plan to rent out the dependent farms to tenants had come to nothing: no one he had considered qualified had applied. As always, he was surrounded by a sea of troubles. A duplex house he was building for rental in the city of Washington was costing more and taking longer than it should have. He was having difficulty re-establishing one of his boundary lines and was certain an effort was being made to cheat him out of a good many acres rightfully his. He attempted to collect debts long overdue, and his shortage of money became so acute that for the first time in his life he made a loan from a bank—and had to ask how to go about it. And he was upset at learning that President Adams was sending another envoy to France on reports that the French Government might at last be inclined to make peace.

Yet the entries in his diary, brief as they were, indicate that the spirit of Mount Vernon had not changed; it was a house always open to people, always ready to welcome guests, whether old friends or virtual strangers. November, 1799, was the last full month in the diary.

1 [November, 1799]. ... Mr. Craik went away after Breakfast....

2. ... Mr. Jno. Fairfax (formerly an overseer of mine) came here before dinner and stayed all Night.

3. ... Mr. Valangin came to dinner.

4. ... A Mr. Teakle from Accomack County dined here & returned as did Doctr. Craik. Mr. Lear returned from Berkeley....

5. ... Set out on a trip to Difficult-run to view some Land I had there & some belonging to Mr. Jno. Gill who had offered it to me in discharge of Rent which he was owing me. Dined at Mr. Nicholas Fitzhughs and lodged at Mr. Corbin Washingtons.

6. Set out from thence after 8 Oclk. being detained by sprinkling Rain, & much appearance of it until that hour. Reached Wiley's Tavern near Difficult Bridge to Breakfast and then proceeded to Survey my own Land—the day clearing & the weather becoming pleasant.

7. Weather remarkably fine. Finished Surveying my own Tract & the Land belonging to Gill—returning, as the Night before to Wileys Tavern.

8. Morning very heavy and about 9 oclock it commenced Raining which it continued to do steadily through the day—notwithstanding which I proceed[ed] to ascertain by actual measurement the qualities. This being finished betwn. 12 & 1 oclock I returned to Wiley's Tavern and stayed there the remainder of the day.

9. Morning & the whole day clear warm & pleasant. Set out a little after 8 Oclock. Viewed my building in the Fedl. City. Dined at Mr. Laws & lodged at Mr. Thos. Peter's.

10. ... Returned home about Noon. Mr. Law, Mr. Barry Mr. White & Doctr. Thornton came to Dinner & stayed all Night....

11. ... The Gentlemen above mentioned went away after breakft....

14. ... Mr. Valangen came to dinner & stayed all night.

15. ... Rode to visit Mr. now Lord Fairfax who was just got home from a Trip to England. Retd. to dinner.

16. ... Doctr. Craik came here in the afternoon on a

A check payable to William Thornton, the architect of the Capitol, was signed by Washington less than a month before his death.

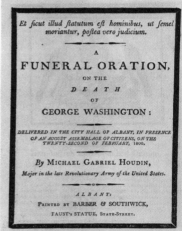

Et ficut illud ftatutum eft hominibus, ut femel moriantur, poftea vero judicium.

A

FUNERAL ORATION,

ON THE

D E A T H

OF

GEORGE WASHINGTON :

DELIVERED IN THE CITY HALL OF ALBANY, IN PRESENCE OF AN AUGUST ASSEMBLAGE OF CITIZENS, ON THE TWENTY-SECOND OF FEBRUARY, 1800.

By MICHAEL GABRIEL HOUDIN,

Major in the late Revolutionary Army of the United States.

A L B A N Y:

PRINTED BY BARBER & SOUTHWICK,

FAUST's STATUE, STATE-STREET.

visit to sick people.

17. ... Went to Church in Alexandria & dined with Mr. Fitzhugh. On my return fd. young Mr. McCarty here on his way back from the Federal City. Young McCarty came to Dinr....

20. ... Mr. McCarty went away after breakfast and Mrs. Summers—Midwife for Mrs. Lewis [Martha's granddaughter Eleanor (Nelly) had married Washington's nephew Laurence Lewis] came here abt. 3 oclk.

21. ... Mrs. Stuart and the two eldest Miss Stuarts came here to dinner.

22. ... Colo. Carrington & Lady came in the afternn.

23. ... Colo. Carrington & Lady went away after Breakfast. Doctr. Craik came to dinner & Doctr. Stuart at Night....

25. ... Doctr. Craik & Doctr. Stuart both went away after Breakfast....

27. ... Doctr. Craik who was sent for to Mrs. Lewis (& who was delivered of a daughter abt. [ ] oclock in the forenoon) came to Breakfast & stayed [to] dinner. Mr. Dublois dined here, and both went away afterwards.

28. ... Colo. & Mrs. Carrington came to Dinner.

29. ... Young D. McCarty came to dinner and Mr. Howell Lewis & wife after dinner.

30. ... Colo. & Mrs. Carrington went away after B[reakfas]t.

Washington's diary continued only through December 13. On December 12 he recorded that snow began to fall about ten o'clock in the morning, soon changing to hail, and then settling down to a cold rain. The next day there was about three inches of snow on the ground; the snow ended early in the afternoon, the sky cleared, and by night the mercury was at 28 degrees. These were probably the last words Washington ever wrote.

On December 12 Washington made his usual horseback ride around the plantation. Before he returned he had been exposed for five hours to the snow, hail, and rain that he had recorded in his diary. When he returned home, Tobias Lear mentioned that his hair and neck were wet, but Washington answered that his great coat had kept him otherwise dry. The next day a sore throat and the falling snow made him decide to remain indoors, and as the day progressed he became somewhat hoarse, although not enough to prevent him from reading aloud from the newspapers in the evening. Sometime after midnight he woke Martha to tell her he was ill, with a throat so excruciatingly sore he could hardly speak and breathed with difficulty, but he would not let her get up in the cold room. At sunrise a servant was sent to call Tobias Lear and an overseer, who Washington wished should bleed him at once.

As soon as the overseer arrived, Washington insisted that he open a vein, and about half a pint of blood was taken. About nine o'clock James Craik, the family doctor, arrived, and after diagnosing the ailment as inflammatory quinsy, bled the patient again and tried various remedies, including blistering his throat to draw the inflammation to the surface. When none of these measures appeared to help, Craik did yet another bleeding, and when the first of two doctors who had been called for consultation arrived, he and Craik opened a vein for the fourth time. Through it all, Washington did not once complain, although he was in constant pain. In the afternoon he spoke to the doctors, thanking them for their attention, and saying that they had better not trouble themselves "but let me go off quietly; I cannot last long."

There were still a few hours left to him that day, December 14, and through them Washington remained completely clear of mind. About ten o'clock at night Lear saw that Washington wanted to speak, and leaned close to hear the low voice. "I am just going. Have me decently buried, and do not let my body be put into the vault in less than two days after I am dead." Lear nodded, but Washington, insistent, asked, "Do you understand me?" "Yes, sir," said Lear. "'Tis well," said Washington. Lear remained holding Washington's hand, but not many minutes later the hand was suddenly withdrawn, and there was a change in the face on the pillow. Lear called to Dr. Craik, who stepped to the bedside and saw in a moment that the last campaign was over.

A rare engraving of Washington appeared as the frontispiece to a funeral oration by a French army officer (opposite); later he was apotheosized in paintings such as the highly romantic version done on glass at left and in innumerable mourning prints (above).

407

Selected Bibliography

Alden, John R. *The American Revolution, 1775–1783.* New York: Harper & Row, 1962.

Bowers, Claude G. *Jefferson and Hamilton: The Struggle for Democracy in America.* Boston: Houghton Mifflin, 1925.

Bryan, William A. *George Washington in American Literature, 1775–1865.* New York: Columbia University Press, 1952.

Cook, Roy Bird. *Washington's Western Lands.* Strassburg, Va.: Shenandoah, 1930.

Cunliffe, Marcus. *George Washington, Man and Monument.* Boston: Little, Brown, 1958.

De Conde, Alexander. *Entangling Alliance: Politics and Diplomacy under George Washington.* Durham: Duke University Press, 1958.

Fitzpatrick, John C. *George Washington, Colonial Traveller, 1732–1775.* Indianapolis: Bobbs-Merrill, 1927.

Flexner, James Thomas. *George Washington: The Forge of Experience, 1732–1775.* Boston: Little, Brown, 1965.

————. *George Washington in the American Revolution, 1775–1783.* Boston: Little, Brown, 1968.

————. *George Washington and the New Nation, 1783–1793.* Boston: Little, Brown, 1970.

————. *George Washington: Anguish and Farewell, 1793–1799.* Boston: Little, Brown, 1972.

Ford, Paul Leicester. *George Washington.* Philadelphia: Lippincott, 1924.

Freeman, Douglas Southall. *George Washington.* 7 vols. New York: Charles Scribner's Sons, 1948–57. (Vol. 7 by John A. Carroll and Mary W. Ashworth.)

Irving, Washington. *Life of George Washington.* 5 vols. New York: G. P. Putnam, 1855–59.

Isely, Bliss. *The Horseman of the Shenandoah: A Biographical Account of the Early Days of George Washington.* Milwaukee: Bruce, 1962.

Knollenberg, Bernhard. *George Washington, the Virginia Period, 1732–1775.* Durham: Duke University Press, 1964.

————. *Washington and the Revolution, a Reappraisal: Gates, Conway, and the Continental Congress.* New York: Macmillan, 1940.

Marshall, John. *The Life of George Washington.* 5 vols. Philadelphia: C. P. Wayne, 1804–7.

Nettels, Curtis P. *George Washington and American Independence.* Boston: Little, Brown, 1951.

Rossiter, Clinton L. *1787: The Grand Convention.* New York: Macmillan, 1966.

Sears, Louis M. *George Washington and the French Revolution.* Detroit: Wayne State University Press, 1960.

Stetson, Charles W. *Washington and His Neighbors.* Richmond: Garrett and Massie, 1956.

Tebbel, John W. *George Washington's America.* New York: E. P. Dutton, 1954.

Thane, Elswyth. *Potomac Squire.* New York: Duell, Sloan and Pearce, 1963.

Washington, George. *Diaries, 1748–1799.* Edited by John C. Fitzpatrick. 4 vols. Boston: Houghton Mifflin, 1925.

————. *The Writings of George Washington.* Edited by Jared Sparks. 12 vols. Boston: American Stationers' Co.: 1834–37.

———— *The Writings of George Washington from the Original Manuscript Sources, 1745–1799.* Edited by John C. Fitzpatrick. 39 vols. Washington: U.S. Government Printing Office, 1931–44.

White, Leonard D. *The Federalists: A Study in Administrative History.* New York: Macmillan, 1948.

Whiteley, Emily Stone. *Washington and his Aides-de-Camp.* New York: Macmillan, 1936.

Wilson, Woodrow. *George Washington.* New York: Harper, 1896.

Acknowledgments

Unless otherwise specifically credited below, all documents reproduced in this volume are from George Washington Papers, Library of Congress, Washington, D.C., the greatest collection of Washington documents in existence. In addition the Editors would like to thank the following individuals and institutions for permission to reprint documents in their possession:

Alexander Hamilton Papers, Library of Congress, Washington, D.C., page 284

Detroit Public Library, Detroit, Mich., pages 304-09

Free Public Library, Trenton, N.J., page 298 (top)

Harvard University, Cambridge, Mass., pages 66-67

Henry E. Huntington Library and Art Gallery, San Marino, Calif., pages 169 (center), 314-15 (top), and 376-77 (top)

Historical Society of Pennsylvania, Philadelphia, pages 76 (bottom)-77 (top), and 79 (bottom)-80 (top)

John Carter Brown Library, Brown University, Providence, R.I., pages 118 (bottom)-119, and 120-21 (top)

Massachusetts Historical Society, Boston, pages 118 (top) and 293 (top)

Mount Vernon Ladies' Association of the Union, Mount Vernon, Va., pages 69 (top), 105 (bottom), 186 (top), 375, and 399 (bottom)-400

National Archives, Washington, D.C.
Miscellaneous Papers, pages 338, 349, and 350-51
Papers of the Continental Congress, pages 101 (bottom)-102 (top), 116 (bottom)-117, 121 (bottom)-122 (top), 148 (center), 149 (bottom)-150, 154-56 (top), 156 (bottom)-158 (top), 158 (bottom)-159 (top), 170 (bottom)-172, 173 (bottom)-174 (top), 175 (bottom)-176, 189 (bottom)-190 (top), and 204 (bottom)-205 (top)

New York Public Library, New York, N.Y., pages 393 (bottom)-394

Old South Association in Boston, Boston, Mass., pages 398 (bottom)-399 (top)

Pierpont Morgan Library, New York, N.Y., pages 324-25 (top) and 357-58 (top)

Thomas Jefferson Papers, Library of Congress, Washington, D.C., pages 353 (bottom)-354 (top)

University of Virginia, Charlottesville, page 28 (bottom)

Virginia Historical Society, Richmond, pages 43 (bottom)-46 (top), 60 (bottom)-62 (top), 317-18, 319, 320-21 (top), and 321 (bottom)-322

Wadsworth Atheneum, Hartford, Conn., page 126

The Editors also make grateful acknowledgment for the use of documents from the following works:

Custis, George Washington Parke. *Recollections and Private Memoirs of Washington by his Adopted Son.* New York, 1860. Page 385 (center)

Fitzpatrick, John C., ed. *The Writings of George Washington.* Washington, D.C., 1931-44. Pages 41 (bottom)-43 (top), 46 (center)-48 (top), 49-50 (top), 114 (bottom)-115 (top), 168 (bottom)-169 (top), 209-10 (top), 259, 364-65, 367 (bottom)-369 (top), 369 (bottom)-370, 377 (bottom)-378 (top), and 383 (bottom)-385 (top)

Ford, Worthington Chauncey, ed. *The Writings of George Washington.* New York, 1889. Pages 80 (bottom)-81 (top) and 97 (bottom)-98 (top)

Freeman, Douglas Southall. *George Washington,* vol. III. New York, 1948-57. Pages 102 (bottom)-104 (top)

Letters and Recollections of George Washington... London, 1906. Page 398 (top)

National Intelligencer. 22 October 1862. Pages 159 (bottom)-162 (top) and 166 (bottom)-168 (top)

Reed, William B. *Life and Correspondence of Joseph Reed.* Philadelphia, 1847. Pages 122 (bottom)-124 (top)

Richardson, James D., ed. *A Compilation of the Messages and Papers of the Presidents.* vol. I Washington, 1913. Pages 348 (bottom)-349 (top)

Sparks, Jared, ed. *Writings of George Washington.* Boston, 1836. Page 295 (top)

The Debates and Proceedings in the Congress of the United States; with an Appendix, Containing Important State Papers and Public Documents, and All the Laws of a Public Nature. Washington, 1849. Pages 354 (bottom)-355 (top)

The Journal of Major George Washington, Sent by the Hon. Robert Dinwiddie, Esq.; His Majesty's Lieutenant Governor, and Commander in Chief of Virginia to the Commandant of the French Forces on Ohio... Williamsburg, 1754. Pages 30-40

The Editors also wish to express their appreciation of the many institutions and individuals who made available their pictorial material for use in this volume. In particular the Editors are grateful to:

Mount Vernon Ladies' Association of the Union—Charles C. Wall, Resident Director; Christine Meadows, John Castellani

The Papers of George Washington, University of Virginia, Charlottesville—Donald Jackson, Editor; Dorothy Twohig

Beinecke Rare Book and Manuscript Library, Yale University, New Haven, Conn.

Boston Athenaeum, Boston, Mass.

Anne S. K. Brown Military Collection, Brown University, Providence, R.I.

Richard Storrs Childs, Norfolk, Conn.

Connecticut Historical Society, Hartford

Historical Society of Pennsylvania, Philadelphia

Independence National Historical Park Collection, Philadelphia, Pa.

Lewis Walpole Library, Farmington, Conn.

Library of Congress, Washington, D.C.—Mrs. Carolyn H. Sung

Metropolitan Museum of Art, New York, N.Y.

Museum of Fine Arts, Boston, Mass.

National Broadcasting Company, New York, N.Y.—Daniel W. Jones, Jr.

National Gallery of Art, Washington, D.C.

New Haven Colony Historical Society, New Haven, Conn.

New-York Historical Society, New York, N.Y.

New York Public Library, New York, N.Y.

Valley Forge Historical Society, Valley Forge, Pa.

Washington and Lee University, Lexington, Va.

Henry Francis du Pont Winterthur Museum, Wilmington, Dela.

Yale University Art Gallery, New Haven, Conn.

Finally the Editors thank Susan Storer in New York for assistance in obtaining pictorial material; Sylvia J. Abrams in Washington for copyediting and proofreading; and Mary-Jo Kline in New York for compiling the chronology and bibliography.

Index

Boldface indicates pages on
which illustrations appear.

When
leisure (if th
will give you
of this quarte
my view & rec
I shall certain
ony you, that
join very since
your health,
—and that I a
tionate esteem
J. W.

Colo Humphreys,